TOURISM IN RECENT GLOBAL SCENARIO

TOURISM IN RECENT GLOBAL SCENARIO

By

G.A.H. Rizvi

2008

CYBER TECH PUBLICATIONS
4264/3, Ansari Road, Daryaganj, New Delhi-110002 (India)
Ph.: 011-23244078. Fax: 011-23280028
E-Mail: cyberpublicationsdelhi@yahoo.com

TOURISM IN RECENT GLOBAL SCENARIO

G.A.H. Rizvi

First Edition 2008

Published by :

G.S. Rawat for **Cyber Tech Publications**
4264/3, Ansari Road, Daryaganj, New Delhi-110002 (India)
Ph.: 011-23244078. Fax: 011-23280028
E-Mail: cyberpublicationsdelhi@yahoo.com

Printed at : **Amit Enterprises**, Maujpur, Delhi, (9810878184)

Preface

In the past two decades, the tourism industry has experienced unprecedented growth. Increasing consumer demand for educational and participatory travel experiences has resulted in a variety of specialty niche markets such as nature-based tourism, cultural-heritage tourism, and agritourism. Today, more and more communities seek to link strategic tourism planning with sustainable development. This book is designed to provide organizations and individuals with a development process and training materials to help communities plan, initiate, and expand tourism as a means of long-term economic development. The development concepts are applicable to communities of all sizes and at various stages of tourism development.

This book is intended to help communities expand their economic development potential by developing their travel and tourism industry. It is designed for community groups working on tourism development and for others interested in expanding their knowledge and skills in Tourism.

This book provides knowledge and tools to help your community develop or improve its tourism efforts. Ideally, a community will work through the process as laid out in the manual-taking the time and effort to develop a comprehensive community tourism plan and implementation strategy. However, because communities are in different stages of tourism development and have differing needs; the materials are laid out so that chapters and can be used when and as needed.

—*Author*

Contents

1

Tourism: An Introduction

Tourism is the act of travel for predominantly recreational or leisure purposes, and also refers to the provision of services in support of this act. According to the World Tourism Organization, tourists are people who "travel to and stay in places outside their usual environment for not more than one consecutive year for leisure, business and other purposes not related to the exercise of an activity remunerated from within the place visited".

Tourism, however long its incident duration, has become an extremely popular, global activity. In 2004, there were over 763 million international tourist arrivals.

As a service industry, tourism has numerous tangible and intangible elements. Major tangible elements include transportation, accommodation, and other components of a hospitality industry. Major intangible elements relate to the purpose or motivation for becoming a tourist, such as rest, relaxation, the opportunity to meet new people and experience other cultures, or simply to do something different and have an adventure.

Tourism is vital for many countries, due to the income generated by the consumption of goods and services by tourists, the taxes levied on businesses in the tourism industry, and the opportunity for employment and economic advancement by working in the industry. For these reasons NGOs and government agencies may sometimes promote a specific region as a tourist destination, and support the development of a tourism industry in that area. The contemporary phenomenon of mass tourism may sometimes result in overdevelopment, however alternative forms of tourism such as ecotourism seek to avoid such outcomes by pursuing tourism in a sustainable way.

The terms tourism and travel are sometimes used interchangeably. In this context travel has a similar definition to tourism, but implies a more purposeful journey. The terms tourism and tourist are sometimes used pejoratively to imply a shallow interest in the cultures or locations visited by tourists.

DEFINITION, CLASSIFICATION AND PREREQUISITES

General Definition

One of the earliest definitions of tourism was provided by the Austrian economist Hermann Von Schullard in 1910, who defined it as, "sum total of operators, mainly of an economic nature, which directly relate to the entry, stay and movement of foreigners inside and outside a certain country, city or a region."

Hunziker and Krapf, in 1941, defined tourism as "the sum of the phenomena and relationships arising from the travel and stay of non-residents, in so far as they do not lead to permanent residence and are not connected with any earning activity."

In 1976 Tourism Society of England defined it as "Tourism is the temporary, short-term movement of people to destination outside the places where they normally live and work and their activities during the stay at each destination. It includes movements for all purposes."

In 1981 International Association of Scientific Experts in Tourism defined Tourism in terms of particular activities selected by choice and undertaken outside the home environment.

United Nations Definition

United Nations classified 3 forms of tourism in 1994 in its Recommendations on Tourism Statistics as follows:

1. Domestic tourism, involving residents of the given country traveling only within this country;
2. Inbound tourism, involving non-residents traveling in the given country;
3. Outbound tourism, involving residents traveling in another country.

UN also derived different categories of tourism by combining the 3 basic forms of tourism:

1. Internal tourism, which comprises domestic tourism and inbound tourism;
2. National tourism, which comprises domestic tourism and outbound tourism;
3. International tourism, which consists of inbound tourism and outbound tourism.

New Definition

Intrabound tourism is a new academic terminology coined by the Korea tourism organization and widely accepted in Korea. Intrabound tourism differs from 'domestic tourism' in that the former is more dynamic and comprehensive, encompassing policy-making and implementation of national tourism policies in consideration of the tourism ecosystem consisting of inbound, outbound and intrabound tourism.

Entering into 21st century, the tourism industry has undergone a paradigm shift form the promotion of inbound tourism to the promotion of intrabound tourism since many countries are experiencing a tough competition for inbound tourists. Also realizing that it is impossible to advance the inbound tourism in the absence of active intrabound tourism, national policy makers have shifted their policy priority onto the promotion of intrabound tourism such as the promotion of local tourism to contribute to the local economy.

Examples of such policies are "See America," "Getting Going Canada," and "See Korea Campaign". Taking a Korean case as an example, Korea Tourism Organization has recently launched a nation-wide campaign to promote introbound tourism, named "Guseok Guseok, literally meaning corner to corner..

PREREQUISITES OF TOURISM

Before people are able to experience tourism they usually need at least:

1. disposable income, i.e. money to spend on non-essentials
2. leisure time
3. tourism infrastructure, such as transport and accommodation

Individually, sufficient health is also a condition, and of course the inclination to travel. Furthermore, in some countries there are legal restrictions on travelling, especially abroad. Certain states with strong governmental control over the lives of citizens (notably established Communist states) may restrict foreign travel only to trustworthy citizens. The United States prohibits its citizens from traveling to some countries, for example, Cuba.

HISTORY

Wealthy people have always travelled to distant parts of the world to see great buildings or other works of art, to learn new languages, to experience new cultures, or to taste new cuisine. As long ago as the time of the Roman Republic places such as Baiae were popular coastal resorts for the rich.

The terms tourist and tourism were first used as official terms in 1937 by the League of Nations. Tourism was defined as people travelling abroad for periods of over 24 hours.

TYPES OF TOURISM

Health Tourism and Leisure Travel

The history of European tourism can perhaps be said to originate with the medieval pilgrimage. Although undertaken primarily for religious reasons, the pilgrims in the Canterbury Tales quite clearly saw the experience as a kind of holiday (the term itself being derived from the 'holy day' and its associated leisure activities). Pilgrimages created a variety of tourist aspects that still exist-bringing back souvenirs, obtaining credit with foreign banks (in medieval times utilising international networks established by Jews and Lombards), and making use of space available on existing forms of transport (such as the use of medieval English wine ships bound for Vigo by pilgrims to Santiago De Compostela). Pilgrimages are still important in modern tourism-such as to Lourdes or Knock in Ireland. But there are modern equivalents-Graceland and the grave of Jim Morrison in Père Lachaise Cemetery.

During the seventeenth century, it became fashionable in England to undertake a Grand Tour. The sons of the nobility and gentry were sent upon an extended tour of Europe as an educational experience. The eighteenth century was the golden age of the Grand Tour, and many of the fashionable visitors were painted at Rome by Pompeo Batoni. A modern equivalent of the Grand Tour is the phenomenon of the backpacker, although cultural holidays, such as those offered by Swann-Hellenic, are also important.

Health tourism has always existed, but it was not until the eighteenth century that it became important. In England, it was associated with spas, places with supposedly health-giving mineral waters, treating diseases from gout to liver disorders and bronchitis. Bath was the most fashionable resort, but Buxton, Harrogate, and Tunbridge Wells, amongst others, also flourished. Of course, people visited these places for the balls and other entertainments, just as much as 'the waters'. Continental Spas such as Karlsbad attracted many fashionable travellers by the nineteenth century.

It could be argued that Britain was the home of the seaside holiday. In travelling to the coast, the population was following in the steps of Royalty. King George III made regular visits to Weymouth when in poor health. At the time, a number of doctors argued the benefits of bathing in sea water, and sea bathing as a widespread practice was popularised by the Prince Regent (later George IV), who frequented Brighton for this purpose.

Leisure travel was associated with the industrialization of United Kingdom-the first European country to promote leisure time to the increasing industrial population. Initially, this applied to the owners of the machinery of production, the economic oligarchy, the factory owners, and the traders. These comprised the new middle class. Cox & Kings were the first official travel company to be formed in 1758. Later, the working class could take advantage of leisure time.

The British origin of this new industry is reflected in many place names. At Nice, one of the first and best-established holiday resorts on the French Riviera, the long esplanade along the seafront is known to this day as the Promenade des Anglais; in many other historic resorts in continental Europe, old well-established palace hotels have names like the Hotel Bristol, the Hotel Carlton or the Hotel Majestic-reflecting the dominance of English customers.

Winter Tourism

Winter sports were largely invented by the British leisured classes, initially at the Swiss village of Zermatt (Valais), and St Moritz in 1864. The first packaged winter sports holidays took place in 1902 at Adelboden, Switzerland. Winter sports were a natural answer for a leisured class looking for amusement during the coldest season.

Organized sport was well established in Britain before it reached other countries. The vocabulary of sport bears witness to this: rugby, football, and boxing all originated in Britain, and even tennis, originally a French sport, was formalized and codified by the British, who hosted the first national championship in the nineteenth century, at Wimbledon.

The Fun Ski & Snow Festival, which has been organized annually by Korea tourism organization since 1998 and participated by about 10,000 tourists from Asia, is one of the most successful winter tourism products in Asia. The festival provides a variety of events such as ski and sled competitions, ski and snow board lessons, performances and recreational activities. Majority of the event participants are foreign visitors who come from countries with a warm climate that have no snow. The event offers them opportunities to enjoy winter and winter sports in Korea.

In addition, southern South American countries making up the Patagonia region in Chile and Argentina attract thousands of tourists every year. Skiing is extremely popular in the mountanous areas.

Mass Travel

Mass travel could only develop with two crucial features:

1. improvements in technology allowed the transport of large numbers of people in a short space of time to places of leisure interest, and
2. greater numbers of people began to enjoy the benefits of leisure time.

The pioneer of modern mass tourism was Thomas Cook who, on 5 July 1841, organized the first package tour in history. He arranged for the rail company to charge one shilling per person for a group of 570 temperance campaigners from Leicester to a rally in Loughborough, eleven miles away. Cook was paid a share of the fares actually charged to the passengers, as the railway tickets, being legal contracts between company and passenger, could not have been issued at his own price. There had been railway excursions before, but this one included entrance to an entertainment held in private grounds, rail tickets and food for the train journey. Cook immediately saw the potential of a convenient 'off the peg' holiday product in which everything was included in one cost. He organised packages inclusive of accommodation for the Great Exhibition, and afterwards pioneered package holidays in both Britain (particularly in Scotland) and on the European continent (where Paris and the Alps were the most popular destinations).

He was soon followed by others (the Polytechnic Touring Association, Dean and Dawson etc.), with the result that the tourist industry developed rapidly in late Victorian Britain. Initially it was supported by the growing middle classes, who had time off from their work, and who could afford the luxury of travel and possibly even staying for periods of time in boarding houses.

The Bank Holidays Act 1871 introduced a statutory right for workers to take holidays, even if they were not paid at the time. By the last quarter of the nineteenth century, the tradition of the working class holiday had become firmly established in Britain. These were largely focussed upon the seaside resorts.

The spread of the railway network in the nineteenth century resulted in the growth of Britain's seaside towns by bringing them within easy distance of Britain's urban centres. Blackpool was created by the construction of a line to Fleetwood, and some resorts were promoted by the railway companies themselves-Morecambe by the Midland Railway and Cleethorpes by the Great Central Railway. Other resorts included Scarborough in Yorkshire, servicing Leeds and Bradford; Weston-super-Mare in Somerset, catering for the inhabitants of Bristol; and Skegness, patronised by the residents of the industrial East Midlands. The cockneys of London flocked to Southend-on-Sea, mainly by Thames Steamer, and the South Coast resorts such as Broadstairs, Brighton, and Eastbourne were only a train ride away, with others further afield such as Bournemouth, Bognor Regis and Weymouth.

For a century, domestic tourism was the norm, with foreign travel being reserved for the rich or the culturally curious. A number of inland destinations, such as the English Lake District, and Snowdonia appealed to those who liked the countryside and fine scenery. The holiday camp began to appear in the 1930s, but this phenomenon really expanded in the post-war period. Butlins and Pontins set this trend, but their popularity waned with the rise of overseas package tours and the increasing comforts to which visitors became accustomed at home. Towards the end of the 20th century this market has been revived by the upmarket inland resorts of Dutch company Center Parcs.

Cox & Co, the forebear of Cox & Kings were in existence from 1758 largely entwined with the travel arrangements for the British Army serving around the Empire. While acting as 'agents' for various regiments, they organised the payment, provision, clothing and travel arrangements for members of the armed forces. In the 19th century their network of offices contained a banking and also travel department. The company became heavily involved with affairs in India and its Shipping Agency had offices in France and the Middle East.

Other phenomena that helped develop the travel industry were paid holidays:

- 1.5 million manual workers in Britain had paid holidays by 1925
- 11 million by 1939 (30% of the population in families with paid holidays)

INTERNATIONAL MASS TOURISM

Increasing speed on railways meant that the tourist industry could develop internationally.

To this may be added the development of sea travel. By 1901, the number of people crossing the English Channel from England to France or Belgium had passed 0.5 million per year. Shipping companies were anxious to fill cabin space that was under utilised. For example, P&O found that the majority of their passengers for India and the Far East joined the ship at Marseilles. Consequently, they marketed holidays based upon sea trips from London to Lisbon and Gibraltar. Other companies diverted their older ships to operate cruises in the summer months.

However, the real age of international mass travel began with the growth of air travel after World War Two. In the immediate post-war period, there was a surplus of transport aircraft, such as the popular and reliable Douglas Dakota, and a number of ex military pilots ready to fly them. They were available for charter flights, and tour operators began to use them for European destinations, such as Paris and Ostend.

Vladimir Raitz pioneered modern package tourism when on 20 May 1950 his recently founded company, Horizon, provided arrangements for a two-week holiday in Corsica. For an all inclusive price of £32.10s.-, holiday makers could sleep under canvas, sample local wines and eat a meal containing meat twice a day-this was especially attractive due to the continuing austerity measures in post-war United Kingdom. Within ten years, his company had started mass tourism to Palma (1952), Lourdes (1953), Costa Brava (1954), Sardinia (1954), Minorca (1955), Porto (1956), Costa Blanca (1957) and Costa del Sol (1959).

However it was with cheap air travel in combination with the package tour that international mass tourism developed. The postwar introduction of an international system of airline regulation was another important factor. The bilateral agreements at the heart of the system fixed seat prices, and airlines could not fill blocks of empty seats on underused flights by discounting. But if they were purchased by a tour operator and hidden within the price of an inclusive holiday package, it would be difficult to prove that discounting had taken place-even though it was obvious that it had! This was the origin of the modern mass package tour.

These developments coincided with a significant increase in the standard of living in Britain. At the end of the 1950s, Harold Macmillan could say "you've never had it so good."

Another significant development also happened at the end of this decade. The devaluation of the Spanish peseta made Spain appear a particularly attractive destination. The cheapness of the cost of living attracted increasing numbers of visitors. Mass package tourism has at times been an exploitative process, in which tour operators in a country with a high standard of living make use of development opportunities and low operating costs in a country with a lower standard of living. However, as witness the development of many tourist areas in previously poor parts of the world, and the concomitant rise in standards of living, when there is equality of bargaining power, both parties can gain economic benefits from this arrangement.

Spain and the Balearic Islands became major tourist destinations, and development probably peaked in the 1980s. At the same time, British tour operators developed the Algarve in Portugal. The continuing search for new, cheaper, destinations spread mass tourism to the Greek Islands, Italy, Tunisia, Morocco, parts of the coast of Turkey, and more recently Croatia.

For the worker living in greater London, Venice today is almost as accessible as Brighton was 100 years ago. Consequently, the British seaside resort experienced a marked decline from the 1970s onwards. Some, such as New Brighton, Merseyside have disappeared. Others have reinvented themselves, and now cater to daytrippers and the weekend break market.

RECENT DEVELOPMENTS

There has been a discernible upmarket trend in tourism over the last few decades, especially in Europe where international travel for short breaks is commonplace. Tourists have higher levels of disposable income and greater leisure time. They are also better educated and have more sophisticated tastes. There is now a demand for a better quality product in many quarters. This has resulted in the following trends:-

- The old 'sun, sea, and sand' mass market has fragmented. People want more specialised versions of it, such as 'Club 18-30', quieter resorts with select hotels, self-catering, etc.
- People are taking second holidays in the form of short breaks/city breaks, ranging from British and European cities to country hotels.
- There has been a growth in niche markets catering for special interests or activities, including growth of destination hotels.

The developments in technology and transport infrastructure (particularly the advent of jumbo jets) have placed some types of holiday in the affordable mainstream:-

- The development of a mass cruise holiday market.
- The advent of affordable holidays to long-haul destinations such as Thailand or Kenya.
- The phenomenon of the low budget airline, utilising a new generation of small regional airports.

There have also been changes in lifestyle, which may call into question the current definitions of tourism. Some people (particularly the 45+ and retired) may be adopting a tourism lifestyle, living as a tourist all the year round-eating out several times a week, going to the theatre, daytripping, and indulging in short breaks several times a year.

Much of this results in impulse purchasing. This is facilitated by internet purchasing of tourism products. Some sites have now started to offer dynamic packaging, in which an inclusive price is quoted for a tailor-made package requested by the customer upon impulse.

There have been a few setbacks in tourism, such as the September 11, 2001 attacks and terrorist threats to tourist destinations such as Bali and European cities. Some of the tourist destinations, including the Costa del Sol, the Baleares and Cancún have lost popularity due to shifting tastes. In this context, the excessive building and environmental destruction often associated with traditional "sun and beach" tourism may contribute to a destination's saturation and subsequent decline. This appears to be the case with Spain's Costa Brava, a byword for this kind of tourism in the 1960s and 1970s. With only 11% of the Costa Brava now unblemished by low-quality development (Greenpeace Spain's figure), the destination now faces a crisis in its tourist industry. Sustainable tourism is becoming more popular as people start to realize the devastating effects tourism can have on communities.

Receptive tourism is now growing at a very rapid rate in many developing countries, where it is often the most important economic activity in local GDP.

In recent years, second holidays or vacations have become more popular as people's discretionary income increases. Typical combinations are a package to the typical mass tourist resort, with a winter skiing holiday or weekend break to a city or national park.

On December 26, 2004 a tsunami, caused by the 2004 Indian Ocean earthquake hit Asian countries bordering the Indian Ocean, and also the Maldives. Tens of thousands of lives were lost, and many tourists died. This, together with the vast clean-up operation in place, has stopped or severely hampered tourism to the area.

SPECIAL FORMS OF TOURISM

For the past few decades other forms of tourism, also known as niche tourism, have been becoming more popular, particularly:

- Adventure tourism: tourism involving travel in rugged regions, or adventurous sports such as mountaineering and hiking (tramping).
- Agritourism: farm based tourism, helping to support the local agricultural economy.
- Ancestry tourism: (also known as genealogy tourism) is the travel with the aim of tracing one's ancestry, visiting the birth places of these ancestors and sometimes getting to know distant family.
- Armchair tourism and virtual tourism: not travelling physically, but exploring the world through internet, books, TV, etc.
- Audio tourism: includes audio walking tours and other audio guided forms of tourism including museum audio guides and audio travel books.
- Bookstore Tourism is a grassroots effort to support independent bookstores by promoting them as a travel destination.
- Creative Tourism is a new form of tourism that allows visitors to develop their creative potential, and get closer to local people, through informal participation in hands-on workshops that draw on the culture of their holiday destinations.
- Cultural tourism: includes urban tourism, visiting historical or interesting cities, and experiencing their cultural heritages. This type of tourism may also include specialized cultural experiences, such as art museum tourism where the tourist visits many art museums

during the tour, or opera tourism where the tourist sees many operas or concerts during the tour.

- Coastal Tourism involves tourist products located along Coastal Environments-due to the limited extent of coastal environments they often are amongst the first places to experience coastal tourist congestion for a region.
- Dark tourism: is the travel to sites associated with death and suffering. The first tourist agency to specialise in this kind of tourism started with trips to Lakehurst, New Jersey, the scene of the Hindenburg airship disaster.
- Disaster tourism: travelling to a disaster scene not primarily for helping, but because it is interesting to see. It can be a problem if it hinders rescue, relief and repair work.
- Drug tourism: travel to a country to obtain or consume drugs, either legally or illegally.
- Ecotourism: sustainable tourism which has minimal impact on the environment, such as safaris (Kenya), Rainforests (Belize) and hiking (Lapland), or national parks.
- Educational tourism: may involve travelling to an education institution, a wooded retreat or some other destination in order to take personal-interest classes, such as cooking classes with a famous chef or crafts classes.
- Extreme tourism: tourism associated with high risk.
- Free Independent Traveler: a sector of the market and philosophy of constructing a vacation by sourcing one's own components eg accommodation, transport.
- Gambling tourism, e.g. to Atlantic City, Las Vegas, Palm Springs, California, Macau or Monte Carlo for the purpose of gambling at the casinos there.
- Garden tourism visiting botanical gardens famous places in the history of gardening, such as Versailles and the Taj Mahal.

- Heritage tourism: visiting historical (Rome, Athens, Cracow) or industrial sites, such as old canals, railways, battlegrounds, etc.
- Health tourism: usually to escape from cities or relieve stress, perhaps for some 'fun in the sun', etc. Often to Sanatoriums or "health spas".
- Hobby tourism: tourism alone or with groups to participate in hobby interests, to meet others with similar interests, or to experience something pertinent to the hobby. Examples might be garden tours, amateur radio DX-peditions, or square dance cruises.
- Inclusive tourism: tourism marketed to those with functional limits or disabilities. Referred to as "Tourism for All" in some regions. Destinations often employ Universal Design and Universal Destination Development principles.
- Mass Tourism is an ecotourism policy to minimise the footprint of tourists by concentrating them into a small area. Mass tourism also maximises the ultisation of tourist infrastructure.
- Medical tourism, e.g.:
  * for what is illegal in one's own country, such as abortion or euthanasia
  * for advanced care that is not available in one's own country
  * in the case that there are long waiting lists in one's own country
  * for use of free or cheap health care organisations
- Mystical tourism: Tourism for people that believe feel energy and travel to places to meditate, yoga, special events, ceremonies, mystical rituals.
- Pop-culture tourism: tourism by those that visit a particular location after reading about it or seeing it in a film.

- Perpetual tourism: individuals always on vacation; some of them, for tax purposes, to avoid being resident in any country.
- Pilgrimage Tourism: pilgrimages to ancient holy places (Rome and Santiago de Compostela for Catholics, temples and stupas of Nepal for the Hindus and Buddhist, Mount Athos or Painted churches of northern Moldavia for the Orthodox), religious sites such as mosques, shrines, etc.
- Sex tourism: travelling solely for the purpose of sexual activity, usually with prostitutes
- Shopping tourism promoting shopping festivals as tourist drawcards such as the Dubai, Singapore, Hong Kong and the Gold Coast.
- Solo Travel: travelling alone
- Sport travel: skiing, golf and scuba diving are popular ways to spend a vacation. This could also include travelling to a major international sporting event such as the FIFA World Cup or following a tour such as the Ashes or British and Irish Lions.
- Space tourism: traveling in outer space or on spaceships.
- Vacilando is a special kind of wanderer for whom the process of travelling is more important than the destination.
- Wine tourism, the visiting of growing regions, vineyards, wineries, tasting rooms, wine festivals, and similar places or events for the purpose of consuming or purchasing wine.

TRENDS

The World Tourism Organization (UNWTO) forecasts that international tourism will continue growing at the average annual rate of 4 %. By 2020 Europe will remain the most popular destination, but its share will drop from 60 % in 1995 to 46 %. Long-haul will grow slightly faster than intraregional travel and by 2020 its share will increase from 18 % in 1995 to 24 %.

With the advent of e-commerce, tourism products have become one of the most traded items on the internet. Tourism products and services have been made available through intermediaries, although tourism providers (hotels, airlines, etc.) can sell their services directly. This has put pressure on intermediaries from both on-line and traditional shops.

Space tourism is expected to "take off" in the first quarter of the 21st century, although compared with traditional destinations the number of tourists in orbit will remain low until technologies such as a space elevator make space travel cheap.

Technological improvement is likely to make possible air-ship hotels, based either on solar-powered airplanes or large dirigibles. Underwater hotels, such as Hydropolis, expected to open in Dubai in 2006, will be built. On the ocean tourists will be welcomed by ever larger cruise ships and perhaps floating cities.

Some futurists expect that movable hotel "pods" will be created that could be temporarily erected anywhere on the planet, where building a permanent resort would be unacceptable politically, economically or environmentally.

2

BACKPACKING TRAVEL

INTRODUCTION

The term backpacking is said to have originated in the early 1970s with the advent of low-cost jet airplane fares. During this era it became common for young Westerners, to follow the hippie trail into India and Southeast Asia. This period also gave birth to the first budget guidebooks (see Tony and Maureen Wheeler) and began to change the way that many people looked at the possibilities and opportunities of travel.

More recently, backpacking has become something of a rite of passage in the popular culture of some countries, most notably Australia, Israel and New Zealand where after finishing high school, university or a period in the army they take several months to two year's break in Europe (some of whom work in this region), Asia or the Americas. This can be put down to the light population and geographic isolation of these two countries from much of the world's population and history, the fact that Australia and New Zealand are both affluent English-speaking countries where the majority of their citizens can afford overseas travel, and that both countries have a tradition of students attending university in the home city rather than moving away for college. A substantial amount of young adults from Israel also undertake long-term backpacking trips, particularly after they finish their mandatory military service. Travel of a backpacking nature is also extremely popular with Northern Europeans, particularly the Dutch and British and with small sections of North Americans and Japaneses.

CULTURE

Low-cost options are popular: such as sharing lifts, budget flights, rail/bus passes (or if the backpacking trip is circumglobal, a relatively cheap round-the-world air ticket which permits numerous stops), youth hostels, free hospitality services and buying food at local stores abroad instead of going to restaurants.

Hostels and other budget accommodations in the 'developed' world tend to be communal to some degree, and thus backpacker culture is often highly social and emphasizes the camaraderie of communal life, such as the shared kitchens common in many hostels. When backpackers stay in one place for a while, they often seek a house-share with numerous other backpackers and are likely to share a room to keep the costs down. In the 'developing' world accommodation is normally found in cheap hotels, pensions or guesthouses.

The common language of backpackers is overwhelmingly English in varying levels of fluency while German is arguably the second most common language encountered due to the large presence of backpackers from Germany or Switzerland. (However, German-speakers will usually only speak German informally amongst one another, and will otherwise speak English in most other situations). Britons, Australians, Canadians and Germans typically form among the most common backpacker nationalities in the world, in addition to Israelis, Americans, New Zealanders and numerous other Western European nations such as Switzerland or The Netherlands. Backpackers from Spain are very common in Latin America, where there is little or no language barriers and the cost of travel and living expenses is often very favorable for the Spanish. The same is true of French in West Africa. Per head of population, Australia is thought to have the highest representation of backpackers, although there is no data available to demonstrate this empirically.

Backpacker culture is perhaps typified by the Lonely Planet (Australian) series of guidebooks, which caters to budget travelers both in its regular guides as well as, more specifically, the "On a Shoestring" regional compilations. The Rough Guide

(UK) and Let's Go (USA) series of guidebooks are also popular. In France, the traditional backpacker's guidebook is the Guide du routard.

Traditionally, backpackers do not travel with expensive electronic equipment such as laptop computers and PDAs due to concerns about theft, damage, and additional luggage weight. However, the desire to stay connected coupled with trends in lightweight electronics have given rise to the flashpacking trend.

Some backpackers take a high resolution digital camera and/or high capacity MP3 Player with them on their travels. Blogging from various Internet cafes around the world is also a growing phenomenon, offering a more convenient way to relay information to interested friends and family at home.

AGE OF BACKPACKERS

Backpackers can be of any age to theoretically be part of the backpacker scene and subculture; however, the vast majority of budget travelers are clearly in their 20s. Patrons at most youth hostels are rarely under 18 (some even mandate a minimum age of 18) while guests over 30 constitute a minority. The 'stereotypical' backpacker is often envisioned as a senior college student or recent college graduate about 20 to 25 years of age with no dependents (spouse, children, etc.), therefore making it relatively easy to put typical daily responsibilities on temporary hiatus to go traveling for up to many months at a time. Depending on the part of the world people backpack through, the median age can vary slightly.

Philosophy

Rolf Potts writes in his book Vagabonding about what he sees as the myths that surround conventional travel: Of all the outrageous throwaway lines one hears in movies, there is one that stands out for me. It doesn't come from a madcap comedy, an esoteric science-fiction flick, or a special-effects-laden action thriller. It comes from Oliver Stone's Wall Street, when the Charlie Sheen character-a promising big shot in the stock market-is telling his girlfriend about his dreams.

"I think if I can make a bundle of cash before I'm thirty and get out of this racket," he says, "I'll be able to ride my motorcycle across China."

When I first saw this scene on video a few years ago, I nearly fell out of my seat in astonishment. After all, Charlie Sheen or anyone else could work for eight months as a toilet cleaner and have enough money to ride a motorcycle across China. Even if they didn't yet have their own motorcycle, another couple months of scrubbing toilets would earn them enough to buy one when they got to China.

For many, this sums up the allure of backpacking, promising an "exotic" or "adventurous" experience that is also deemed "authentic," that is, an experience that, because it is self-planned and directed, does not fit within the typical Western-style vacation or travel industry.

This desire to experience "authentic" travel may be a reaction to the commercialization of the travel industry. Many backpackers express disdain towards "packaged" travel experiences including cruise ships and guided or bus tours which typically consist of a large number of tourists led by a guide. In contrast, backpacker philosophy encourages self-reliance and individuality, like overcoming the language barrier without the help of a translator or making all of one's own travel arrangements (to present two examples). John Gregory sums up this philosophy as:

Those spending big bucks for guided travel get peace-of-mind in return. They are guaranteed no worries, no hassles, an experience as close as possible to being home, without being home. They get an hour and fifteen minutes for the guaranteed-open museum, then a two-hour sightseeing ride that catches all the picture-postcard highlights.

They break for lunch at a "recommended" restaurant, where the food is reasonable and ordering is easy. And as the next bus pulls in they re-board theirs to repeat the routine, ending with an easy check-in at a reasonable hotel, populated with plenty of other tourists, pretty much like themselves.

While all travel is good for the human spirit, budget backpacking is unparalleled for meeting people and experiencing worlds on their own intimate terms. There are many travelers who have the resources for pampered-class but choose to strap on a backpack and see the world via the seat-of-their-pants, because they know it's the best way to experience cultures and interact with local people

In the United States among many other Western countries, this backlash against the large-scale commercial travel industry as expressed in the philosophy of backpacking has made some inroads into mainstream culture, such as in the popular travel guide writer Rick Steves who, like Tony and Maureen Wheeler of Lonely Planet, spun his experiences as a backpacker in the 1970s into a successful guidebook series.

In addition to notions of authenticity, some backpackers value the sense of freedom and independence in this mode of travel. Especially on extended trips, there is often only a rough itinerary, which can be changed at will. If a backpacker does not like a place, she can move on. If she likes it, she is free to stay and kick back for a while. Travel directions may change when a backpacker meets other independent travelers and learns about destinations she had not considered before or joins up with new friends. The semblance of "gypsy" life has its own romantic allure.

Of course, while backpack travel is carefree in this respect, it is more complicated in that backpackers have to plan everything and deal with all adversities themselves. There is no cruise director taking care of them. However, some backpackers also view this as a positive: It is a challenge and adventure, and the sometimes intense problem-solving in unfamiliar surroundings helps to hone their life skills.

WORKING ON THE ROAD

Many backpackers gain temporary work (usually low-paid, unskilled, casual, and sometimes in violation of local labor laws) in the countries they visit. For instance, London's pubs are well known for the number of Australian bartenders working in them; "Irish pubs" around the world hire Irish backpackers. In Australia, fruit picking is a popular job among backpackers, although it can be physically demanding. Although while staying in one place for a long duration, say while working and living in semi-permanent accommodation it could be questioned whether you are still backpacking in the form of the adjective.

Backpackers are also commonly employed by hostels, where English-language proficiency and familiarity with hostel operations are considered assets. Hostels around the world are increasing their revenue by inaugurating work and travel programs, where hostelers can work for accommodation by performing basic hostel upkeep and operational duties.

CRITICISM

Backpacker philosophy is sometimes criticized for being hypocritical. Some travelers have been known to forego finding "authentic" contact with a culture, and instead congregate only with other travelers in international hostels or guesthouses.

In addition, backpackers are sometimes blamed for the commercialization of the destinations they travel to. By definition, any "undiscovered paradise" cannot remain pristine under the demand of thousands of visitors. This can often lead to the overuse of certain natural and cultural resources, a vice backpacking shares with other forms of tourism. A notable example of this phenomenon is Byron Bay in Australia, which was a largely quiet backpacker town in the 1970s and is now considered one of the most popular destinations in the 2000s with a bias for yuppies. This is sometimes said to actually pervert the backpacking culture itself: while backpackers seek genuineness and "authentic" cultural interactions, thus often looking for places with as few other foreigners as possible, they very often tend to meet in so-called "backpacker paradises"- places where all backpackers meet and that, eventually, end-up being modern-day "hippie-resorts". Examples include San Pedro de Atacama, a formerly isolated village in Chile and now a town dependent on tourism. This phenomenon is perhaps not unlike the phenomenon of gentrification that happens in urban ecologies.

A third layer of criticism is economic. Backpackers' pursuit of "cheap" travel destinations is only possible through the imbalance of living costs between Western and developing nations. Thus, backpacking can be seen as an inherently exploitative activity that benefits from the poverty of destination countries. Bolivia and Cambodia are notable examples of very inexpensive countries which backpackers visit and have the ability to stay comfortably for months even on a relatively small budget, all the while contributing little to the local have-nots. A more recent example includes the collapse of the peso currency in Argentina in the early 2000s, which quickly made that country a very attractive destination for budget backpackers. However, backpackers, involved as they are in an inherently pragmatic project, rarely give this concern any more thought than it deserves.

The idea that the passing of money from the more affluent to the less affluent is "exploitative" is not as compelling as it may have been in decades past. A more plausible economic criticism, from the point of view of the local economy, is that backpackers do not spend as much money as packaged or luxury tourists.

ADVANTAGES

In their defense, some backpackers say that budget travel pumps money into the economies of Third World countries, increasing their standard of living and creating jobs, and doing this in a way that is inherently more egalitarian than mainstream tour companies, who often operate with minimal contact with third party vendors or average citizens. Backpacking in comparison, frequently makes use of local food vendors, merchants and accommodations, and thus does more to benefit the local economy. The lower cost to the budget-conscious young Western tourist and the increased patronage to local merchants actually makes the economics of backpacking a win-win situation in many cases.

Backpackers are accused of traveling to exotic places only to associate with other backpackers. That perception is probably correct but requires some explanation. Generally backpackers are from developed countries, speak fluent English (even if from a non-English speaking country). When these backpackers arrive in developing countries they congregate at the hostels and guesthouses in the center of town where they tend to not blend in. In these areas the best English speakers among the locals tend to be touts who will prey upon the backpackers to visit the factories that they "own", to buy jewels to smuggle back and resell in their home countries, to purchase their services as a "guide" and to undertake illegal activities such as gambling, prostitution and drug use.

Most backpackers would like to interact with locals, but have a hard time fending off the touts, as bargaining and negotiating hassle are key factors of backpacking in parts of the world. Locals with the intent of approaching a backpacker are generally not as aggressive as the touts. Backpackers would consider it obtrusive to approach a local in English and ask to join the local in their home for dinner for instance. The inability to travel beyond the areas covered by public transportation further strain the situation.

'DEVELOPED' AND 'DEVELOPING' WORLD DESTINATIONS

It is worth noting that there is a notable difference between backpacking travel in the developed world, typically Australia, New Zealand, North America and Europe where hostel are commonly used, than in the developing world, typically South and South-East Asia, Africa and Latin America. In such developing nations travel is cheaper, but often harder. Equally where backpacking is popular, whole industries have established to tend to the needs of backpackers offering services to make their lives easier (laundry, visa applications, train tickets) and goods from 'home' countries not commonly available such as Falafel for Israelis, Marmite/vegemite for British/Australian. Plus bars/restaurants showing sporting events from 'back home' and bootleg copies of movies. Well know examples of such places would be the Khaosan Road in Bangkok, Anjuna in Goa and Antigua in Guatemala. In backpacker hot-spots, many bars and restaurants are set up primary for backpackers with few locals patronizing them-this again fosters the social aspect of backpacking travel.

Favourite

Classically, Western Europe is a very common backpacker destination because of the availability of public transport and the large number of hostels and other budget accommodations. However, since the fall of the Berlin Wall and the dissolution of the Soviet states, Eastern Europe has become a rapidly growing destination for budget travelers. Originally this meant cities such as Prague and Budapest, but more recently Croatia, Slovenia, the Balkans, and the Baltic Republics have become a popular stops on the backpacking circuit

Long-term backpacker destinations are places in the developing world with low costs of living such as Goa (India), Essaouira (Morocco), or Thailand. Australia's East Coast is also a very popular destination for many backpackers. Latin America is quickly becoming a hot-spot for backpackers, who are drawn to the continent by the often favorable exchange rates and unique culture and beauty. Machu Picchu, Patagonia, the Triple Frontier and the cities of Buenos Aires, Rio de Janeiro, La Paz and Cusco are often the highlights for travelers to this continent and see the most 'traffic'.

As mentioned above, certain destinations are so popular on the backpacking circuit that some cities house "backpacker ghettos," whole districts where large numbers of travellers congregate to find cheap accommodation, street food, and share travel information. The most famous of these is the Khaosan Road area of downtown Bangkok.

It is true to say that most backpacking follows established routes with terms such as the 'gringo trail' in Latin America and the 'Banana Pancake' or trail' in Southeast Asia used. These routes and popular countries generally focus on three factors. One reputation, what is the current hot destination? Two popular sights that everyone seems to want to see: Machu Picchu, the Sydney Opera House, Prague, etc. And finally round the world air travel routing and airline hubs. It is easy to argue that Thailand's huge popularity is in no small measure a result of (it's ease of travel and natural beauty aside) the fact it is an obvious stop-off between Europe and Australia. Consider the Philippines which has no overland connections, is not a major stop-off and holds similar attributes to Thailand is far less popular. The same is true of Eastern Europe's and Central America's proximity to affluent Western Europe and North America. Africa and notably, West Africa see relativity few backpackers since including them in a round-the-world ticket is difficult and expensive.

Avoided

While largely a matter of nationality, personal taste and the current political situation, some generalizations can be made about the destinations many backpackers avoid. For example, a fair number of backpackers, like many other tourists, avoid countries where there is a perceived danger of terrorism, food poisoning or hassle in the way of getting a visa or repeatedly being accosted to purchase goods/services. Some countries, wising up to what's good for their travel economy, have tried to address these issues. Morocco, which at some point had one of the worst reputations in this regard, is reported to have clamped down on hustling and touting aimed at foreign travelers. In Asia and Eastern Europe visa regulations are being greatly relaxed encourage more travelers. In Egypt, Turkey and Pakistan huge efforts are made to safe-guard travelers from terrorism and countries such as Syria and Iran, while holding terrible reputations abroad are welcoming of backpackers (once issued with a visa).

High Costs

Regions with a high cost of living, such as Scandinavia for example, are avoided by many long-term backpackers because of the expense. Other destinations have high costs for transportation, such as Polynesia, and are also avoided by the majority of backpackers. This rule applies to a lesser degree to many destinations in Western Europe, where costs are generally high enough to discourage extensive (three months and longer) budget travel. Travel to popular but extremely expensive cities such as New York City or London is generally limited to just several days, and backpackers tend to try and fit as much daily sight-seeing as possible in such locations.

Infrastructure

While not an absolute, countries without developed infrastructure, especially in the form of public transportation, are more difficult for backpackers to travel in because of the serious limits on mobility. This includes many African countries and the greater part of Central Asia.

Some travellers also avoid the United States of America for similar reasons, because of the general lack of public transport, the expense of renting a car and the lack of hostels in many destinations, which are largely relegated only to the most major cities, the California Coast, parts of New England, and parts of Florida. Hostels in the United States are also generally expensive in comparison to many other countries, often between $US20-30 per night.

This has given the United States a reputation for being relatively 'unfriendly' towards backpacking culture even though it is a highly desirable, varied, and generally safe country to be explored for foreign backpackers. The prevalence of motel chains, catering primarily to private motorists, may contribute to the relatively small number of backpacker hostels in the USA. These same problems are also present to an extent in parts of Canada, where the centrally-located provinces generally have few options for backpackers.

People who wish to travel the United States extensively and as cheaply as possible often decide to purchase an economical van with improvised bedding within the vehicle. Even this option is becoming increasingly expensive however, as oil prices in the 2000s remain stubbornly high. This lifestyle also may discourage many solo backpackers, as they must pay many bills entirely by themselves and establish few social connections.

Instability

While the desire to travel at low cost and the desire to travel with convenience and security are often at odds, some countries are generally avoided by backpackers because of the general political instability. In the most extreme cases, such as Iraq, Somalia or North Korea opportunities for travel may be severely curtailed or an outright impossibility. Other areas are avoided by many backpackers because of the perceived general hostility of the political climate, including some parts of the Middle East and Central Asia, Myanmar and parts of Central Africa.

These are generalizations made by the majority of the community and are disputed by many others (Myanmar being a recent example of debate), especially travelers drawn to "dangerous" destinations.

Crime, Dangers and Victimization

Some countries are largely avoided by backpackers due to a substantially increased risk of being kidnapped or mugged of their possessions, to the point where the benefits of travel may not compensate for their dangers. Colombia in South America is a notable example, which has the unfortunate reputation of having one of the highest number of kidnappings per capita in the world. Many other South American cities, such as Rio de Janeiro, São Paulo and Lima, also have high crime rates. Moreover, African cities such as Johannesburg or Nairobi are also discouraged on the backpacker circuit due to their high crime rates and perceived danger of visiting.

Generally a backpacker will keep his main funds and important documents in the hostel or guesthouse room or safe to minimize damage if robbed or lost during the day. Backpackers are thus most vulnerable when traveling between locations when they are carrying all their belongings and items most often go missing on public transport or at bus/train stations. Traveling by day will always minimize this risk as does being careful and/or in a group. It seems backpackers universally trust other backpackers based on the logic that someone wouldn't come all the way from [Stockholm, Berlin, Sydney, etc.] just to steal from other tourists (Although the wisdom of this logic is drawn into question due to the desperate financial woes often encountered by poorly planned backpackers). On the whole dangers while backpacking, when put in perspective and if using common sense are not overly great (certainly lower than that of the dangers of road traffic accidents, in many parts of the world), but unfortunately some travelers are either over confident, don't exercise common sense or (the minority) unlucky and fall victim to some annoyance.

Health is another issue of concern for backpackers with sometimes poor health facilities away from urban hubs and prevalence of diseases such as in some regions, malaria. More common, however are minor ailments like sun burn, diarrhea or food poisoning, which seems to be an unfortunate caveat of third world travel.

Crowds

Many backpackers try to avoid crowds of other (ordinary) tourists. The first rule is to avoid traditional package holiday destinations such as Benidorm or Cancún because it goes against the backpacker's image. Such places may also be undesirable because of high costs, inauthentic culture, limited sightseeing options and exclusively prebooked accommodation.

Language Barriers

While a matter of personal taste, willingness to learn foreign languages, and other stipulations, countries where the English language is not widely understood or holds little sway in everyday life can or cannot be seen as a hinderence for independent travel. This may include a significant part of Latin America, many parts of Africa, Central Asia, and more rural areas of East Asia. However, this can also be seen as challenging, so it can just as well draw many backpackers to these regions.

HOTEL

The 4-star Manor House Hotel at Castle Combe, Wiltshire, England. Built in the fourteenth century, the hotel has 48 rooms and 365 acres (1.5 km^2) of gardens. The Las Vegas Strip is lined with the world's largest hotels, most of which have a 4-or 5-star rating and over 2,000 rooms each.

A hotel is an establishment that provides paid lodging, usually on a short-term basis. Hotels often provide a number of additional guest services such as a restaurant, a swimming pool or childcare. Some hotels have conference services and meeting rooms and encourage groups to hold conventions and meetings at their location.

Hotels differ from motels in that most motels have drive-up, exterior entrances to the rooms, while hotels tend to have interior entrances to the rooms, which may increase guests' safety and present a more upmarket image.

In Australia, a hotel may also be an establishment that serves alcoholic drinks, and usually meals in a casual setting but which does not necessarily provide accommodation. This type of establishment would more usually be called a pub or bar in other countries. In general use in Australia the terms '"hotel" and pub are usually taken to be synonymous.

In India, the word may also refer to a restaurant since the best restaurants were always situated next to a good hotel.

Origins of the Term

The word hotel derives from the French hôtel, which referred to a French version of a townhouse, not a place offering accommodation (in contemporary usage, hôtel has the meaning of "hotel", and hôtel particulier is used for the old meaning). The French spelling (with the circumflex) was once also used in English, but is now rare. The circumflex replaces the 's' once preceding the 't' in the earlier hostel spelling, which over time received a new, but closely related meaning.

Services and Facilities

Basic accommodation of a room with only a bed, a cupboard, a small table and a washstand has largely been replaced by rooms with en-suite bathrooms and, more commonly in the United States than elsewhere, climate control. Other features found may be a telephone, an alarm clock, a TV, and broadband Internet connectivity. Food and drink may be supplied by a mini-bar (which often includes a small refrigerator) containing snacks and drinks (to be paid for on departure), and tea and coffee making facilities (cups, spoons, an electric kettle and sachets containing instant coffee, tea bags, sugar, and creamer or milk). In the United Kingdom a hotel is required by law to serve food and drinks to all comers within certain stated hours; to avoid this requirement it is not uncommon to come across "private hotels" which are not subject to this requirement.

However, in Japan the capsule hotel supplies minimal facilities and room space.

Classification

The cost and quality of hotels are usually indicative of the range and type of services available. Due to the enormous increase in tourism worldwide during the last decades of the 20th century, standards, especially those of smaller establishments, have improved considerably. For the sake of greater comparability, rating systems have been introduced, with the one to five stars classification being most common.

Boutique Hotels

"Boutique Hotel" is a term originating in North America to describe intimate, usually luxurious or quirky hotel environments. Boutique hotels differentiate themselves from larger chain or branded hotels by providing an exceptional and personalized level of accommodation, services and facilities.

Boutique hotels are furnished in a themed, stylish and/or aspirational manner. Although usually considerably smaller than a mainstream hotel (ranging from 3 to 100 guest rooms) boutique hotels are generally fitted with telephone and wi-fi Internet connections, honesty bars and often cable/pay TV. Guest services are attended to by 24 hour hotel staff. Many boutique hotels have on site dining facilities, and the majority offer bars and lounges which may also be open to the general public. Of the total travel market a small percentage are discerning travelers, who place a high importance on privacy, luxury and service delivery. As this market is typically corporate travelers, the market segment is non-seasonal, high-yielding and repeat, and therefore one which boutique hotel operators target as their primary source of income.

Famous Hotels

Some hotels have gained their renown through tradition, by hosting significant events or persons, such as Schloss Cecilienhof in Potsdam, Germany, which derives its fame from the so-called Potsdam Conference of the World War II allies Winston Churchill, Harry Truman and Joseph Stalin in 1945. Other establishments have given name to a particular meal or beverage, as is the case with the Waldorf Astoria in New York City, USA, known for its Waldorf Salad or the Raffles Hotel in Singapore, where the drink Singapore Sling was invented. Another example is the Hotel Sacher in Vienna Austria, home of the Sachertorte. There are also hotels which became much more popular through films like the Grand Hotel Europe in Saint Petersburg, Russia when James Bond stayed there in the Blockbuster, Goldeneye. Cannes hotels such as the Carlton or the Martinez become the center of the world during Cannes Film Festival (France).

A number of hotels have entered the public consciousness through popular culture, such as the Ritz Hotel in London, UK ('Putting on The Ritz') and Hotel Chelsea in New York City, subject of a number of songs and also the scene of the alleged stabbing of Nancy Spungen by her boyfriend Sid Vicious. Hotels that enter folklore like these two are also often frequented by celebrities, as is the case both with the Ritz and the Chelsea. Other famous hotels include the Beverly Hills Hotel, the Hotel Bel-Air and the Chateau Marmont, in California, Watergate complex in Washington DC, the Hotel Astoria in Saint Petersburg, Russia, the Hotel George V and Hôtel Ritz in Paris, Palazzo Versace hotel on the Gold Coast, Queensland, Australia, Hotel Hermitage and Hotel de Paris in Monaco (in the French Riviera), Peninsula Hotel in Hong Kong and Hotel Leningradskaya in Moscow.

Unusual Hotels

Many hotels can be considered destinations in themselves, by dint of unusual features of the lodging and/or its immediate environment:

Treehouse Hotels

Some hotels, such as the Costa Rica Tree House in the Gandoca-Manzanillo Wildlife Refuge, Costa Rica, or Treetops Hotel in Aberdare National Park, Kenya, are built with living trees as structural elements, making them treehouses.

The Ariau Towers near Manaus, Brazil is in the middle of the Amazon, on the Rio Negro. Bill Gates even invested and had a suite built there with satellite internet/phone.

Another hotel with treehouse units is Bayram's Tree Houses in Olympos, Turkey.

Cave Hotels

Desert Cave Hotel in Coober Pedy, South Australia and the Cuevas Pedro Antonio de Alarcón (named after the author) in Guadix, Spain, as well as several hotels in Cappadocia, Turkey, are notable for being built into natural cave formations, some with rooms underground.

Capsule Hotels

Capsule hotels are a type of economical hotels that are quite common in Japan.

Ice Hotels

Ice hotels, such as the Ice Hotel in Jukkasjärvi, Sweden, melt every spring and are rebuilt out of ice and snow each winter.

Snow Hotels

The Mammut Snow Hotel in Finland is located within the walls of the Kemi snow castle, which is the biggest in the world. It includes The Mammut Snow Hotel, The Castle Courtyard,

The Snow Restaurant and a chapel for weddings, etc. Its furnishings and its decorations, such as sculptures, are made of snow and ice.

There is snow accommodation also in Lainio Snow Hotel in Lapland (near Ylläs), Finland.

Garden Hotels

Garden hotels, famous for their gardens before they became hotels, includes Gravetye Manor, the home of William Robinson and Cliveden, designed by Charles Barry with a rose garden by Geoffrey Jellicoe.

Underwater Hotels

As of 2005, the only hotel with an underwater room that can be reached without Scuba diving is Utter Inn in Lake Mälaren, Sweden. It only has one room, however, and Jules' Undersea Lodge in Key Largo, Florida, which requires scuba diving, is not much bigger.

Hydropolis is an ambitious project to build a luxury hotel in Dubai, UAE, with 220 suites, all on the bottom of the Persian Gulf, 20 meters (66 feet) below the surface. Its architecture will feature two domes that break the surface and an underwater train tunnel, all made of transparent materials such as glass and acrylic.

Other unusual Hotels

The Library Hotel in New York City is unique in that its ten floors are arranged according to the Dewey Decimal System.

The Rogers Centre, formerly SkyDome, in Toronto, Canada is the only stadium to have a hotel connected to it, with 70 rooms overlooking the field.

The Burj al-Arab hotel in Dubai, United Arab Emirates, built on an artificial island, is structured in the shape of a sail of a boat.

The RMS Queen Mary in Long Beach, California is the only 1930s ocean liner still in existence. Its elegant first-class staterooms are now used as a hotel. The Oriental Pearl Tower in Shanghai houses an extremely expensive hotel with only 20 rooms.

World-record Setting Hotels

Tallest

The tallest hotel in the world is the Burj al-Arab in Dubai, United Arab Emirates, at 321 metres, which however will soon be surpassed by the nearby Rose Rotana Suites at 333 meters (1,091 feet). The Ryugyong Hotel in Pyongyang was intended to reach 330 meters (1,083 feet), but is unlikely to be completed; it has been under construction since 1987 and was abandoned in 1992. The highest hotel rooms are in the Grand Hyatt in the Jin Mao Building in Shanghai, the highest floor being at around 350 m.

Largest

The largest hotel in the world is the MGM Grand Las Vegas in Las Vegas, Nevada, USA with a total of 6,276 rooms as of December 20, 2006. On December 18, 2006 Guinness World Records listed the First World Hotel in Genting Highlands, Malaysia as the worlds largest hotel.

It has a total of 6,118 rooms and is part of the Genting Highlands Resort and Casino. The First World Plaza which is joined to the two hotel towers boasts 500,000 square feet of indoor theme park, shopping centres, casino gaming areas, and eateries. Previously, Guinness had listed the MGM Grand Las Vegas in Las Vegas, Nevada, USA with 5,005 rooms as the largest hotel in the world.

Oldest

According to the Guinness Book of World Records, the oldest hotel still in operation is the Hoshi Ryokan, in Awazu, Japan. It opened in 717, and features hot springs.

Hotel Occupations

The owner, chairman, or CEO of a hotel or hotel group is known as a hotelier.

Living in Hotels

The American billionaire Howard Hughes lived much of his life in hotels. He moved with his entourage from hotel to hotel and from Beverly Hills to Boston before deciding to move to Las Vegas and become a casino baron. Less than a month after his November 27, 1966 arrival, Hughes made a public offer to buy the Desert Inn. The hotel's 8th floor became the nerve center of his empire and the 9th floor penthouse became Hughes's personal residence. Hughes moved to the Bahamas, Vancouver, London and several other locations-always taking up residence in the top floor penthouse of the hotel. Between 1966 and 1968, he also purchased several other hotel-casinos from the Mafia: Castaways, New Frontier, The Landmark Hotel and Casino, Sands and Silver Slipper.

Coco Chanel made the Hôtel Ritz in Paris her home for more than thirty years, until the day of her death, at 87, in a suite now named "Coco Chanel Suite".

King Peter II of Yugoslavia spent much of the Second World War at Claridge's, a hotel in London. His son, Aleksandar Karadordevic, was born in the hotel. Prince Felix Yusupov lived in the Hotel Vendôme in Paris.

Alois Brunner, Austrian Nazi war criminal, is believed to have lived in the Meridian Hotel in Damascus, Syria, under the name Georg Fischer.

Sultan Said Bin Taimur of Muscat lived at Dorchester Hotel in London after he was deposed by Qaboos of Oman in 1970, He died in the hotel in 1972.

Eleftherios Venizelos, Greek statesman and diplomat, lived in the Hôtel Ritz Paris while he was in exile in France from 1935-1936.

Hotels in Fiction

Hotels have been chosen by authors as settings for crime fiction, farce and mystery works. A hotel is perfect as a mysterious, anonymous setting where various characters may gather. Hotels also feature in films, television series, songs and even theme park rides.

RESORT

A resort is a place used for relaxation or recreation, attracting visitors for holidays or vacations. Resorts are places, towns such as Newport, Rhode Island or St. Moritz, Switzerland, or larger regions, like the Adirondack Mountains or the Jersey Shore. A resort is not merely a commercial establishment operated by a single company, although in the late twentieth century this sort of faciltiy became more common. Such a self-contained resort attempts to provide for all or most of a vacationer's wants while remaining on the premises, such as food, drink, lodging, sports, entertainment, and shopping. The term "resort" sometimes is misused to identify a hotel that does not provide the other amenities required of a full resort. However, a hotel is frequently a central feature of a resort, such as the Grand Hotel at Mackinac Island, Michigan. Towns that contain resorts-or where tourism or vacationing is a major part of the local activity-are often called resort towns.

The Walt Disney World Resort is a prominent example of a modern, self-contained commercial resort. Resorts exist throughout the world, increasingly attracting visitors from around the globe. Thailand, for instance, has become a popular destination. Resorts are especially prevalent in Central America and the Caribbean.

Closely related to resorts are convention and large meeting sites. Generally these occur in cities where special meeting halls, together with ample accommodations as well as varied dining and entertainment are provided.

TYPES OF RESORTS

Resort at a Destination

A commercial establishment at a resort destinaton such as a recreational area, a scenic or historic site, a theme park, a gaming facility or other tourist attraction competes with other businesses at that destination.. Examples would be hotels in and around Disney World, resorts in St. Martin in the Caribbean, and establishments at Aspen, Colorado in the USA.

Destination Resort

A destination resort is a resort that contains, in and of itself, the necessary guest attraction capabilities-that is to say that a destination resort does not need to be near a destination (town, historic site, theme park, or other) to attract its public. Consequently, another characteristic of a destination resort is that is offers food, drink, lodging, sports, entertainment, and shopping within the facility so that guests have no need to leave the facility throughout their stay. Commonly these facilities are of higher quality than would be expected if one were to stay at a hotel or eat in a town's restaurants. Some examples are Atlantis in the Bahamas, Costa do Sauípe in the Northeastern Brazil, Laguna Phuket in Thailand and Sun City near Johannesburg in South Africa.

All-inclusive Resort

An all-inclusive resort is a resort that, besides providing all of the common amenities of a resort, charges a fixed price that includes most or all items. At a minimum, most inclusive resorts include lodging, unlimited food, drink, sports activities, and entertainment for the fixed price.

Historical Resorts

A famous resort of the ancient world was Baiae, Italy, popular over 2,000 years ago. Capri, an island near Naples, Italy, has attracted visitors since Roman times.

3

Tourism in India

INTRODUCTION

India is one of the popular tourist destinations in Asia. Bounded by the Himalayan ranges in the north, and surrounded on three sides by water (the Arabian Sea, Bay of Bengal, and the Indian Ocean), with a long history and diverse culture, India offers a wide array of places to see and things to do. In 2004, foreign tourists visiting India spent 15.4 billion USD-the ninth highest in the world. India is also ranked among the top 3 adventure tourism destinations.

In India there are a good number of tourist destinations to see. The tourists from all over the world come here to see the cultural diversity in unity. India is most popularly known for its this very virtue. Following are the few famous tourist destinations of the India:

TAJ MAHAL

Perhaps India's best-known site is the Taj Mahal, one of the world's greatest architectural achievements. It was built between 1631 and 1653 by Emperor Shah Jahan in honor of his wife, Arjumand Banu, more popularly known as Mumtaz Mahal. The Taj Mahal serves as her tomb. Taj Mahal is a 3 hour drive from Delhi.

THE GOLDEN TRIANGLE

One of the popular tourist circuits is called the Golden Triangle: the cities Delhi; Agra (site of the Taj Mahal); and

Jaipur. Delhi is approximately 200 kilometers away from Agra, and 250 kilometers from Jaipur.

WILDLIFE SANCTUARIES

India also has a large variety of protected wildlife. The country's protected wilderness consists of 75 National parks of India and 421 Sanctuaries, of which 19 fall under the purview of Project Tiger. Its climatic and geographic diversity makes it the home of over 350 mammals and 1200 bird species, many of which are unique to the subcontinent. Some well known national wildlife sanctuaries include Corbett, Kanha, Sariska, Periyar, Ranthambore, and Bharatpur.

STATEWISE TOURIST DESTINATIONS

Andhra Pradesh

Andhra Pradesh is very good place for tourism. Andhra Pradesh is India's fifth largest state. AP is also known as the "Rice Granary of India". The main languages spoken in Andhra Pradesh are Telugu, Hindi, Urdu and English. The weather is mostly tropical. June to September are the monsoon months and travel is not advised during this time. NOvember to January are the best time to visit. Andhra Pradesh has a rich cultural heritage. Andhra Pradesh has a variety of attarctions including beaches,hills,wildlife,forests and temples.

People coming to Andhra Pradesh visit:

- Hyderabad
- Tirupati
- Vizag
- Nagarjuna sagar
- Vijaywada
- Warangal

Delhi

Delhi... The capital of the vast, mystic subcontinent that is India. A fine blend of old and new, ancient and modern in every stream of life is the soul of Delhi. A melting pot of cultures and traditions, religions and castes Delhi is true to its democratic nature. Delhi has ruled... always from the mythological days to the present, the Aravali ridges and the Yamuna river stand a mute witness to it.

The rulers left behind their trade marks in the architecture. Tughlakabad fort and the Qutab Minar, the Jama Masjid and the Lotus temple, The Humayun's tomb and the Red Fort, and India Gate and the Magnificent President's house. Delhi is famous for its wide roads and crisp winters. One of the few places in India where colours of nature changes with the seasons.

From Kerala to Kashmir and from Gujarat to Assam all the mouth watering delicacies and shopping goods are found in Delhi. The cosmopolitan nature of the city has only added to the beauty and glory of it. Big gardens, wide roads, ancient structures, and power of politics is what Delhi is all about.

Goa

Goa is another popular destination, famous for its excellent beaches, churches, and temples.

Goa is a tiny emerald land on the west coast of India situated between the borders of Maharastra and Karnataka and is better known to the world as the former Portuguese enclave on Indian soil. With the rule of the Portuguese for over 450 years and the consequential influence of the Latin culture, Goa presents a somewhat different picture to the foreign visitor than any other part of the country. Not only is the proportion of Christians (almost all of whom are Catholics) in the total population of Goa much higher than that obtaining in most of the other States; the general way of living is also markedly different.

Western influence is evident in the dress and food habits, and the general life of the people is quiet and peaceful. A striking feature of Goa is the harmonious relationship between the two principal religious communities, the Hindus and the Catholics, who have lived together peacefully for generations The Bom Jesus cathedral is another famous attraction in Goa.

Jammu and Kashmir

The Manasbal Lake near Srinagar, Jammu and Kashmir is 2000 meters above sea level.

Tourist destinations in Jammu and Kashmir include:

- Srinagar
- Jammu
- Leh
- Amarnath
- Vaishno Devi

Other cities of interest in Northern India include Gwalior, Khajuraho, Varanasi, Mathura, and Haridwar. Moving south, many places are a mix of ancient historic sites as well as industrial/technological hubs. Some of these are listed below.

Karnataka

The southern state of Karnataka offers:

- Bangalore, the IT capital of India, is also significant for its history
- Mysore, about 140 km from Bangalore, has palaces, KRS Dam, several temples, a Hindu temple atop Chamundi Hills, Chamundeswari Temple.
- Srirangapatna, where nearby fortresses can be found (Tipu's)
- Hampi the city of ruins (1500s when the Muslim kings destroyed the prosperous Vijayanagar empire)
- The Belur and Halebidu temples are famed for their sculptural beauty.
- Sravanabelagola has a Jain temple dedicated to king Bahubali. The statue is massive and a MahaMasthakaAbhishekham performed one every year, attracts a huge number of pilgrims
- Sringeri, located in the western ghats, has a wonderful temple dedicated to Sarada devi.

- The Western Ghats offer many other places of exceptional beauty like Agumbe, Horanadu etc.
- Madikeri, Kodagu, Talakaveri, Kemmanagundi all places of immense natural beauty.

Kerala

Kerala, nicknamed as "God's own country", is one of the most beautiful states in Southern India. Shown here is Munnar, in Kerala.

Kerala is an evergreen lush state, tucked away in the southern corner of India. It is one of the most haunted visits of tourists in India. The state has its own tourism brand name-"God's Own Country", which has super-brand status. The state was nicked as one of the "10 paradises of the world" by the National Geographic traveller, the only other Indian place listed being the Taj Mahal.

Kerala is famous for its backwaters and lagoons. There are also several beautiful beaches along the coastline of Kerala. There are also hill stations and tropical rainforests with exquisite flora and fauna including endangared animals like elephant, tiger, nilgiri thar and lion-tailed macaque. Recently, a new brand of tourism was introduced called Monsoon Tourism, aimed at beckoning tourists to enjoy the beauty of the state's hauntigly beautiful rainy season extending from June to September.

Kerala is also known for its Ayurveda, the ancient medicinal system of India. The government of Kerala offers tourism packages related to Ayurvedaand promotes health tourism since treatment charges are low in Kerala.

On the cultural front, the several unique and colourful festivals of Kerala like Onam, Thrissur Pooram, the snake boat races etc. provide great attraction to tourists. The classical artforms Kathakali, Mohiniyattam etc. are also a delight. The martial artform Kalaripayattu is the parent form of all famous martial arts like karate and kungfu. The Kerala Cuisine is also world famous. Also Kerala's rich history of maritime trade from ancient times has left a number of interesting historical monuments.

The major attractions in Kerala include:

- Kumarakom, Kuttanad, Kumbalanghi and other backwater locations.
- Vembanad Lake and the housboats of Alappuzha
- Beaches like Kovalam,Marari etc.
- Hill stations at Thekkady and Munnar
- The city of Kochi with its Chinese fishing nets, Bolgatty Palace, Mattanchery Jewish Synagogue, Jew Street, Fort Kochi etc.
- Enchanting waterfalls at Athirappilly and Vazhachal
- Periyar Tiger Reserve, Iravikulam National Park, Thattekad Bird Sanctuary and other forests
- Its historical monuments like Bakel Fort, Edakal cave of Wayanad
- Kerala Kalamandalam, deemed university teaching classical artforms
- Kalady, birthplace of Adi Sankaracharya, Sabarimala Temple, Guruvayur Temple, Malayatoor Church and other pilgirimage centres

Orissa

Orissa has been a preferred destination from ancient days for people having interest in spirituality, religion, culture, art and beauty of the nature. Ancient and medieval architecture, pristine sea beaches, nature at her beautiful best, the classical and ethnic dance forms and a variety of festivals, all in combine attract tourists from far off places to explore this state to a have a divine exposure of love and hospitality. Orissa has kept alive Buddhism and the Buddha in its ancient womb. The spirit of Buddhism still haunts the very air of Orissa. Rock-edicts that have challenged time stand huge and over-powering by the banks of the river Daya. The silent stones sing out songs of peace and non-violence. The torch of Buddhism is still ablaze in the sublime triangle at Udayagiri, Lalitgiri & Ratanagiri, on the banks of river Birupa. The surrounding hills of Langudi and Kayama stand as mute witness to the quirks and twists of history. Precious fragments of a glorious past come alive in the shape of stupas, rock-cut caves, rock-edicts, excavated monastries, viharas, chaityas and sacred relics in caskets. Rock-edicts of Ashoka are a bonus for your eyes. Orissa is the home for various tribal communities who have contributed uniquely to the multicultural and multilingual character of the state. Their handicrafts, different dance forms, jungle products and their unique life style blended with their healing practices have got world wide attention.

Pondicherry

- Aurobindo Ashram
- Auroville

Rajasthan

Rajasthan has a rich history and culture making it one of the most popular tourist destinations in India. Shown here is the Hawa Mahal in Jaipur, Rajathan.

Rajasthan, the "Land of the Kings", is one of the most attractive tourist destinations in Northern India. The vast sand dunes of the Thar Desert attract millions of tourists from around the globe every year. Major visitor attractions in Rajathan include:

- Jaipur-The capital of Rajasthan, famous for its rich history and royal architecture
- Jodhpur-fortress-city at the edge of the Thar Desert, famous for its blue homes and architecture
- Jaisalmer-famous for its golden fortress
- Barmer-Barmer and surrounding areas offer perfect picture of typical Rajasthani villages.
- Bikaner-famous for its medieval history as a trade route outpost
- Mount Abu
- Pushkar-It has the only Brahma temple in the world

Sikkim

Originally know as Suk-Hem, which in the local language means "peaceful home", Sikkim was an independent kingdom till the year 1974, when it became a part of the Republic Of India. The capital of Sikkim is Gangtok, located approximately 185 kilometres from New Jalpaiguri, the nearest railway station to Sikkim. Although an airport is under construction at Dekiling in East Sikkim, the nearest airport to Sikkim would be Bagdogra. Sikkim is the land of Orchids and mystic culture and colourful tradition. Sikkim is well know among trekkers and adventure lovers, as West Sikkim has a lot to give them. Some must-visit places within Sikkim include: 1.NIT (National Institute Of Tibetology) 2.Hanuman and Ganesh Tok 3.Nathula pass 4.Baba Harbajan Mandir 5.Seven View Points 6.Rumtek Monastery 7.Lachen and Lachung 8.Pelling 9.Pemayantzy 10.Uttaray 11.Dzongri 12.Chewa-bhanjang 13.Barsay 14.Legship-Hot water spring 15.Khorong Hotwater spring 16.Samdrupsey at Namchi

Places near Sikkim include Darjeeling also know as the Queen of hills and Kalimpong. Darjeeling, other than its world famous "Darjeeling tea" is also famous for its refined "Prep schools" founded during the British Raj. A few of the top Schools in the District are: 1.St.Paul's School-Known as Eton of the East. It is 190 years old, thus one of the oldest schools in India. 2.Mt.Hermon School. 3.St.Joseph's School-where the H.M of Bhutan and the Late H.M of Nepal did their schooling. 4.Loreto Convent-where Late Mother Teresa served for many years. 5.Dr.Graham's Homes. 6.St.Joseph's Convent. 7.St.Augustine's School.

Kalimpong is famous for its Flora cultivation and is home to many internationally known Nurseries.

4

MEDICAL TOURISM

INTRODUCTION

Medical tourism or medical travel, is the act of traveling to other countries to obtain medical, dental, and surgical care. The term was initially coined by travel agencies and the media as a catchall phrase to describe a rapidly growing industry where people travel to other countries to obtain medical care. Leisure aspect of traveling may be included on such a medical travel trip. It includes medical services (inclusive of elective procedure and complex specialised surgeries) like knee/hip replacement, heart surgery, dental procedures and different cosmetic surgeries. Many companies like Medical Excursions, Inc. inspect the overseas facilities and then help the North Amercian patients to find qualified affordable and high class medical service providers.

DESCRIPTION

A combination of many factors has led to the recent increase in popularity of medical travel: the high cost of healthcare in industrialized nations, the ease and affordability of international travel, and the improvement of technology and standards of care in many countries of the world.

A large draw to medical travel is the convenience in comparison to that of other countries. Some countries that operate from a public health-care system are so taxed that it can take a considerable amount of time, to get needed medical care. The time spent waiting for a procedure, such as a hip replacement, can be a year or more in Britain and Canada; however, in Singapore, Bangkok or Bangalore, a patient could feasibly have an operation the day after their arrival.

Reasons pushing medical travel include lower healthcare costs as well as the search for medical expertise and safety.

According to research found in an article by the University of Delaware publication, UDaily:

> *"the cost of surgery in Bolivia, Argentina, India, Thailand or South Africa can be one-tenth of what it is in the United States or Western Europe, and sometimes even less. A heart-valve replacement that would cost US$200,000 or more in the U.S., for example, goes for $10,000 in India-and that includes round-trip airfare and a brief vacation package. Similarly, a metal-free dental bridge worth $5,500 in the U.S. costs $500 in India or Bolivia, a knee replacement in Thailand with six days of physical therapy costs about one-fifth of what it would in the States, and Lasik eye surgery worth $3,700 in the U.S. is available in many other countries for only $730. Cosmetic surgery savings are even greater: A full facelift that would cost $20,000 in the U.S. runs about $2,500 in South Africa or $ 2,300 in bolivia."*

To understand the phenomenon of Medical travel, we can compare the average costs of cosmetic surgeries between the industrialized nations and the most popular countries in latin america which are specialized in medical tourism and cosmetic surgery tourism (Argentina, Bolivia, Brazil, Costa Rica, India, Mexico). All the prices have been provided us by the offices affiliated with the ministries of health in USA, Europe (France, Spain, Switzerland), Argentine, Bolivia, brazil, Costa Rica, India, and Mexico.

Medical tourists can come from anywhere in the world and may seek essential healthcare services such as cancer treatment and brain and transplant surgery as well as complementary or 'elective' services such as aesthetic treatments (cosmetic surgery).

Popular Medical travel worldwilde destinations are: Singapore, India, Thailand, Brunei, Cuba, Hong Kong, Hungary, India, Israel, Jordan, Lithuania, Malaysia, The Philippines, Thailand, Singapore, and recently, UAE.

Popular Cosmetic Surgery travel destination are:Argentina, Bolivia, Brazil, Costa Rica, Mexico and Turkey.

	USA	Europe	Argentine	Bolivia	Brazil	Costa Rica	India	Mexico
Rhinoplasty	$ 6,000	$ 5,500	$ 2,300	$ 1,200	$ 2,100	$ 2,000	$ 1,500	$ 1,700
Face Lift	$ 15,000	$ 12,500	$ 4,300	$ 2,600	$ 4,500	$ 4,200	$ 2,900	$ 4,500
Breast Augmentation	$ 8,000	$ 7,500	$ 3,700	$ 2,500	$ 3,800	$ 3,400	$ 2,900	$ 3,900
Breast Reduction	$ 9,000	$ 8,000	$ 3,900	$ 2,400	$ 3,600	$ 3,200	$ 3,000	$ 3,700
Complete Liposuction	$ 13,500	$ 11,000	$ 4,500	$ 2,700	$ 4,700	$ 3,800	$ 3,200	$ 4,800
Gluteal Augmentation	$ 9,000	$ 9,000	$ 4,000	$ 3,000	$ 4,200	$ 3,800	$ 3,200	$ 4,500

In Europe Belgium and Poland are also breaking into the business. South Africa is taking the term "medical tourism" very literally by promoting their "medical safaris": Come to see African wildlife and get a facelift in the same trip. However, feelings towards medical tourism are not always positive. In places like the US, where most have insurance and access to quality health care, medical tourism is viewed as risky. In some parts of the world, wider political issues can influence where medical tourists will choose to seek out healthcare; for example, in late 2006 some patients from the Middle East were choosing to travel to Singapore or Hong Kong for health care rather than to the USA.

While the tourism component might be a big draw for some Southeast Asia countries that focus on simple procedures, India is positioning itself the primary medical destination for the most complex medical procedures in the world. India's commitment to this is demonstrated with an ever growing number of hospitals that are attaining the US Joint Commission International accreditation.

Singapore positions itself as a medical hub where healthcare services, medicine, biomedical research and pharmaceutical manufacturing converge. Singapore has made international news for many complex surgeries in specialties such as neurology, oncology and organ transplants procedures. Currently Singapore boasts the largest number of US Joint Commission accredited hospitals in the region.

On the other hand, in South America, countries such as Argentina, Bolivia, Brazil lead on plastic surgery medical skills relying on the vast experience their surgeons have in treating the style-obsessed. It is estimated that 1 in 30 Argentinians had taken plastic surgery procedures, making this population the most operated in the world after the US and Mexico.

In Bolivia the situation is impressive. According to the "Sociedad Boliviana de Cirugia Plastica y Reconstructiva", more that 70% women who belong to the middle and upper class had taken plastic surgery procedure.

There are companies emerging to offer global healthcare options that will allow North American patients to take full advantage of dramatic reductions in air travel and access world class healthcare at a fraction of the cost. Companies that focus on 'Medical Value Travel' typically will have experienced nurse case managers to assist patients with pre-and post-travel medical issues. They will also help provide resources for follow-up care upon the patient's return. While these services will initially be of interest to the self-insured patient, several studies indicate that the rapid growth of Health Savings Accounts will also drive interest to healthcare in other countries.

Because standards are everything when it comes to healthcare, there is a parallel issue around hospital accreditation. Potential medical tourists may be assisted in making their choices by whether or not hospitals have been assessed and accredited by reputable external accreditation bodies. In the USA, JCI (Joint Commission International) fulfills such a role, while in the United Kingdom and Hong Kong, the Trent Accreditation Scheme is a key player.

INDIA

India is one of the most touted destinations in the world for medical tourists. It is known in particular for heart surgery and hip resurfacing, areas of advanced medicine in which India is generally considered a global leader. Probably no country has been in the news for medical tourism than India in 2005-06, and the government and private hospital groups both seem committed to a goal of making the subcontinent a world leader in the industry. Indian medical industry's main appeal is low-cost treatment. Most estimates claim treatment costs in India start at around a tenth of the price of comparable treatment in America or Britain. Morever Indian Hospitals also provides more personalized care than available in west.

For example, in April Madras Medical Mission, a Chennai-based hospital, successfully conducted a complex heart operation on an 87-year-old American patient at a reported cost of $8,000 (□7,000, £4,850) including the cost of his airfare and a month's stay in hospital.

The patient claimed that a less complex operation in America had earlier cost him $40,000. Take the rising popularity of "preventive health screening". At one private clinic in London a thorough men's health check-up that includes blood tests, electro-cardiogram tests, chest x-rays, lung tests and abdominal ultrasound costs £345 ($574, □500). By comparison, a comparable check-up at a clinic operated by Delhi-based healthcare company Max Healthcare costs $84.

A lady from Vero beach, FL, who was featured in CBS 60 min in April 2005, went to India for hip surgery. In USA only hip replacements are possible, but India allows hip resurfacing that does not need the full hip replacement rather saves part of the hip to achieve the same result as the hip replacement.--Shyamvaran 00:57, 16 January 2007 (UTC)

Escorts Heart Institute and Research Center in Delhi and Faridabad, India performs nearly 15,000 heart operations every year, and the post-surgery mortality rate is only 0.8 percent, which is less than half of most major hospitals in the United States.

Medical Tourism in India is one of the best options available to people across the globe. Millions come to India every year to get treated and then enjoy their recuperative holidays across India. People from different walks of life cut across America, United Kingdom, Pakistan, Sri Lanka, Europe, Maldives, Germany and numerous other countries come to India to have their treatments done with peace of mind.

India provides world class medical facilities with hospitals and specialized multi specialty health centers providing their expertise in the areas of Cosmetic Surgery, Dental care, Heart Surgeries, Coronary Bypass, Heart Check up, Valve replacements, Knee Replacements, Eye surgeries, Indian traditional treatments like Ayurvedic Therapies and much more, practically covering every aspect of medicine combining modern treatments with traditional experience.

Estimates of the value of medical tourism to India go as high as $2 billion a year by 2012. In 2003, Indian finance minister Jaswant Singh called for India to become a "global health destination". However, the biggest stumbling block preventing the rapid growth of India as a healthcare destination is its poor infrastructure and lack of quality hotels.

SINGAPORE

Singapore's healthcare services built on a heritage of excellent quality, safety and trustworthiness, coupled with advanced research and international accreditation, and is Asia's leading medical hub. Nine hospitals and two medical centres in Singapore have obtained Joint Commission International (JCI) accreditation. JCI is the main hospital accreditation agency in the United States.

According to statistics at the official website, www.singaporemedicine.com, 374, 000 visitors came to Singapore purely to seek healthcare in 2005.

Many of these patients come from neighbouring countries such as Indonesia and Malaysia. However, patient numbers from Indo-China, South-Asia, the Middle East and Greater China to Singapore are seeing fast growth. On top of that, patients from developed countries such as United States also choose Singapore as their medical travel destination for relatively affordable quality healthcare services in a clean cosmopolitan city for a peace of mind.

Singapore made news for many complex and innovative procedures such as the separation of conjoined twins and tooth-in-eye surgery. The successful separation of the 10-month-old nepalese conjoined twins in 2001 puts Singapore's medical expertise onto the World's headlines. Singapore has since accomplished many more milestones both in Asia and in the world arena.

Recently, Singapore also hosted the first International Medical Travel Conference (IMTC) from 12th-15th December 2006. The four-day event attracted participants and media from 21 countries, setting pace and platform for the development of the budding medical travel industry.

The conference aims to bring together thought leaders to examine some of the fundamentals, issues and challenges involved in the burgeoning international medical travel industry. Curiously however major media did not pay attention to this awkwardly managed event.

However, up to late 2006 Singapore Hospitals have only chosen to accredit themselves through Joint Commission International (JCI), a US-based group, and this approach may have little appeal to potential health tourists based in other parts of the world. In time, Singapore Hospitals may look towards other European or Asian-based systems of hospital accreditation in an attempt to broaden their credibility and appeal.

THAILAND

Medical tourism is a growing segment of Thailand's tourism and health-care sectors. Lower labor costs translate into significant cost savings on procedures, compared to hospitals in the United States, and a higher, more personalized level of nursing care than Westerners are accustomed to receiving in hospitals back home. In 2005, one Bangkok hospital took in 150,000 treatment seekers from abroad. In 2006, medical tourism was projected to earn the country 36.4 billion baht.

One patient who received a coronary artery bypass surgery at Bumrungrad International hospital in Bangkok said the operation cost him US$12,000, as opposed to the $100,000 he estimated the operation would have cost him at home in the US.

Hospitals in Thailand are a popular destination for other Asians. Another hospital that caters to medical tourists, Bangkok General Hospital, has a Japanese wing and Phyathai Hospitals Group has interpreters for over 22 languages, besides the English speaking medical staff. When Nepal Prime Minister Girija Prasad Koirala needed medical care in 2006, he went to Bangkok.

While it is not commonly known outside Thailand, the modern Thai medical system had its origins in the United States when Prince Mahidol of Songla, the King's father, earned his MD degree from Harvard Medical School in the early 20th century. Prince Mahidol and another member of the Thai Royal Family paid for an American medical education for a group of Thai men and women.

Prince Mahidol also convinced the Rockefeller Foundation to provide scholarships for Thai citizens to study medicine and nursing. Funds from the Rockefeller Foundation were also used to help build modern medical training facilities in Thailand. The men and women who studied medicine and nursing as a result of Prince Mahidol's efforts became the first educators for the modern Thai medical system.

Today many Thai physicians hold US professional certification. A number of Thai hospitals have relationships with facilities in the US. The US Consular information sheet gives the Thai healthcare system high marks for quality, particularly facilities in Bangkok. In Thailand, there is modern infrastructure, with clean, safe streets. According to the US Consular information sheets, the crime rate in Bangkok is lower than that of many US cities.

Personal safety is another factor to consider when traveling abroad both for vacation as well as healthcare. Thailand offers everything from cardiac surgery to organ transplants at a price much lower than the US or Europe, in a safe, clean environment.

Thailand has long been a destination for medical tourists, and has a growing number of hospitals with JCAHO accreditation. Over one million people per year travel there for everything from cosmetic surgery to cutting edge cardiac treatment. Don Ho, the famous Hawaiian entertainer, recently received cutting-edge adult stem cell cardiac treatment at a Bangkok hospital. Six weeks later he had recovered sufficiently from his nonischemic cardiomyopathy and was able to return to the stage.

MEDICAL TRAVEL: RISKS AND REWARDS

Medical tourism does carry risks that local medical procedures do not. Should complications arise, patients might not be covered by insurance or be able to seek adequate compensation via malpractice lawsuits, though it should be noted that the malpractice insurance is a considerable portion of the cost in the West.

For some living in remote rural areas, travel to another country is almost as expensive as travel to a large city in their own country.

Nations such as India or Thailand have different infectious diseases, and different prevalence of the same diseases, than home nations such as the US, Canada, UK. Exposure to foreign diseases without having built up natural immunity can be a hazard for weakened individuals, specifically for gastrointestinal diseases (e.g Hep A, amoebic dysentery, bacteria) which could weaken progress, mosquito transmitted diseases, and influenza, TB, etc. (75% of South Africans have latent TB)

Also, travel soon after surgery can increase the risk of complications, as can vacation activities. For example, scars will be darker and more noticeable if they sunburn while healing. Long flights can be bad for those with heart (thrombosis) or breathing related problems (low oxygen environment), not to mention uncomfortable.

However, because in poor tropical nations diseases run the gamut, doctors seem to be more open to the possibility of any disease, including HIV, TB, and typhoid, there are cases in the West where patients were consistently misdiagnosed for years because it is perceived to be "rare" in the West, a famous case of the misdiagnosis and death of a CDC researcher from TB, something that few would rule out in India or Thailand.

5

Asia Pacific Tourism Industry: Current Trends and Future Outlook

INTRODUCTION

Over the last decade, the Asia Pacific region has been the fastest growing tourism region in the world, Tourism is one of the most important sectors in a large number of Asia Pacific countries. Increases in economic growth, disposable income and leisure time, political stability, and aggressive tourism campaigns, among other factors, have fueled the significant growth of tourism. This paper reviews the growth and development of the tourism industry in the Asia Pacific region. The future outlook is bright for the tourism sector, and the region is expected to maintain a high rate of growth well into the next century.

The Asia and Pacific region will be the focus of the worldwide tourism industry in the new millennium. Over the last decade, tourist arrivals and receipts rose faster than any other region in the world, almost twice the rates of industrialized countries. Between 1980 and 1995, tourist arrivals and receipts in the Asia Pacific region rose at an average annual rate of 10% and 15% respectively, higher than any region in the world (World Tourism Organization 1996a). Statistics from the World Tourism Organization (WTO) for 1996 show that tourist arrivals and receipts accounted for a 15.2% and 19.4% share of the world's total respectively, a significant increase from 1985 as shown in Tables I and 2 (WTO 1997a). The Asia Pacific region has been gaining market share at the expense of the Americas and

European regions, which saw a decline in their respective shares during the same period. The WTO 1996b) projects that by the year 2010, the region will surpass the Americas to become the world's number two tourism region, with 229 million arrivals. It is an indication that the growth of tourism in the Asia Pacific region in the next decade will be nothing short of spectacular.

Mass travel, which first began in the 1950s when millions of Americans and Europeans traveled the world, has blossomed in Asia. The region is now regarded as a major generator and receiver of tourism. A wealthy new middle class of Asians are taking to the skies and joining their European and American counterparts on their pleasure, business, and adventure trips around the globe. The rapid growth of the tourism industry has been attributed to a number of factors including among others, strong economic growth, increase in disposable income and leisure time, easing of travel restrictions, successful tourist promotion, and a recognition by the host governments that tourism is a powerful engine of growth and a generator of foreign exchange earnings.

It is the purpose of this paper to provide a basic discussion of the economic importance of tourism and review the major trends that shaped the growth and development of the tourism industry in the Asia Pacific region. A comparison of the tourism industry performance will also be made between selected Asia Pacific countries, and with other regions of the world, to highlight the trends and changes. The definition of the Asia Pacific region in this paper corresponds to the definition used by the WTO which includes North-East Asia, South-East Asia, and Oceania.

ECONOMIC IMPORTANCE

Tourism is one of the most important sectors in the economies of Asia Pacific countries. Currently, tourism is the most important sector and major source of foreign exchange earnings in Thailand, Australia, and New Zealand. It is ranked second in Hong Kong, Malaysia and the Philippines, and ranked third in Singapore and Indonesia. For example, in New Zealand, the tourism industry employs more than 200,000 people, with projections of a 14% annual growth till the year 2000 (Chan 1995). In Hong Kong, tourism employs 12% of the workforce and contributes about 7% to the economy (Boxall 1996). The tourism sector in Thailand supports over 1.5 million jobs and contributes 5% to the economy (Asian Business 1996). Tourism is also gaining importance in China. By the year 2000, China expects to receive 55 million visitors with foreign exchange earnings of US$14 billion, which will contribute 5% to China's economy, making tourism one of the most significant components of the national economy (Beria 1996). In Singapore, the healthy overall balance of payments is attributed to the huge surplus achieved by the tourism sector which contributes about 10% to the economy (International Monetary Fund 1996a). Despite Singapore's open economy, and its vulnerability to external shocks and import leakages, tourism has made a significant contribution to output, employment, and income.

Based on 1988 input-output tables, Khan et al. (1995) estimated that tourism contributed 11.9% to Singapore's GDP (Gross Domestic Product) in 1992, while employment accounted for 13.4% of the labor force. The employment effect of a million dollars in tourist expenditures would create 25 new jobs. The results ts showed that every dollar of tourist expenditure would generate S$1.97 of output and S$1.05 in income. The income multiplier for tourism was larger when compared to Hong Kong, Indonesia and Malaysia, while the tourism output multiplier was greater relative to other sectors of the Singapore economy.

Comparisons with previous studies (Schymyck 1983; Toh and Low 1990) showed an increase in the contribution of tourism over time, a strong indication of the significance of tourism in the Singapore economy. The estimated economic impact of tourism is also significant in South Korea. According to Lee and Kwon (1995), the total impact of tourism receipts of US$4.7 billion in 1993, generated US$11.7 of output, US$2.4 billion in income, and created 350,000 full time jobs. The secondary impacts were also found to have a considerable effect on the economy. The findings suggested that tourism should be promoted as a strategic export industry.

It is no surprise that the key to the success of tourism in the Asia Pacific region is a clear recognition by the host governments of the important role of tourism in the economic development of the country. Tourism serves as an important means to increase economic growth, raise the quality of life, create employment, and improve the overall balance of payments by helping to offset deficits in other sectors. Many Asia Pacific countries show a net surplus in their tourism balance of payment account as shown in Table 3 (WTO 1997a; IMF 1997). Japan, Taiwan, and South Korea are major tourist generating countries in the region and this is reflected by the deficits in their respective travel balance of payments accounts.

Mak and White (1992) attributed the travel account deficits for these high income countries to a higher allocation of disposable income to leisure travel. The relaxation of travel restrictions in Taiwan also had a significant impact on its travel account, due to the large increase in outbound travel. On the other hand, China, Thailand, and Singapore are major receivers of tourists, enjoying a huge surplus. As a percentage of exports, tourism contributes more than 13/n to the economies of Australia, New Zealand, and Thailand, again reflecting its ranking as the top export. Its contribution to the GDP is significantly greater in Singapore (10%) and Hong Kong (7%).

Almost all Asian nations are committing substantial manpower and resources to attract more arrivals whose expenditures represent significant contributions to national income and foreign exchange earnings. For example, Singapore has unveiled a new tourism blueprint titled "Tourism 21" that is expected to turn the nation into a world class tourism business center and the tourism capital of the East. Plans call for increasing arrivals and receipts by 6.4% and 6.6% annually to 10 million and US$11.4 billion, respectively, by the year 2000 (Boey 1996). Even Indonesia and Malaysia have raised their commitments towards developing the tourism sector. Indonesia plans to make tourism the nation's number one foreign exchange earner by the year 2004, when arrivals will hit 11 million and receipts reach US$15 billion from current levels of 4.3 million and US$5.4 billion, respectively (Travel Trade Gazelle 1997). In the current Seventh Malaysia Plan, which ends in the year 2000, a number of strategies were formulated to turn tourism into a top revenue earner for the country.

Millions of dollars will be allocated for tourism infrastructure in an effort to increase arrivals and receipts to 12.5 million and US$6.3 billion, respectively, by the end of this decade (Pacific Area Travel Association News 1996). With increasing competition for the tourist dollar, the national tourism organizations of New Zealand, Thailand, Australia and Hong Kong, among others, have also allocated an increase in tourism funding to tap the emerging tourism markets that promise new income and employment opportunities.

TOURISM GROWTH FACTORS

A number of factors are responsible for the rapid growth and development of the tourism industry in the Asia Pacific region. These include the strong economic growth, increase in income, breakdown of political barriers, easing of travel restrictions, liberalization of air transport, and focused marketing campaigns. These factors are expected to accelerate the growth of tourism over the next decade.

Economic Growth

The rapid growth of the tourism industry is a reflection of the region's booming and diversified economies. Economic growth has ranged between an average of 6% to 9% in the last decade, in contrast to 3% to 4% growth achieved by the rest of the world. Only the industrialized countries of Australia, Japan, and New Zealand show a lower rate of growth than the rest of the region. China, which has achieved double-digit growth over the last 5 years, is poised to become one of the world's largest economies and surpass Japan in the next decade. The region is expected to maintain its growth at a rate between 6% to 8% over the next decade (IMF 1996b).

Strong economic growth in Asia is attributed to a focus on market reforms, export oriented industries, stable currencies, diversification of the economy, and massive injection of foreign capital. Billions of dollars are being poured into the tourism infrastructure to accommodate a burgeoning Asian tourism industry. This has intensified trade, investment, and travel within the region and with the rest of the world. Asian governments have also sought to avoid extremes of inflation and unemployment, and are keeping budget deficits small or running surpluses. It is no wonder that the region has attracted much attention from the rest of the world regarding its success. The opening up of Indochina, Myanmar, and China to tourism, and given the increasing number of companies setting u p bases and new businesses in the region the volume of business travel will rise. This will provide ample marketing opportunities for travel-related businesses.

Increase in Income and Leisure Time

As a result of strong economic growth, disposable incomes have soared in Asian countries and along with it, the propensity to travel. Leisure consciousness has been enhanced with travel no longer seen as a luxury. In fact, it is now seen as an affordable commodity to be enjoyed by all who choose to engage in a variety of leisurely pursuits. Some Asians may see travel as a status symbol, while others see it as relief from the pressures of work. The introduction of a 5-day workweek in China will provide Chinese residents with more leisure time that will likely be devoted to travel. A number of Asian countries have recorded significant growth in real per capita income over the last Syears with Singapore (7.3%), Thailand (6.8%), China (10.3%), 5. Korea (6.7%), and Indonesia (7.1%) showing the highest growth (IMF 1997).

Rising incomes have created a middle class of sophisticated and affluent Asians who are better educated, have more disposable income, and who appreciate the value of leisure. Research by Mak and White (1992) has shown travel propensity and tourism spending to be positively correlated a ed with per capita income among the major Asia Pacific countries. This means that increases in income levels will enable a greater proportion of Asians to travel overseas. Unlike previous generations, this generation of primarily young travelers are intent on enjoying the fruits of their labor.

Although price conscious, they still demand high qualify products. Since Asians are more likely to travel in groups and families, more travel products and services, such as tour packages that incorporate activities, must be designed to cater to their needs. This may include travel to exotic places, soft-adventure travel, cruises, and sports related tours, among others. Disposable incomes will continue to rise, and thus fuel the demand for leisure travel. The trend among Asia Pacific countries is towards more frequent regional holidays to various destinations and resorts within the region.

Political Stability/Breakdown of Political Barriers

In recent years, the Asia Pacific region has become politically more stable than it has ever been, especially in the Philippines, where tourism was adversely affected by terrorism, civil strife, and natural disasters in the last decade. However, the political, social and economic reforms of the current government have reversed the fortunes of the tourism industry. Tourism investments in the Philippines over the last 3 years were estimated at U5$6.27 billion, with a large portion of the funds allocated towards resort development. To encourage more investment, the Philippines Department of Tourism is urging financial institutions to provide funding to investors involved in tourism-related projects (Shaw 1997). Investors are showing confidence not only in the Philippines but also in Vietnam, Indonesia, and China.

These nations, which were off-limits to foreigners at one time, are witnessing rapid hotel and resort developments. Even areas which were closed or long considered inaccessible in parts of China and Indonesia are now open to tourism. The opening of borders to both inbound and outbound travel, and the breakdown of political barriers, will provide tourists with opportunities to pursue their leisure interests. For example, South Korea's normalization of relations with China also is expected to boost arrivals from Seoul to major cities in China when non-stop air traffic routes are inaugurated.

Easing of Travel Restrictions

Historically, the demand for and freedom to travel increases when travel restrictions are lifted or eliminated. With strong demand for travel, a number of Asia Pacific countries have lifted some travel restrictions. The lifting of restrictions in South Korea and Taiwan in the late 1980s, for example, contributed to a surge in the demand for outbound travel. More recently, the Taiwanese government's open door policy and the institution of a 5-day visa-free entry program to 15 countries also helped to increase arrivals to Taiwan by 10% in 1995 over the previous year (Wieman 1996a). Similarly, the Malaysian government's decision to allow tourists a 3-day visa-free stay in Malaysia, and Indonesia's granting of unilateral visa-free entry are steps in the right direction The general trend is towards a reduction of travel barriers to promote tourism.

Table 1. World Tourism Arrivals by Regions, 1985-1996

(in thousands)

Region	1985	% Share	1990	% Share	1996*	% Share
Africa	9,710	2.9	15,090	3.3	19,593	3.3
Americas	66,430	20.1	93,570	20.4	115,572	19.5
Asia Pacific	30,843	9.4	53,109	11.6	89,774	15.2
Europe	213,795	64.9	286,708	62.4	347,329	58.7
Middle East	6,240	1.9	7,577	1.6	15,121	2.5
South Asia	2,540	.8	3,179	.7	4,475	.8
World	329,558	100%	459,233	100%	591,864	100%

Source: World Tourism Organization, 1997

* preliminary data

Liberalization of Air Transport

Traditionally, Asian countries have safeguarded their national flag carriers to protect them from foreign competition.

However, the situation is changing as governments realize that such restrictive policies are counterproductive to tourism. Singapore and Taiwan have already signed open skies agreements with the United States and similar agreements are expected between the U.S. and Malaysia, S. Korea and New Zealand (Dhaliwal 1997). Liberalization of air transport will only serve to enhance trade and tourism growth in the region. It will to lead to more multilateral open skies agreements between countries.

In other parts of the region, Thailand and Australia are showing more tourism growth as a result of liberalized internal aviation policies. Indonesia, the Philippines and South Korea have followed suit with similar aviation policies. Indonesia's limited open skies policy invites foreign airlines to fly to new international destinations and participate in code sharing agreements with Indonesian airlines. As a result of liberalized air policies in the Philippines, new international gateways have emerged, and more inter-island services initiated. This will save travel time, increase convenience, and enable the promotion of more resorts in the islands. Liberalization of aviation policies have also sparked the creation of new carriers and subsidiaries of major carriers such as Silkair (Singapore), Dragonair (Hong Kong), and Sempati (Indonesia). These airlines have launched new routes to secondary destinations, especially in China, Indonesia, Thailand, and Malaysia, to serve the emerging and growing tourism market in secondary cities.

Technology

Technological developments have significantly impacted the travel industry in the Asia Pacific region and will continue to do so over the next decade. Developments in large and more fuel efficient aircraft such as the Boeing 777, Boeing 747, and Airbus A340 have lowered operating costs, increased airline seat capacity, and raised the comfort and safety of air travel. These aircraft facilitate travel over longer distances and fly non-stop over trans-Atlantic and Pacific routes. Lower operating costs, coupled with cheaper airfares, have reduced the cost of travel, thereby making air travel the dominant mode of travel in the region. Most of the new wide bodied jets built over the next decade will be delivered to Asia Pacific airlines to meet their increasing demand for capacity.

Technological developments are also impacting the way in which the product is delivered to the customer. Ticketless travel will find its way into the major hubs in Asia this year. Singapore Airlines will introduce ticketless travel on selected regional routes while Malaysian Airlines will introduce it on domestic routes. Air New Zealand and Ansett Australia are also planning ticketless travel by the end of this year. Ticketless travel will speed up customer service, provide convenience, improve efficiency, and decrease distribution costs

Ticketless travel can save airlines up to 30% of their distribution costs if it is implemented and standardized successfully (Klyne 1997). With the availability of computer-based interactive information and product buying systems, tourists can view the facilities and destinations on the Internet, video, or CD-ROM and make

direct purchases. The National Tourism Organizations (NTOs) of the Asia Pacific countries have also created custom-made destination promotion pages on the World Wide Web in order to reach a global audience. New technological developments and production efficiencies will continue to create more leisure time that will be devoted to travel.

FOCUSED MARKETING AND THEMED CAMPAIGNS

In light of the increasingly competitive situation in the Asia Pacific region, traditional methods of marketing a destination to the masses has yielded to more focused marketing segmentation strategies and themed campaigns.

Thailand started the trend towards international and nationwide events when it launched "Visit Thailand Year 1987" to celebrate the Thai King's 60th birthday. The success of the campaign was reflected in visitor arrival figures, which jumped 24% in 1987 (Corben l996). Since then, the success of nationwide campaigns have been emulated all across Asia. In 1997, China will organize a second "Visit China Year 1997" to complement its recovery of sovereignty of Hong Kong. The theme for the campaign is" Visit China-A Completely New Experience" with major events planned throughout the country. These marketing campaigns are designed to enhance the destination image by focusing on the rich cultural, historical, and natural heritage of the country. Through creative and innovative p roduct differentiation strategies, each country has created a diverse destination product with a unique guest appeal that will enrich the visitor experience, provide quality, and maximize the value of the visitor's leisure time. Increased emphasis will be placed on niche marketing, whereby specific market segments are identified through visitor profile studies and then targeted by matching the destination product to appeal to the segment. For example, in 1995, the Korea National Tourist Corporation used its "Discover Korea: A Different Asia" campaign to emphasize the differences that South Korea had to offer over other Asian countries; its unique traditional culture, delicious cuisine, exceptional shopping, and four distinct seasons.

For the Japanese market, the theme was "Korea: The Nearest Country" capitalizing on its proximity to Japan. The success of the campaign was reflected in tourism receipts which jumped 46.6% over 1994 (Price 1995). Capitalizing on this trend, Malaysia has developed a new "Malaysia: Fascinating Destinations" theme to showcase eight different destinations within the country, each with its own attraction and appeal. The campaign is aimed at the North American, European, East Asian, and Australian markets. To complement existing promotional campaigns, some Asian countries have entered into joint marketing ventures and cooperative endeavors with neighboring countries and other NTOs.

For example, Singapore and Indonesia jointly promote Bintan Island in Indonesia, with plans for more initiatives covering other Indonesian islands. Singapore and Indonesia have also identified seven target markets in the U.S., Europe, and Asia in which both countries will spend US$800,000 over the next 2 years to promote both destinations (Business Times 1996). NTOs have also forged alliances with the private sector to promote destinations. For example, by setting up an alliance with major travel agencies in South Korea, the New Zealand Tourism Board was able to design and promote New Zealand tour packages aimed at the mature traveler from S. Korea. Palmer and Bejou (1995) noted that alliances between the private and p ublic sectors will attract more visitors that can benefit both sectors.

The value of forming alliances has also been recognized in tourism marketing (Gunn 1988; Stevens 1988). Joint promotions and marketing with members of ASEANTA (Association of South East Asian Nations Tourism Organization) and travel missions led by PATA (Pacific Area Travel Association) have also been successful. Both organizations have been instrumental in promoting the travel interests of members through trade shows, seminars, education and training, research, and destination marketing and sales promotion. For example, the collaborative efforts of ASEANTA paid off during" Visit ASEAN Year 1992," when visitor arrivals increased 9.5% to a record 21.86 million (WTO 1996a).

TRENDS IN THE TOURISM INDUSTRY

Trends in Arrivals and Receipts

Economic growth, increasing competition, easing of travel restrictions, and aggressive promotion strategies adopted by the NTOs contributed to the growth in arrivals in 1996. Most of the Asia Pacific countries saw an increase in arrivals (Table 4). Japan, which experienced a drop in arrivals in 1995 due to its lack of appeal, increasing cost, and strong currency, rebounded in 1996 with a 22% growth in arrivals. South Korea failed to meet its target of 4 million arrivals.

The decline in arrivals were attributed to rising costs of vacationing in the country. Japan, which is S. Korea's largest market, accounting for over 40% of all visitors, declined 8.4% to 1.52 million visitors. Many Japanese visitors also chose to visit Hong Kong before the hand over to China. Malaysia experienced a decline in arrivals, primarily from its Asian markets, due to health-related concerns of a cholera outbreak. Political stability in the Philippines, easing of restrictions in China, concerns over the hangover of Hong Kong to China, and improving economic conditions in Australia and Indonesia, led to double-digit growth rates in arrivals in these countries.

Paralleling the growth in arrivals, tourism receipts also showed significant growth for most of the Asia Pacific countries, especially for Japan, Australia, and New Zealand, which exceeded 20%. Higher receipts were also recorded for Hong Kong, China, Indonesia, and the Philippines. On the other hand, South Korea and Singapore saw a decline in receipts, due to increasing cost concerns. The strong Singapore currency, a declining length of stay, and growing competition from regional destinations contributed to the decline. Tourism receipts for Asia Pacific countries are expected to grow at a faster rate than arrivals, due to rising affluence and increased spending by visitors.

Table 4.: Trends in International Tourism in Selected Asia Pacific Countries, 1996

Country	Arrivals* 1996 (000)	Arrivals 1995 (000)	% Change 96/95	Receipts* 1996 (US$mil.)	Receipts 1995 (US$mil.)	% Change 96/95
Australia	4,167	3,726	11.8	8,690	7,100	22.4
China	22,765	20,034	13.6	10,200	8,730	16.8
Hong Kong	11,703	10,200	14.7	10,836	9,604	12.8
Indonesia	5,034	4,324	16.4	6,087	5,228	16.4
Japan	2,114	1,731	22.1	4,069	3,226	26.1
Malaysia **	7,138	7,469	-4.4	3,926	3,910	.4
New Zealand	1,508	1,409	7.0	2,663	2,163	23.1
Philippines	2,054	1,760	16.7	2,790	2,450	13.9
Singapore	6,608	6,422	2.9	7,916	8,377	-5.5
South Korea	3,684	3,753	-1.8	5,430	5,587	-2.8
Taiwan	2,358	2,332	1.1	3,546	3,287	7.9
Thailand	7,192	6,951	3.5	8,491	7,664	10.8

*preliminary results

**includes Singaporeans traveling by road to Malaysia

Source: World Tourism Organization, 1997

TRENDS IN OUTBOUND TRAVEL

In 1996, the Asia Pacific region surpassed North America for the first time in generating visitors. Outbound travel grew 8% to record 94 million international visitors, while North Americans made 92 million trips abroad. The Asia Pacific region received 74% of the visitors generated, followed by Europe (14%), and the Americas (10%). It is a dramatic increase from the 69% share recorded in 1985 (WTO 1997b). Falling airfares, high cost of domestic travel in some countries, rising affluence, increase in business travel, and more competitive packages, contributed to increasing number of Asians traveling overseas to regional destinations (Mak and White, 1992). Intraregional travel, which is characterized by more frequent short-haul trips, has been growing at a higher rate than long-haul travel. Between 1985 and 1995, intraregional travel grew at an average annual rate of 12%, compared to 10% for long-haul travel (WTO 19971,). Japan by far, is still the largest tourist generating market in the region, but the emerging markets of China, S. Korea, Hong Kong, Taiwan, Singapore, and Thailand, are generating most of the region's new international travelers.

The increase in demand for travel has created new marketing opportunities in ecotourism, adventure travel, dive travel, cruises, golf tours, arts and entertainment, and meetings and incentives, among others. Tourism marketers must focus on attracting these high yield markets by differentiating their products and customizing them to individualized needs. Since the Asia Pacific region covers a great diversity of cultures, lifestyles and preferences, more innovative and creative marketing strategies have to be designed for each source market of visitors. The increasing sophistication the Asian visitors also requires travel products to offer quality, comfort, convenience, relaxation, independence, and unique learning experiences that maximize the value of their leisure time.

FUTURE OUTLOOK

The Asia Pacific region will still maintain its status as the fastest growing region in the world and most forecasts point to the region's healthy long-term prospects. The WTO's (1996b) forecast reveals the region emerging as the world's number two region behind Europe in 2010 with 229 million international arrivals, growing at an annual rate of 7.6%. The rapid growth of tourism will create new marketing opportunities in the cruise line industry, timesharing, meetings and incentives, ecotourism, and dive travel. Japan will continue to be the principal visitor generating market, while China has the potential to be the next major visitor generating market. Major events that will boost the status of the region include the Commonwealth Games in Malaysia in 1998, the 2000 Olympic Games in Sydney and soccer's World Cup in Korea and Japan in 2002. Forecasts by the World Travel and Tourism Council (1995) for the Asia Pacific region reveal that by the year 2005, travel and tourism will generate US$1.9 trillion in gross output, and account for 11.6% of GDP. Further, the industry will create an additional 105 million new and indirect jobs. To support this growth, US$553 billion in capital investments will be needed for the infrastructure and superstructure.

Strong economic growth will continue to increase disposable incomes and stimulate the desire to travel. This will increase the demand for air travel which is expected to grow at an annual rate of 8.6% till 2000 and 7.1% from 2000 to 2010. By 2010, the Asia Pacific region will control half of the world's total passenger traffic. Japan will dominate the traffic with over 90 million passengers, followed by Hong Kong, China, and Singapore. The fastest growing travel markets by 2000 will be Vietnam, China, Taiwan, Indonesia, and Thailand (Air Transport Action Group 1995). To accommodate the demand for air travel, airlines in the region will take delivery of more than US$100 billion worth of aircraft. As of March 1996, Asia Pacific airlines had firm orders and options for a total of 575 aircraft (Muqbil 1996). New airports are opening in Hong Kong, Korea, and Malaysia, while expansions in Singapore and Indonesia will help to alleviate capacity and congestion problems. Billions of dollars will be spent in capital investments to meet the increasing demands of a burgeoning tourism and hotel industry. Joint promotions and alliances between NTOs and the private sector, will create a stronger collective tourism product that will increase arrivals and enhance tourism growth.

Finally, the recent devaluation of the regional currencies will also have major implications for the tourism industry in the region. Inbound travel will increase as visitors will be attracted by the higher purchasing power in countries where currencies have been devalued. More specifically, visitor expenditures will increase as a result of a higher length of stay and attractive prices. In the short term, devaluation may have some negative impact on outbound travel and operating costs, but the long-term benefits will outweigh the costs.

Since the beginning of the 1960s, space tourism has been investigated world-wide. NASA has just finished a space tourism feasibility study in co-operation with the Space Transportation Association with promising results. In Japan, different space tourism scenarios are investigated in the context of industrial research for about 10 years with respect to the transportation and accommodation of tourists. In Europe and Germany, space hotel concepts are investigated and several studies analyse future advanced low cost space transportation systems which represent the key technology to make future space tourism affordable for the public. This wide variety of studies indicates, that space tourism is considered to have a considerable economic potential in the mid to long-term. Currently, tourism on Earth represents one of the biggest industrial sectors with an annual market volume of about $3400 Billion (estimate for the year 1995). If it would be possible to shift only a few percent from this amount to a future space tourism market, the size of the global civil space industry could be doubled (for comparison: presently, the global, civil, governmental space budgets amount to about $30 Billion). In this context it is notable, that initial national and international market research analyses indicate, that e.g. 4.3% of the Germans are willing to spent an annual salary for a holiday-trip into space (several $10000). Because of the presently very high space transportation costs in the order of several $10 Million, space tourism will not be feasible in the short-term due to the fact that it is not affordable. However, suborbital flights-perhaps already in the next decade-could represent precursor activities which allow a short stay in space by ascending vertically into space or by landing after one Earth orbit at the departure airport. In this case, the target "ticket prices" are in the range of $10.000 to $100000 comparable in the best case with a Concorde flight from Europe to America. Furthermore, this study presents possible future space transportation concepts of the next generations, which have a significant cost reduction potential and could allow a "space-ticket" price into Earth orbit in the range of a few $100000. These space transportation systems are fully reusable and have very high launch rates, comparable to the operation of present aircraft-fleets within the commercial airline business. The $1 billion effort of NASA 's X-33 development program also aims in this direction. Furthermore, this study discusses the economic feasibility of future tourism on the Moon and Mars and presents the Space Hotel Berlin and Space Hotel Europe concepts, which allow the accommodation of about 50 tourists. TheSpace Hotel Berlin concept is mainly based on existing technologies by the use and integration of modified habitation modules (e.g. derived from COF) from the International Space Station to a ring-shaped structure. By rotating this ring-structure at different velocities, a wide variety of artificial gravity levels can be achieved. First economic analyses show that in the case of a 100% capacity utilisation, one overnight stay in the Space Hotel Berlin (without the transportation of tourists from Earth) would cost about $100000. Finally the fascinating entertainment opportunities of future space tourism are outlined.

6

SPACE AND INTERNATIONAL TOURISM

INTRODUCTION

According to current reports in the media, travelling to outer space should become possible for everyone by the beginning of the next century. In April 1998, the newspaper Berlin Morgenpost reported that the international Hilton Hotel corporation is planning the construction of a 5-star hotel, the "Lunar Hilton," on the Moon. A team of British architects was commissioned to develop plans for the gigantic building project. The luxury hotel with 5000 beds and a height of 325 metres provides its own beach at its private "ocean," and should be equipped with all the amenities one can expect from a first class hotel.

However, the short-term realisation of this utopian project of the Hilton Group will most likely take a little more time, and for the first half of the 21st century it must be regarded as pure science fiction. Apart from the technical feasibility of some of the construction plans, economic analyses performed by DLR and the Technical University of Berlin show that the transportation of humans and building materials to the Moon would be extraordinarily expensive, even if very optimistic economic conditions in space operations are assumed [LAssMANN94, REICHERT97a]. With the announcement of its spectacular project, the Hilton Corporation competes with three Japanese corporations, Shimizu, the construction firm Nishimatsu, and Obayashi, all of which have already invested millions into futuristic colonising concepts for the moon.

Life-cycle cost analyses performed in [ESA99, REICHERT97b/c/d] for the planet Mars indicate, that the transportation of humans would require ticket prices in the range of hundreds of millions of dollars, even if very favourable economic conditions in space operations are assumed. In addition, one must consider that after the successful completion of the Apollo program no transportation infrastructure is currently available that would allow humans to be transported beyond the Earth orbital. The creation of such a new infrastructure would require investments of billions of dollars. The Moon and Mars are therefore not likely to play a role in international tourism in the first half of the next century, although Mars represents one of the most promising travel destination because of its many similarities to Earth and its potential of possible former life forms.

Therefore future space tourism will focus for a long time on Earth orbit which can be reached more easily. Figure 2 shows the expected roadmap for space tourism for the next decades with its four sub-scenarios. It is likely, that the space tourism business is initiated by very short suborbital flights, followed by short Earth orbital tourism in advanced, reusable spacecraft which allow several orbits around Earth. Before extended stays in space hotels will become a reality in the far future, touristic trips to existing orbital facilities (e.g. the international space station) might represent an intermediate step.

Already since the mid-sixties, several important analyses of Earth orbital space tourism have been carried out [EHRICKE67]. Various scenarios of transportation and accommodation of tourists in space have been analysed in the frame of industrial research in Japan, increasingly over the last 10 years [COLLINS97, MATSUMOTO97]. In the United States, NASA and the American "Space Transportation Association " have completed a study of the feasibility of space tourism with some promising results [O'NEIL97] in 1998. Furthermore, DASA (DaimlerChrysler Aerospace) investigates touristic spacecraft and space hotel concepts and supported the first international symposium on space tourism in the spring of 1997, which took place in Bremen (Germany) and attracted more than 100 experts from around the world. The symposium also found a significant echo in the media. Moreover, in 1998/99, the general feasibility and economics of space tourism played also a considerable role in an ESA study under the lead of DLR [ESA98, ESA99, REICHERT98]. All of these activities indicate that space tourism is gaining more and more attention and significance. Today, it is already possible to book atmospheric parabolic flights in aeroplanes for the short-term simulation of zerogravity, and to reserve future passenger flights into suborbital space, even though the technology for the latter has not been developed yet.

INDUSTRIAL SIGNIFICANCE

According to an estimate of the World Travel Tourism Council, annual global expenditures in the terrestrial tourism sector amount to about 3400 billion US dollars for the year 1995. Tourism thus globally represents one of the largest industries. If it would be possible to shift only a few percent of the world-wide terrestrial tourist expenditures to a future space tourism market, this could double the civil space budgets to 60 billion dollars. This would create up to half a million new jobs also in the high technology space industry, if it is assumed that a sales volume of $50000 to $250000 creates one job.

If a space tourism business can be established in the future, the scientific and operational know-how-globally gained after decades of research and experience in manned space flight (e.g. by astronaut training centers or institutions of aerospace medicine)-could be applied to the space flight preparation and medical supervision of future space tourists. Furthermore, touristic spaceflights could be planned, controlled and monitored by existing space operation centers in Europe, the USA or Russia. As soon as a space tourism market is established, large commercially oriented industrial conglomerates will cooperate in strategic alliances to operate and expand the space tourism business comparable to the terrestrial tourism and telecommunications industries. The main motivation for an industrial investment in the space tourism sector will be the potential of very high achievable profits, which can be expected due to multi-billion dollar market potential.

THE MARKET FOR SPACE TOURISM

As soon as the "space ticket" can be purchased for some $10000-in the best of all cases a ticket price comparable to that of a transatlantic flight with the Concorde-one can expect that a global space tourism market will be established. This has been confirmed by first national and international polls and market analyses (e.g. in the US, Japan, Europe) which indicate that a remarkable segment of clients would be already willing to make considerable financial commitments for short trips into space. For example, 4.3% of all Germans are willing to pay several $10000-which is roughly comparable to an annual income-for a space trip. This could be a ticket price which might be achievable with future generations of spacecraft, and it is comparable to the cost of a vacation on a cruise ship which already attracts a steady clientele. Figure 4 shows the expected number of passengers for a space trip as a function of the ticket costs according to international polls performed in the US, Japan, and Europe. With current costs of several ten million dollars to transport a human into space, space tourism is not affordable and finds no acceptance in the public.

However, with declining space travel ticket prices the situation will change. Once a ticket price of $ 1000 is obtainable, a passenger volume of about 20 million is expected, and even with a ticket price of $ 50000 a passenger rate of 1 million per year can be expected.. Nevertheless, the above mentioned polls have to be critically assessed with respect to their accuracy and credibility. Therefore, more detailed and representative polls and market research in this area have to be carried out.

Generally, any average person in good health and with appropriate preparation is able to go on a space trip. NASA, for example, just recently decided to send 77-year old former astronaut and Senator John Glenn into space with the Space Shuttle (Fig. 5). He took part in important medical research experiments from which especially the older generation will profit.

THE FASCINATION OF SPACE TRAVEL

The fact, that a significant portion of the public is willing to spend a lot of money on space trips proofs that these are regarded as very promising and fascinating. The confrontation with the high technology of space missions, the heroic myth of astronauts, and the possibility of orbiting planet Earth in just a little more than 80 minutes with a speed of about 30000 kilometres per hour (compared to the 80 days needed a hundred years ago) will represent for each tourist an unforgettable adventure and event. Furthermore, for the first time in his life, the tourist in a space hotel will experience an entirely different environment. Depending on the rotational velocity of the Space Hotel Berlin various levels of artificial gravity can be obtained, ranging from customary terrestrial gravity (1G) to Mars gravity (1/3 G) and even Lunar gravity (1/6 G), i.e. a human being will weigh only one sixth of his or her earthly weight.

In the central node of the Space Hotel Berlin there will be nearly zero gravity. Here the tourist can experience weightlessness. How does one behave if one can not get from A to B in a normal way and "above" or "below" are without meaning. Many of the questions that astronauts were asked-how they manage eating, sleeping, and personal hygiene-can be explored by tourists themselves. The zerogravity area also offers fascinating opportunities for entirely new sorts of entertainment, games and sports.

For example a ball game in zero-gravity and three-dimensional space. Or one can imagine a swimming pool. The water would not be in a basin, but would float as wobbly water bubbles in space, some of which are several meters in diameter, and one can swim and dive through them. One can imagine that some tourists may want to use the zero-gravity zones for future medical therapies: This could represent a first step towards a future space hospital. Furthermore, the Coriolis force, which only appears within rotating systems, will baffle the tourist, since it will push him, like a magic force, into a certain direction, depending on his direction of movement. Probably, the predominant part of the vacation will be spent with the breathtaking view each tourist will have from the panoramic window of each apartment onto the blue home planet from a distance of 400 kilometres. Even if initially concentrating on his home city and country, soon the tourist will discover earth with its thin and precious atmosphere and a wide variety of picturesque structures on its surface as a totality without national borders. On the other hand, the view of the infinite expanse of outer space will dramatically symbolise that we owe our human existence, history and future a singular, beautiful, tiny "grain of sand" which we call Earth.

After returning to Earth, the consciousness of many tourists may have changed; it will be expanded and globalised with many potentially positive social consequences, which could help, for example, to lower the dangers for environmental pollution, local conflicts, and war. Once space tourism is affordable to the broad public, space activities-especially manned space programs-will develop and increase in a way that is hardly imaginable today. A wide variety of space station concepts have been investigated for decades (fig. 17) and first concepts for gigantic, circular cities in orbit are available. Perhaps many humans increasingly will harbour the wish to visit the more remote planetary worlds of Mars and of the Earth's Moon some day, according to the Russian space pioneer Ziolkowksy who proclaimed around the year 1900: "Earth is the cradle of humanity, but one cannot always remain in the cradle."

INTERNATIONAL CULTURAL TOURISM CHARTER

The Charter Ethos

At the broadest level, the natural and cultural heritage belongs to all people. We each have a right and responsibility to understand, appreciate and conserve its universal values.

Heritage is a broad concept and includes the natural as well as the cultural environment. It encompasses landscapes, historic places, sites and built environments, as well as bio-diversity, collections, past and continuing cultural practices, knowledge and living experiences. It records and expresses the long processes of historic development, forming the essence of diverse national, regional, indigenous and local identities and is an integral part of modern life. It is a dynamic reference point and positive instrument for growth and change. The particular heritage and collective memory of each locality or community is irreplaceable and an important foundation for development, both now and into the future. At a time of increasing globalisation, the protection, conservation, interpretation and presentation of the heritage and cultural diversity of any particular place or region is an important challenge for people everywhere. However, management of that heritage, within a framework of internationally recognised and appropriately applied standards, is usually the responsibility of the particular community or custodian group.

A primary objective for managing heritage is to communicate its significance and need for its conservation to its host community and to visitors. Reasonable and well managed physical, intellectual and/or emotive access to heritage and cultural development is both a right and a privilege. It brings with it a duty of respect for the heritage values, interests and equity of the present-day host community, indigenous custodians or owners of historic property and for the landscapes and cultures from which that heritage evolved.

THE DYNAMIC INTERACTION BETWEEN TOURISM AND CULTURAL HERITAGE

Domestic and international tourism continues to be among the foremost vehicles for cultural exchange, providing a personal experience, not only of that which has survived from the past, but of the contemporary life and society of others. It is increasingly appreciated as a positive force for natural and cultural conservation. Tourism can capture the economic characteristics of the heritage and harness these for conservation by generating funding, educating the community and influencing policy. It is an essential part of many national and regional economies and can be an important factor in development, when managed successfully. Tourism itself has become an increasingly complex phenomenon, with political, economic, social, cultural, educational, bio-physical, ecological and aesthetic dimensions. The achievement of a beneficial interaction between the potentially conflicting expectations and aspirations of visitors and host or local communities, presents many challenges and opportunities. The natural and cultural heritage, diversities and living cultures are major tourism attractions. Excessive or poorly-managed tourism and tourism related development can threaten their physical nature, integrity and significant characteristics. The ecological setting, culture and lifestyles of host communities may also be degraded, along with the visitor's experience of the place.

Tourism should bring benefits to host communities and provide an important means and motivation for them to care for and maintain their heritage and cultural practices. The involvement and co-operation of local and/or indigenous community representatives, conservationists, tourism operators, property owners, policy makers, those preparing national development plans and site managers is necessary to achieve a sustainable tourism industry and enhance the protection of heritage resources for future generations.

ICOMOS, the International Council on Monuments and Sites, as the author of this Charter, other international organisations and the tourism industry, are dedicated to this challenge.

OBJECTIVES OF THE CHARTER

The Objectives of the International Cultural Tourism Charter are:

- To facilitate and encourage those involved with heritage conservation and management to make the significance of that heritage accessible to the host community and visitors.
- To facilitate and encourage the tourism industry to promote and manage tourism in ways that respect and enhance the heritage and living cultures of host communities.
- To facilitate and encourage a dialogue between conservation interests and the tourism industry about

the importance and fragile nature of heritage places, collections and living cultures, including the need to achieve a sustainable future for them.

- To encourage those formulating plans and policies to develop detailed, measurable goals and strategies relating to the presentation and interpretation of heritage places and cultural activities, in the context of their preservation and conservation.

In addition,

- The Charter supports wider initiatives by ICOMOS, other international bodies and the tourism industry in maintaining the integrity of heritage management and conservation.
- The Charter encourages the involvement of all those with relevant or at times conflicting interests, responsibilities and obligations to join in achieving its objectives.
- The Charter encourages the formulation of detailed guidelines by interested parties, facilitating the implementation of the Principles to their specific circumstances or the requirements of particular organisations and communities.

PRINCIPLES OF THE CULTURAL TOURISM CHARTER

Principle 1

Since domestic and international tourism is among the foremost vehicles for cultural exchange, conservation should provide responsible and well managed opportunities for members of the host community and visitors to experience and understand that community's heritage and culture at first hand.

The natural and cultural heritage is a material and spiritual resource, providing a narrative of historical development. It has an important role in modern life and should be made physically, intellectually and/or emotively accessible to the general public. Programmes for the protection and conservation of the physical attributes, intangible aspects, contemporary cultural expressions and broad context, should facilitate an understanding and appreciation of the heritage significance by the host community and the visitor, in an equitable and affordable manner.

Individual aspects of natural and cultural heritage have differing levels of significance, some with universal values, others of national, regional or local importance. Interpretation programmes should present that significance in a relevant and accessible manner to the host community and the visitor, with appropriate, stimulating and contemporary forms of education, media, technology and personal explanation of historical, environmental and cultural information.

Interpretation and presentation programmes should facilitate and encourage the high level of public awareness and support necessary for the long term survival of the natural and cultural heritage. Interpretation programmes should present the significance of heritage places, traditions and cultural practices within the past experience and present diversities of the area and the host community, including that of minority cultural or linguistic groups. The visitor should always be informed of the differing cultural values that may be ascribed to a particular heritage resource.

Principle 2

The relationship between Heritage Places and Tourism is dynamic and may involve conflicting values. It should be managed in a sustainable way for present and future generations.

Places of heritage significance have an intrinsic value for all people as an important basis for cultural diversity and social development. The long term protection and conservation of living cultures, heritage places, collections, their physical and ecological integrity and their environmental context, should be an essential component of social, economic, political, legislative, cultural and tourism development policies.

The interaction between heritage resources or values and tourism is dynamic and ever changing, generating both opportunities and challenges, as well as potential conflicts. Tourism projects, activities and developments should achieve positive outcomes and minimise adverse impacts on the heritage and lifestyles of the host community, while responding to the needs and aspirations of the visitor.

Conservation, interpretation and tourism development programmes should be based on a comprehensive understanding of the specific, but often complex or conflicting aspects of heritage significance of the particular place. Continuing research and consultation are important to furthering the evolving understanding and appreciation of that significance.

The retention of the authenticity of heritage places and collections is important. It is an essential element of their cultural significance, as expressed in the physical material, collected memory and intangible traditions that remain from the past. Programmes should present and interpret the authenticity of places and cultural experiences to enhance the appreciation and understanding of that cultural heritage.

Tourism development and infrastructure projects should take account of the aesthetic, social and cultural dimensions, natural and cultural landscapes, bio-diversity characteristics and the broader visual context of heritage places. Preference should be given to using local materials and take account of local architectural styles or vernacular traditions.

Before heritage places are promoted or developed for increased tourism, management plans should assess the natural and cultural values of the resource. They should then establish appropriate limits of acceptable change, particularly in relation to the impact of visitor numbers on the physical characteristics, integrity, ecology and biodiversity of the place, local access and transportation systems and the social, economic and cultural well being of the host community. If the likely level of change is unacceptable the development proposal should be modified.

There should be on-going programmes of evaluation to assess the progressive impacts of tourism activities and development on the particular place or community.

Principle 3

Conservation and Tourism Planning for Heritage Places should ensure that the Visitor Experience will be worthwhile, satisfying and enjoyable.

Conservation and tourism programmes should present high quality information to optimise the visitor's understanding of the significant heritage characteristics and of the need for their protection, enabling the visitor to enjoy the place in an appropriate manner.

Visitors should be able to experience the heritage place at their own pace, if they so choose. Specific circulation routes may be necessary to minimise impacts on the integrity and physical fabric of a place, its natural and cultural characteristics.

Respect for the sanctity of spiritual places, practices and traditions is an important consideration for site managers, visitors, policy makers, planners and tourism operators. Visitors should be encouraged to behave as welcomed guests, respecting the values and lifestyles of the host community, rejecting possible theft or illicit trade in cultural property and conducting themselves in a responsible manner which would generate a renewed welcome, should they return.

Planning for tourism activities should provide appropriate facilities for the comfort, safety and well-being of the visitor, that enhance the enjoyment of the visit but do not adversely impact on the significant features or ecological characteristics.

Principle 4

Host communities and indigenous peoples should be involved in planning for conservation and tourism.

The rights and interests of the host community, at regional and local levels, property owners and relevant indigenous peoples who may exercise traditional rights or responsibilities over their own land and its significant sites, should be respected. They should be involved in establishing goals, strategies, policies and protocols for the identification, conservation, management, presentation and interpretation of their heritage resources, cultural practices and contemporary cultural expressions, in the tourism context.

While the heritage of any specific place or region may have a universal dimension, the needs and wishes of some communities or indigenous peoples to restrict or manage physical, spiritual or intellectual access to certain cultural practices, knowledge, beliefs, activities, artefacts or sites should be respected.

Principle 5

Tourism and conservation activities should benefit the host community.

Policy makers should promote measures for the equitable distribution of the benefits of tourism to be shared across countries or regions, improving the levels of socio-economic development and contributing where necessary to poverty alleviation.

Conservation management and tourism activities should provide equitable economic, social and cultural benefits to the men and women of the host or local community, at all levels, through education, training and the creation of full-time employment opportunities.

A significant proportion of the revenue specifically derived from tourism programmes to heritage places should be allotted to the protection, conservation and presentation of those places, including their natural and cultural contexts. Where possible, visitors should be advised of this revenue allocation.

Tourism programmes should encourage the training and employment of guides and site interpreters from the host community to enhance the skills of local people in the presentation and interpretation of their cultural values.

Heritage interpretation and education programmes among the people of the host community should encourage the involvement of local site interpreters. The programmes should promote a knowledge and respect for their heritage, encouraging the local people to take a direct interest in its care and conservation. Conservation management and tourism programmes should include education and training opportunities for policy makers, planners, researchers, designers, architects, interpreters, conservators and tourism operators. Participants should be encouraged to understand and help resolve the at times conflicting issues, opportunities and problems encountered by their colleagues.

Principle 6

Tourism promotion programmes should protect and enhance Natural and Cultural Heritage characteristics.

Tourism promotion programmes should create realistic expectations and responsibly inform potential visitors of the specific heritage characteristics of a place or host community, thereby encouraging them to behave appropriately.

Places and collections of heritage significance should be promoted and managed in ways which protect their authenticity and enhance the visitor experience by minimising fluctuations in arrivals and avoiding excessive numbers of visitors at any one time.

Tourism promotion programmes should provide a wider distribution of benefits and relieve the pressures on more popular places by encouraging visitors to experience the wider cultural and natural heritage characteristics of the region or locality.

The promotion, distribution and sale of local crafts and other products should provide a reasonable social and economic return to the host community, while ensuring that their cultural integrity is not degraded.

7

ECONOMIC IMPACTS OF TOURISM

- Negative economic impacts from tourism
- How tourism can contribute to economic development

The tourism industry generates substantial economic benefits to both host countries and tourists' home countries. Especially in developing countries, one of the primary motivations for a region to promote itself as a tourism destination is the expected economic improvement.

As with other impacts, this massive economic development brings along both positive and negative consequences.

> *According to the World Tourism Organization, 698 million people traveled to a foreign country in 2000, spending more US$ 478 billion. International tourism receipts combined with passenger transport currently total more than US$ 575 billion-making tourism the world's number one export earner, ahead of automotive products, chemicals, petroleum and food.*
>
> ***Source:** WTTC*

NEGATIVE ECONOMIC IMPACTS OF TOURISM

There are many hidden costs to tourism, which can have unfavorable economic effects on the host community. Often rich countries are better able to profit from tourism than poor ones. Whereas the least developed countries have the most urgent need for income, employment and general rise of the standard of living by means of tourism, they are least able to realize these benefits. Among the reasons for this are large-scale transfer of tourism revenues out of the host country and exclusion of local businesses and products.

Leakage

The direct income for an area is the amount of tourist expenditure that remains locally after taxes, profits, and wages are paid outside the area and after imports are purchased; these subtracted amounts are called leakage. In most all-inclusive package tours, about 80% of travelers' expenditures go to the airlines, hotels and other international companies (who often have their headquarters in the travelers' home countries), and not to local businesses or workers. In addition, significant amounts of income actually retained at destination level can leave again through leakage.

A study of tourism 'leakage' in Thailand estimated that 70% of all money spent by tourists ended up leaving Thailand (via foreign-owned tour operators, airlines, hotels, imported drinks and food, etc.). Estimates for other Third World countries range from 80% in the Caribbean to 40% in India.

Source: *Sustainable Living*

Of each US$ 100 spent on a vacation tour by a tourist from a developed country, only around US$ 5 actually stays in a developing-country destination's economy. The figure below shows how the leakage happens.

There are two main ways that leakage occurs:

Import Leakage: This commonly occurs when tourists demand standards of equipment, food, and other products that the host country cannot supply. Especially in less-developed countries, food and drinks must often be imported, since local products are not up to the hotel's (i.e. tourist's) standards or the country simply doesn't have a supplying industry. Much of the income from tourism expenditures leaves the country again to pay for these imports.

The average import-related leakage for most developing countries today is between 40% and 50% of gross tourism earnings for small economies and between 10% and 20% for most advanced and diversified economies, according to UNCTAD.

> *Even in developed regions, local producers are often unable to supply the tourism industry appropriately even if good will is present: the 64-room hotel "Kaiser im Tirol" in Austria, an award-winning leader in sustainable practices, cannot find organic food suppliers in the local farming networks in the appropriate quantity, quality and reliability, as production cycles and processes are not compatible with its needs.*
>
> **Source:** *Austrian Preparatory Conference for the International Year of Ecotourism, September 2001*

Export leakage Multinational corporations and large foreign businesses have a substantial share in the import leakage. Often, especially in poor developing destinations, they are the only ones that possess the necessary capital to invest in the construction of tourism infrastructure and facilities. As a consequence of this, an export leakage arises when overseas investors who finance the resorts and hotels take their profits back to their country of origin.

> *A 1996 UN report evaluating the contribution of tourism to national income, gross levels of incomes or gross foreign exchange, found that net earnings of tourism, after deductions were made for all necessary foreign exchange expenditures, were much more significant for the industry. This report found significant leakage associated with: (a) imports of materials and equipment for construction; (b) imports of consumer goods, particularly food and drinks; (c) repatriation of profits earned by foreign investors; (d) overseas promotional expenditures and (e) amortization of external debt incurred in the development of hotels and resorts. The impact of the leakage varied greatly across countries, depending on the structure of the economy and the tourism industry. From the data presented in this study on the Caribbean, St. Lucia had a foreign exchange*

leakage rate of 56% from its gross tourism receipts, Aruba had 41%, Antigua and Barbuda 25% and Jamaica 40%.

Source: *Caribbean Voice*

Enclave Tourism: Local businesses often see their chances to earn income from tourists severely reduced by the creation of "all-inclusive" vacation packages. When tourists remain for their entire stay at the same cruise ship or resort, which provides everything they need and where they will make all their expenditures, not much opportunity is left for local people to profit from tourism.

The Organization of American States (OAS) carried out a survey of Jamaica's tourist industry that looked at the role of the all-inclusives compared to other types of accommodation. It found that 'All-inclusive hotels generate the largest amount of revenue but their impact on the economy is smaller per dollar of revenue than other accommodation subsectors.'

It also concluded that all-inclusives imported more, and employed fewer people per dollar of revenue than other hotels. This information confirms the concern of those who have argued that all-inclusives have a smaller trickle-down effect on local economies.

The cruise ship industry provides another example of economic enclave tourism. Non-river cruises carried some 8.7 million international passengers in 1999. On many ships, especially in the Caribbean (the world's most popular cruise destination with 44.5% of cruise passengers), guests are encouraged to spend most of their time and money on board, and opportunities to spend in some ports are closely managed and restricted.

OTHER NEGATIVE IMPACTS

Infrastructure Cost

Tourism development can cost the local government and local taxpayers a great deal of money. Developers may want the government to improve the airport, roads and other infrastructure, and possibly to provide tax breaks and other financial advantages, which are costly activities for the government. Public resources spent on subsidized infrastructure or tax breaks may reduce government investment in other critical areas such as education and health.

Increase in Prices

Increasing demand for basic services and goods from tourists will often cause price hikes that negatively affect local residents whose income does not increase proportionately. A San Francisco State University study of Belize found that, as a consequence of tourism development, the prices for locals increased by 8%.

Tourism development and the related rise in real estate demand may dramatically increase building costs and land values. Not only does this make it more difficult for local people, especially in developing countries, to meet their basic daily needs, it can also result in a dominance by outsiders in land markets and in-migration that erodes economic opportunities for the locals, eventually disempowering residents. In Costa Rica, close to 65% of the hotels belong to foreigners. Long-term tourists living in second homes, and the so-called amenity migrants (wealthy or retired people and liberal professionals moving to attractive destinations in order to enjoy the atmosphere and peaceful rhythms of life) cause price hikes in their new homes if their numbers attain a certain critical mass.

Economic Dependence of the Local Community on Tourism

Diversification in an economy is a sign of health, however if a country or region becomes dependent for its economic survival upon one industry, it can put major stress upon this industry as well as the people involved to perform well. Many countries, especially developing countries with little ability to explore other resources, have embraced tourism as a way to boost the economy. In The Gambia, for instance, 30% of the workforce depends directly or indirectly on tourism. In small island developing states, percentages can range from 83% in the Maldives to 21% in the Seychelles and 34% in Jamaica, according to the WTO. Over-reliance on tourism, especially mass tourism, carries significant risks to tourism-dependent economies. Economic recession and the impacts of natural disasters such as tropical storms and cyclones as well as changing tourism patterns can have a devastating effect on the local tourism sector.

Malta has only 380,000 residents, but received 1.2 million tourists in 1999. As 25% of GDP (and indirectly 40%), tourism generated more than $650 million in foreign exchange earnings. Malta's high dependence on tourism and a limited number of export products makes its trade performance vulnerable to shifts in international demand.

Source: *Washington Times*

Seasonal Character of Jobs

The seasonal character of the tourism industry creates economic problems for destinations that are heavily dependent on it. Problems that seasonal workers face include job (and therefore income) insecurity, usually with no guarantee of employment from one season to the next, difficulties in getting training, employment-related medical benefits, and recognition of their experience, and unsatisfactory housing and working conditions.

Other Industry Impacts Affecting Tourism

Economic crises, like the Asian crisis that hit Thailand, Malaysia and Indonesia a few years ago, can be devastating to inbound tourism flows. The financial turmoil triggered a sharp fall in tourism flows to affected countries during 1997 and 1998. In the Philippines, the crisis and the temporary closure of Philippine Airlines affected inbound arrivals significantly as there was a decline of almost 3.3% in 1998.

Source: *Hotel-online*

HOW TOURISM CAN CONTRIBUTE TO ECONOMIC CONSERVATION

The main positive economic impacts of tourism relate to foreign exchange earnings, contributions to government revenues, and generation of employment and business opportunities. These are discussed briefly here; further information on economic contributions from tourism can be found at the World Travel & Tourism Council's home page.

Foreign Exchange Earnings

Tourism expenditures and the export and import of related goods and services generate income to the host economy and can stimulate the investment necessary to finance growth in other economic sectors. Some countries seek to accelerate this growth by requiring visitors to bring in a certain amount of foreign currency for each day of their stay and do not allow them to take it out of the country again at the end of the trip.

> *An important indicator of the role of international tourism is its generation of foreign exchange earnings. Tourism is one of the top five export categories for as many as 83% of countries and is a main source of foreign exchange earnings for at least 38% of countries.*
>
> ***Source:*** *World Tourism Organization*

Contribution to Government Revenues

Government revenues from the tourism sector can be categorized as direct and indirect contributions. Direct contributions are generated by taxes on incomes from tourism employment and tourism businesses, and by direct levies on tourists such as departure taxes. Indirect contributions are those originated from taxes and duties levied on goods and services supplied to tourists.

The United States National Park Service estimates that the 273 million visits to American national parks in 1993 generated direct and indirect expenditures of US$ 10 billion and 200,000 jobs. When visits to land managed by other agencies, and to state, local, and privately-managed parks, are added, parks were estimated to bring around US$ 22 billion annually to the US economy. These expenditures also generate significant tax revenues for the government.

The World Travel and Tourism Council estimates that travel and tourism's direct, indirect, and personal tax contribution worldwide was over US$ 800 billion in 1998-a figure it expects to double by 2010. (Source: WTTC/Michigan State University Tax Policy Center)

Employment Generation

The rapid expansion of international tourism has led to significant employment creation. For example, the hotel accommodation sector alone provided around 11.3 million jobs worldwide in 1995. Tourism can generate jobs directly through hotels, restaurants, nightclubs, taxis, and souvenir sales, and indirectly through the supply of goods and services needed by tourism-related businesses. According to the WTO, tourism supports some 7% of the world's workers.

Stimulation of Infrastructure Investment

Tourism can induce the local government to make infrastructure improvements such as better water and sewage systems, roads, electricity, telephone and public transport networks, all of which can improve the quality of life for residents as well as facilitate tourism.

Contribution to Local Economies

Tourism can be a significant, even essential, part of the local economy. As the environment is a basic component of the tourism industry's assets, tourism revenues are often used to measure the economic value of protected areas. For example, Dorrigo National Park in New South Wales, Australia, has been estimated to contribute 7% of gross regional output and 8.4% of regional employment. The importance of tourism to local economies can also be illustrated by the impacts when it is disrupted: the catastrophic 1997 floods that closed Yosemite National Park in California cause locally severe economic losses to the areas around the park. In the most heavily impacted county, Mariposa County, 1997 personal income was reduced by an estimated US$1,159 per capita (US$18 million for the entire county)-a 6.6% decline. The county was also estimated to have lost US$1.67 million in county occupancy and sales tax revenues, and 956 jobs, a significant number in a county of fewer than 16,000 residents.

There are other local revenues that are not easily quantified, as not all tourist expenditures are formally registered in the macro-economic statistics. Money is earned from tourism through informal employment such as street vendors, informal guides, rickshaw drivers, etc. The positive side of informal or unreported employment is that the money is returned to the local economy, and has a great multiplier effect as it is spent over and over again. The World Travel and Tourism Council estimates that tourism generates an indirect contribution equal to 100% of direct tourism expenditures.

8

SUSTAINABLE TOURISM: A LOCAL AUTHORITY PERSPECTIVE

INTRODUCTION

A primary challenge of local governance, both today and in decades ahead, is to steer increasingly external, global forces on local development so that development achieves the shared vision of the local population. In cities, towns and villages throughout the world, the primary responsibility for this steering process rests with the institution of local government and its diverse local authorities.

As providers of social services, builders of economic infrastructure, regulators of economic activity, and managers of the natural environment, local authorities have many direct instruments at their disposal to influence development. Yet in addition to their direct roles in the development process, perhaps the most important role that local authorities can play in a global economy is that of facilitator among the diverse interests seeking to influence the direction of local development. Only with such a facilitator can a community of diverse interests define a shared vision and act consistent with this vision.

The role of local authorities as facilitators in the development process is reinforced through municipal international cooperation (MIC). With globalisation, the governance challenges facing local authorities in different parts of the world have increased in their similarities, transcending the national political and economic systems upon which different communities rely.

These shared challenges of governance have instigated thousands of local authorities to establish municipal international cooperation projects and to join international local government organisations (LGOs) to advocate for local self-governance and control over the development process.

Even prior to the UN Conference on Environment and Development, but particularly since the adoption of Agenda 21, many local authorities and their LGOs have focused on the unique challenges of governance for sustainable development. At the local level, sustainable development is achieved by steering local development activities to simultaneously achieve three objectives:

increased local social welfare;

greater, and more equitably distributed, local economic wealth; and

enhanced integrity of local ecosystems.

Thousands of local authorities, in partnership with their communities and supported by MIC activities, have instigated Local Agenda 21 processes to create a shared vision for local development that is consistent with the sustainable development concept. In response to these visions, local authorities have been adapting their practices and activities to steer local development along the sustainable development path. Local Agenda 21 processes, in conjunction with decentralisation policies originating at the national level, are transforming local governance and reorienting the process of local development in communities throughout the world.

Tourism is one of the many external forces influencing the direction and options for local development. The question of whether tourism can be sustainable-that is, whether it can contribute to local sustainable development-is rightfully addressed in the context of the Local Agenda 21 process.

A truly legitimate and practical discussion on sustainable tourism must take place in and with the communities that are being influenced by tourist industry development. It must create accountability of the tourism industry to locally-defined development visions. This paper provides an general call for the tourism industry, through both its local and transnational agents, to join and support the Local Agenda 21 processes in communities where tourism is a fundamental development force.

The true proof of "sustainable tourism" will be the sustainable development of local communities that serve as tourist destinations. It is time for the sustainable tourism debate to focus on this challenge. Local authorities worldwide welcome the leadership of the UN Commission on Sustainable Development, and the interest of the tourism industry, to reduce tourism's negative impacts and to increase the positive contribution of tourism business and consumption activity to local sustainable development.

INDUSTRY INITIATIVES FOR SUSTAINABLE TOURISM PROBLEMS

Tourism is a recognised global industry-one of the largest industries in the world. Like any global industry, tourist business activities can have considerable impact on local development trends. The local impacts of the tourism industry are diverse and are often unique to the tourism sector.

Tourist activities, as traditionally defined by the tourism industry, fundamentally involve the transportation and hosting of the tourism consumer in a local community, i.e., "tourist destination," where the tourist product is consumed. No other global industry structures itself in such a way that the consumer is brought to the product, rather than the product being delivered to the consumer in his or her own community. This structural difference produces unique social impacts upon the local tourist community, including the interruption of local customs and lifestyles, the spread of infectious diseases, changes in local demographics, and changes in local housing and labor markets.

The primary product of tourism is not something produced by the industry. The product is often the heritage, wealth, and expected legacy of the community that serves as the tourist destination. The business activity of the tourism industry is to promote the "salable" or appealing aspects of the community, transport non-residents into the community, manage the hospitality for and guide the activities of these visitors, and provide them with goods and services to purchase during their stay. If these business activities degrade the community's heritage and wealth, then the community suffers more directly than the consumer, who can return to his or her own community without responsibility for or awareness of the impacts of his tourist activities.

Tourism activities can, in particular, degrade the social and natural wealth of a community. The intrusion of large numbers of uninformed foreigners into local social systems can undermine pre-existing social relationships and values. This is particularly a problem where tourism business is centered in traditional social systems, such as isolated communities or indigenous peoples.

Tourism in natural areas, euphemistically called "eco-tourism," can be a major source of degradation of local ecological, economic and social systems. The intrusion of large numbers of foreigners with high-consumption and high-waste habits into natural areas, or into towns with inadequate waste management infrastructure, can produce changes to those natural areas at a rate that is far greater than imposed by local residents. These tourism-related changes are particularly deleterious when local residents rely on those natural areas for their sustenance. Resulting economic losses can encourage socially deleterious economic activities such as prostitution, crime, and migrant and child labour.

SOLUTIONS

Solutions to adverse tourism impacts are to be found in the shared interest of local communities, tourism businesses, and tourism consumers to maintain the natural wealth and social heritage of the tourist destination. In the first instance, therefore, an institutional mechanism must be established, relative to each destination, to articulate and develop this sense of shared interest.

To secure the legitimacy of these mechanisms, the participation of all interested local groups or interests must be guaranteed. Dialogue must take place in an open and transparent way.

Experience demonstrates that if dialogue among interested parties is to have a real impact on development, it must generate accountability among these parties with regards to future investments, practices and policies. Consensus or decisions arising from dialogue must be reflected in institutional action. Only through such accountability can interests maintain a commitment to continued dialogue and a common agenda for local tourism development.

Experience demonstrates that this accountability should be reciprocal between individual or private interests and societal or public interests. Without such reciprocal accountability, local communities are typically forced to choose, in conflict, between private and public benefits, even if ample "win-win" development choices exist. On the one hand, accountability requires that property owners are provided with opportunity to retain the economic value of their property, either through sale or income generating activity. On the other hand, private market relationships, including property ownership, do not provide sufficient basis for social accountability related to "public goods," including ecological integrity and social heritage. Private property titles do not recognize the concepts of ecological integrity or social heritage. Excessive reliance upon private property ownership as a guide in development has in fact contributed to the deterioration of public goods.

Within such a framework of accountability, numerous instruments are available to guide local tourist development on a sustainable path. These instruments include:

heritage preservation requirements for site developments and building designs;

programs to exchange land and development rights from non-suitable to suitable development areas;

private heritage and green space stewardship programs;

tax benefits accruing to property owners exercising sustainable development practices;

tourism taxes and development fees to support construction and maintenance of required infrastructure.

However, without true commitment to the sustainable tourism agenda, these instruments are not themselves sufficient to prevent the steady erosion, by legally sanctioned private actions, of local natural wealth and social heritage. Therefore, support from the international, national, provincial and local levels of industry and government, is essential to the success of this agenda.

Agents and Partnerships for Change

Fortunately, in more than 2,000 communities in 64 countries Local Agenda 21 partnership forums already exist to serve as a mechanism for sustainable tourism dialogue. Where these forums are weak or have not yet addressed tourism issues, the tourist industry, local government organisations (LGOs) and concerned NGOs can serve as a catalyst for dialogue. A particular opportunity exists in those countries where Local Agenda 21 national campaigns (in more than 20 countries) or where National Councils for Sustainable Development (NCSDs-in about 70 countries) have been established. NCSDs can play a key role in providing country-level support to local review of the sustainable tourism agenda. Through their international facilitating body, the Earth Council, a comprehensive effort between industry, NGOs, LGOs and NCSDs can be established.

Of additional interest at the local level is the potential role of local tourism offices or Convention and Visitor Bureaus (CVBs) that have been created through public-private partnerships to promote local tourist attractions. Where motivated to support sustainable tourism development, the CVBs could serve as facilitators of working groups, within the context of Local Agenda 21 activities, on sustainable tourism development. Where CVBs or their related international body(ies) have made no express commitment to sustainable development, local authorities, as primary funders of CVBs, are in an excellent position to mobilise their awareness and support.

Internationally, alliances between LGOs and various tourism industry trade associations, trade unions and consumer organisations can support awareness raising and local demonstration projects that may serve as models for other local communities on a country or regional basis.

INFLUENCING CONSUMER BEHAVIOR TO PROMOTE SUSTAINABLE TOURISM

Problems

Tourism-related consumption has three stages of impact. First, prior to departure, tourists purchase travel-related clothing and equipment, which may be produced under conditions that undermine the social and ecological sustainability of the producing communities. Second, when tourists travel long distances to tourist destinations, they create considerable atmospheric pollution and other impacts on the global environment. Third, upon arrival at the tourist destination, tourists often continue their accustomed habits of consumption, even though these destinations may not have the infrastructure required to manage those consumption patterns. This paper will focus on the second and third stages of impact.

In addition to high altitude emissions from long distance air travel, air travel produces considerable negative local environmental impacts, including ground level emissions of VOCs and particulates, disposal of fuel, hazardous chemicals and solid waste, noise pollution, and wildlife and habitat disruption. Marine dumping of wastes from cruise ships is an increasing concern.

However, with nearly 600 million international travelers in 1997, surprisingly little public information is available on the environmental and social impacts of long distance travel. For instance, individual travelers receive far greater information about the impacts of their local automobile use than of their air or cruise ship transportation. Motor vehicle pollution is typically more highly regulated than aircraft and ship pollution.

Following arrival at tourist destinations, the tourism industry typically strives to host tourists according to the standards and amenities of their country of origin. These hospitality standards mimic-and encourage-the high consumption lifestyles of developed countries. For instance, luxury hotel rooms, with high levels of energy and water consumption, are given the highest rankings or "stars" in international hotel rankings. These "luxury" consumption standards, using current technologies, are themselves globally unsustainable (i.e., in an equitable world).

The most immediate observable impacts of introducing these high consumption practices into lower consumption communities are:

degradation of local water and soil quality, with direct impacts on local health and economies, as a result of the lack of adequate water, drainage, waste water, and waste management infrastructure to manage the higher volumes of waste produced by higher levels of consumption;

reduced access by local residents to land, housing and marine resources through, among other things, reallocation of these community resources to foreign tourist residents and inflation of local prices;

destruction of traditional sources of income.

Solutions

The most direct way to reduce the adverse impacts of tourism-related travel is to increase opportunities for people to engage in appealing tourism activities in their own cities, regions or countries. In various cities of the world, this local tourism concept is known as "green tourism." Green tourism-in contrast to "eco-tourism," which relies on travel to distant locations-seeks to provide recreational attractions and hospitality facilities to local people within their local regions, thereby reducing tourism-related travel. While green tourism has the positive economic effect of stimulating local economic activity, it reduces the flow of foreign currency to developing nations-and any resulting economic benefits that may accrue to developing towns and cities from these revenue flows. However, short of definitive actions by the tourism industry and host countries/communities to reduce the negative environmental impacts of foreign travel and the negative social impacts of foreign tourist enclaves in developing nations, green tourism advocates will continue to build support among tourism consumers.

Solutions to tourism-related pollution in the travel and tourism industry are technologically available. Overcoming economic barriers to their implementation may require government regulation, the development of economic instruments, and industry self-regulation.

The industry has every opportunity to institute voluntary initiatives and self-regulation to address green tourism advocates and those calling for government regulation. The growing effort among international hotel chains, for instance, to offer guests the option of reusing their bedroom towels and linens demonstrates the ability of the industry to respond in one area of impact. However, more comprehensive efforts are required to tangibly resolve accelerating environmental and social impacts. In this regard, the establishment of formal environmental management systems (EMSs) in each business establishment provides a way for tourism businesses to identify their adverse social and environmental impacts and to institute a programme for continuous reductions of those impacts. EMS registration programmes such as ISO 14001 and European EMAS regimes offer extensive guidance to tourism businesses, and deserve the active support of international tourism industry associations.

Ultimately, the solution to adverse environmental impacts arising from local tourist consumption is the establishment of waste reduction programs and appropriate waste management systems and infrastructure, particularly in developing country destinations. Again a choice exists between voluntary and regulatory measures. National governments and tourism businesses, which receive disproportional economic benefits from tourism, share an interest in maintaining tourism related hard currency inflows, and should either directly provide such infrastructure or ensure that funds are made available to local authorities for this purpose. Without such support, powers should be provided to local authorities to increase local revenues from tourism, through local airport taxes, hotel and service taxes, and development fees, to finance infrastructure construction and maintenance. Only through such economic instruments can the public costs of tourism activity be "internalised" in the local tourist economy.

Local revenue measures need to be carefully coordinated across municipal jurisdictions on a regional basis to ensure coordinated infrastructure development. Without a coordinated regional infrastructure development approach, pollution from communities without infrastructure can undo the environmental benefits of infrastructure investments in neighboring communities. Where statutory regional planning bodies do not exist to provide coordination, Local Agenda 21 forums may provide a flexible mechanism for multi-jurisdictional coordination.

Tourist businesses can make a significant voluntary contribution to resolving the social costs of tourism by:

providing local resident employment and training opportunities, including in traditional trades and crafts;

establishing purchasing guidelines that favor local goods and services procurement;

making donations and investments in local recreational facilities, parks, cultural facilities and security operations (which also serve to improve local tourist amenities as well);

establishing local profit-sharing arrangements.

Failing necessary voluntary measures, local governments can institute economic incentives and regulatory measures to reward best practices and prevent severe social impacts that need to be resolved at public expense. Ultimately, in the face of private establishments that demonstrate no long-term commitment to maintaining the preconditions for tourism-which include public safety, environmental quality, infrastructure maintenance, and economic justice-local authorities need to use all powers available to protect the cultural and environmental wealth that make an attractive tourist destination.

Agents and Partnerships for Change

A partnership approach to addressing negative impacts of tourism consumption requires, above all, assumption of responsibility and voluntary action by the tourism industry. For example, within the framework of a voluntary EMS approach, partnerships can be established between local governments, airport authorities, regional air quality agencies, airlines, trade unions, NGOs and resident associations to develop an action programme to reduce local airport pollution. Following the model of the "Responsible Care" programme in the chemical industry, these partnerships could be supported by international travel and tourism organisations and related industry associations. Measures to reduce high altitude pollution by aircraft require similar initiatives by the industry and government at the national and international levels.

Of critical importance is the creation of mechanisms to inform and involve tourism consumers in making educated choices about their activities as tourists in distant tourist destinations. Ideally, these efforts would ensure that tourism consumers, as with industry, begin to recognise and understand tourist destinations as living communities that deserve their support and respect. Communications from tourism consumers to tourism industry and to local authorities about their desire to reduce the adverse impacts of their tourism activities can be essential to mobilizing changes in industry and government practices. International consumer advocacy organisations and trade unions can play an important role in informing consumers about tourism development activities that violate basic principles of sustainable development. Provision of such information to LGOs can facilitate local authority responsiveness to identified problems.

Other actions to reduce the adverse local impacts of tourism consumption at local tourist destinations can be developed within the context of the Local Agenda 21 activities outlined in sections B and D.

PROMOTING BROAD-BASED SUSTAINABLE DEVELOPMENT

Many of the technologies and measures required for sustainable development in the tourism sector are clear. Resources exist within the tourism industry-which annually generates hundreds of billions of dollars-to apply these technologies and to make development within the sector more equitable. However, as the experiences of hundreds of local authorities demonstrate, through their engagement in broad-based sustainable development planning through Local Agenda 21, the appropriate application of technologies and resources requires effective and truly accountable development partnerships. If industry and government are to protect and sustain the social, cultural and environmental wealth that attracts tourists, they must build more ambitious and committed partnerships to plan, manage and invest in this wealth.

In this respect, the primary barrier to sustainable development through tourism is an over reliance on market mechanisms to guide tourism development and consumption decisions. The market-which treats cultural and environmental wealth as free, "public goods" and which responds to degradation of this wealth as a "free rider"-provides instruments to guide development, but is insensitive to many requirements of sustainable tourism. Furthermore, in a global market such as tourism, the problem of "leakage", whereby the economic benefits of local tourism activity flow out of the local community and country back to a foreign corporate headquarters, is another indication of the inadequacy of simple market-driven approaches.

Sustainable tourism development requires a partnership among the stakeholders of the local tourist destination. This partnership must use both market and non-market instruments to implement a shared sustainable development vision. Without such a partnership, advocacy for sustainable development becomes a conflictive struggle between an industry which seeks to respond only to market forces and a public sector which, when accountable, acts to protect public goods and wealth for future generations.

Therefore, the key problem at this stage of the "sustainable tourism" debate is the creation of tangible, working local partnerships. These local partnerships must be encouraged and supported by national governments and industry, and not undermined by "higher level" agreements. To succeed, local residents and their local authorities need to more fully recognise the significant adverse impacts of tourism development and must be informed about opportunities for reduced impact tourism development. Tourism businesses need to recognise and support the social conditions (e.g., security, public health) and the cultural and environmental wealth that make a community an attractive tourist destination.

Solutions

The UN Commission on Sustainable Development has repeatedly recognised Local Agenda 21 planning as an effective partnership mechanism for implementing Agenda 21 in cities and local communities. Experience with Local Agenda 21 activities in hundreds of communities since 1990 has highlighted a number of principles for effective sustainable development planning. These principles can also provide the basis for effective partnerships for sustainable tourism planning and development in local tourist destinations. These partnerships can be established either within or independent from existing Local Agenda 21 activities.

The principles for Local Agenda 21 planning are as follows:

Participation and Transparency, that involves local residents, representing all major groups of society, in Local Agenda 21 planning and makes information aboutsustainable development easily available to the general public.

Partnerships that build collective responsibility for planning, decision making,problem solving, project implementation and evaluation.

Accountability that holds all partners answerable for their actions.

Systemic Approach that addresses the underlying causes of social, economic and ecological problems in an integrated way, focusing on the entire systems that are affected, rather than only problem symptoms.

Ecological Limits, that are defined by Earth's carrying capacity and that serve as the limits for development.

Equity and Justice, that are secured locally through the provision of equal opportunities and human rights, and globally through development cooperation partnerships between developed and developing nations.

Concern for the Future, that requires long-term planning and action that addresses both immediate needs and long-term trends.

These principles can be applied, in working partnerships, to evaluate and improve efforts to address sensitive tourism development issues, such as:

inequitable distribution of tourism revenues and "leakage" of revenues to foreign shores;

displacement of pre-existing local settlements by tourism developments;

equal access to local coastal and recreational resources and controversies over uses and long-term protection of those areas;

concerns related to lack of foreign tourist sensitivity to cultural traditions and sites.

Agents and Partnerships for Change

The primary partnerships for sustainable tourism development will be local partnerships, addressing the unique development goals and needs of each community. Where Local Agenda 21 activities are underway, a Sustainable Tourism Working Group could be established within the existing Local Agenda 21 planning structures to facilitate planning and action.

Notwithstanding the primacy of local partnerships, the transnational nature of tourism requires transnational partnerships to support sustainable tourism planning activities at the local and national levels. The Local Agenda 21 process has established a new mechanism for such transnational partnership, called "Local Agenda 21 Charters." Initiated by the Netherlands Ministry of Foreign Affairs, in cooperation with the International Union of Local Authorities, the International Council for Local Environmental Initiatives, and Towns & Development, the Local Agenda 21 Charters process provides a mechanism for local communities to factor issues of global responsibility within their Local Agenda 21 activities. Two local authorities, typically on a North-South and East-West basis, establish a "Charter" agreement that specifies areas of mutual support to jointly address relevant issues of global equity and sustainability. Presently, 20 local authorities have established the first Local Agenda 21 Charters.

Ultimately, tourism consumers must be rallied to the sustainable tourism agenda, thereby shaping both the market and public policy. Tourism consumers in existing Local Agenda communities may find the Local Agenda 21 Charters mechanism useful in supporting sustainable development in popular tourist destinations. Existing "twinning" or "sister city" relationships with cities that are located in tourist regions can provide the basis for a possible Local Agenda Charters relationship.

COASTAL IMPACTS OF TOURISM

Problems

Economic development activities in any sensitive natural area pose a particular challenge for sustainable development. Coastal areas host the most productive marine ecosystems and serve as spawning grounds for the oceans. The degradation of coastal areas in many countries, with the resulting impacts upon coastal settlements and fisheries, justifies strict local controls on further coastal development.

Coastal zones are dynamic in nature, responding to daily tidal changes as well as long term events such as sea level rising. This dynamic quality offers a defense from extreme weather events. Rigid infrastructure from coastal development can inhibit the ability of coastal ecosystems to respond to changes.

Since coastal areas are the most highly populated regions on Earth, their protection requires unique attention and the effective management of numerous competing interests.

In many coastal areas, tourism development is destroying or marginalising dwindling habitats for marine animals and spawning fish, as well as the livelihoods of traditional fishing families and villages. Unregulated water sport activities and machinery are adding to this toll. Lack of effective waste water treatment for tourist facilities is making a significant contribution to coastal water pollution. Excessive private tourist development is denying equitable human access to beaches and coastal waters, cutting off local populations from their coastal heritage. Inappropriate development in high risk storm areas is costing families, local economies and governments billions of dollars annually.

Solutions

As a first measure towards the sustainable management of coastal areas, governments at all levels, working in partnership with private foundations and investors, should establish designated coastal areas where development will be forever restricted. Protection of these areas should be stringently enforced. In areas where coastal development can be socially and environmentally justified, tourism development should be designed as a form of low-impact economic activity relative to other development alternatives.

The reputation and viability of the sustainable tourism concept depends upon the definition and implementation of clear management objectives for each coastal area. These objectives should clearly designate ecologically and socially/ culturally sensitive areas as well as high risk areas.

Appropriate tourism uses should be designated for each area according to levels of sensitivity and risk. Education programs should be established to inform tourists about these management objectives.

The aims of any sustainable tourism development in coastal areas should be to:

recognise the economic value of existing coastal ecosystems, towns and heritage sites by providing opportunity for local revenue-generation through managed tourist use of these areas;

design tourism developments, in cooperation with local stakeholders, to suit the unique ecological and social characteristics of each coastal site;

use tourism investment to develop and upgrade the watershed, solid waste and waste water management systems for coastal cities and towns;

ensure equitable access to coastal areas by all people, with a specific emphasis on using tourism development as a means to upgrade and manage traditional social uses, for example, through the designation of special natural/cultural heritage sites.

In addition sound planning and management to achieve the above aims, the following opportunities for low-impact tourism development could be considered:

application of low-impact building and transportation designs, materials and technologies;

control of waste production through recycling and efficiency measures;

co-investment by the tourism industry, government and local residents to upgrade existing settlements and urban infrastructure, including drainage and sewerage infrastructure.

Agents and Partnerships for Change

The planning and management of coastal development typically requires the cooperation of local stakeholders-including property owners, residents, local business groups, and local authorities-and government agencies at the national and sub-national levels. In general, some institutional mechanism will need to be established to facilitate cooperation and consensus-building among these actors. As coastal areas typically extend beyond the jurisdictions of individual local authorities, regional coastal management agencies are often established through inter-municipal cooperation or sub-national action to provide effective multi-jurisdictional coordination. Alternatively, private foundations or regional/national NGOs have frequently been used as a mechanism for coastal area planning.

Under ideal circumstances, tourism industry representatives, including property owners, will be directly involved in coastal planning and management schemes. In such cases, the tourism industry, in particular transnational businesses, needs to make a good faith commitment not to circumvent local/regional planning and management discussions by directly lobbying national government for special permissions and considerations.

Ultimately, actions to reduce the adverse impacts of tourism on coastal areas will reflect the principles of Local Agenda 21 planning outlined earlier.

9

Rural Tourism and Sustainable Development

INTRODUCTION

Rural tourism is a segment of the total tourist industry which is particularly important in Hungary, in a country with no spectacular natural attractions, without seaside, high mountains, rainforest or herds of exotic animals. However, its attractive cultural landscapes with small villages, thermal springs, rivers and lakes, combined with the traditional hospitality, are able to offer pleasant experiences to the kind of tourist who is looking for relaxation and recreation in a calm setting.

On one hand, rural tourism development can play an important role in the diversification of the Hungarian tourist supply and in the creation of a more complex and colourful country image. On the other hand, rural tourism is not only the end, but the means to stimulate economic growth, to increase the viability of underdeveloped regions, and to improve the living standards of local populations.

If rural tourism is to fulfil all these roles, it has to be developed in a way that ensures the long-term sustainability of the resources and that of the development progress itself. But what is a sustainable way of development in rural tourism ? How can sustainability be monitored and promoted in rural destinations ? This paper attempts to answer these questions by presenting the current situation of Hungarian rural tourism through indicators that are considered to be relevant for this type of tourism.

SUSTAINABLE TOURISM DEVELOPMENT

The concept of sustainable development was introduced by the World Commission on Environment and Development in the Brundtland Report in 1987, defining sustainable development as "development that meets the needs of the present without compromising the ability of future generations to meet their own needs".

Tourism is one of the foremost economic activities around the world, having transported more than 617 million people internationally and generated 448 billion USD in receipts in 1997 (WTO, 1998). It is a major economic force, having generated in 1996 an estimated 3,153.3 billion USD in gross output, creating employment for app. 255 million people, producing app. 10.7 per cent of world gross domestic product, investing app. 766 billion USD in new facilities and equipment annually, and contributing more than app. 653.3 billion USD to global tax revenue (WTTC, 1996).

The volume and significance of tourism clearly shows that it is not enough to develop new forms of "alternative" tourism in order to minimise the negative and maximise the positive impacts of tourism development. The whole sector must be developed and managed in a way that it does not damage the natural and socio-cultural environment and this is the responsibility of the world-wide tourism industry.

Though the Brundtland report made no special reference to tourism, since its publication, the role of tourism in the process of continuously misusing the Earth's resources has been analysed and the concept of sustainable tourism appeared.

Sustainable tourism has several-often seriously debated-definitions. According to the definition of the Federation of Nature and National Parks, sustainable tourism is "all forms of tourism development, management and activity that maintain the environmental, social and economic integrity and well-being of natural, built and cultural resources in perpetuity"

(FNNP, 1993). A publication by the Tourism Concern and the World Wide Fund for Nature defines sustainable tourism as tourism which "operates within natural capacities for the regeneration and future productivity of natural resources; recognises the contribution that people and communities, customs and lifestyles, make to the tourism experience; accepts that these people must have an equitable share in the economic benefits of tourism; and is guided by the wishes of local people and communities in the host areas" (Tourism Concern & WWF, 1992).

Though the existing definitions usually differ in their focus or level of elaborateness, the main message of the Brundtland Report seems to be more and more accepted by the tourism industry all over the world. However, the notion of sustainability is a very complex one and it has many ramifications (Mowforth & Munt, 1998).

Ecological sustainability, which means that tourism development does not cause irreversible changes in a given destination's ecosystem, is the most commonly accepted dimension, since there is an obvious need all over the world to protect natural resources from the negative impacts of tourism activities. The general growth of environment-awareness has significantly contributed to this trend. Social sustainability refers to the ability of a community to absorb tourism (both the industry and the tourists themselves) without the creation of social disharmony. Cultural sustainability in the context of tourism assumes that a given community is able to retain or adapt their own distinctive cultural traits against the pressure of both the so-called "tourist culture" and the "residual culture" of the visitors (Jafari, 1987).

Economic sustainability refers to a level of economic gain from tourism that is sufficient to provide an appropriate income for the local community (compared to the inconvenience caused by the activities of the tourism sector) and to cover all the costs of any special measure taken to satisfy the tourists (thus a precondition of economic sustainability is the attractiveness of an area and the perceived high quality of its tourist supply:

without being in a competitive position in the world market, no destination can be economically sustainable). The different aspects of sustainability do not compete, but must be seen as equally important. High level of economic profitability must not be considered as a tool to cover over the damage done to social or natural resources, but the relative fragile nature of these latter must not create a planning environment where economic considerations are not being taken (properly). Sustainable tourism development has to be economically viable and naturally and culturally sensitive at the same time.

As we could see, inappropriate tourism development results in increasing stress on destinations and consequently in negative changes in the destinations' physical, economic and socio-cultural characteristics. In order to avoid or minimise unfavourable impacts, decision-makers must be aware of all the factors that play a role in the development process. In the measurement of the progress that an individual destination is making towards sustainable tourism development, sustainability indicators are commonly accepted as one set of useful tools.

INDICATORS OF SUSTAINABILITY

"Indicators measure information with which decision-makers may reduce the chances of unknowingly taking poor decisions" (WTO, 1996). In other words, indicators are a set of useful measures of those factors that are important to the decision-makers (the relative significance of these factors depend on their relevance to the development objectives of a given destination, and on their importance to tourists)."Indicators are both a tool for management today and an investment in the future, since they reduce the risk of inadvertent damage to the resource base on which the [tourist] industry depends" (WTO, 1996).

Based on different guidelines and recommendations (Tourism Concern & WWF, 1992; McCool & Watson, 1994; Murphy, 1994; Howie, 1996; Swarbrooke, 1996; WTO, 1996; Mowforth & Munt, 1998), the indicators suggested for the purpose of this study are the following (Table 1):

Table 1-Indicators of Sustainability in Rural Tourism

Indicator	Measure
1. Stress	- Number of visitors/tourists (per annum/ season)
2. Social stress	- Ratio of visitor/tourist numbers to local population (per annum/season)
3. Attractiveness	- List of natural and cultural resources
	- Rate of attractiveness of natural and cultural resources
4. Planning process	- Existence of local/regional plan for development
5. Tourism planning process	- Existence of local/regional plan for tourism development
6. Area protection	- Category of protection
	- Percentage of protected area compared to the whole territory of the destination
7. Local involvement	- Ratio of the number of locally owned tourist businesses to the total number of tourist businesses
8. Local control	- Existence of formal measures (public hearing, community meeting, local referendum) to ensure local control over development planning and implementation
9. Employment	- Number of jobs created in tourism (full-time equivalent)
	- Ratio of local employee number to the number of guest workers
10. Tourism contribution to the local economy	- Proportion of total tax income generated by tourism only
11. Economic diversity	- Share of different economic activities in the total tax income
12. Energy consumption	- Ratio of renewable energy sources to non-renewable energy sources (consumption)
13. Waste management	- Percentage of households with proper sewage system
	- Percentage of waste receiving treatment

14. Education and training	- Percentage of local people involved in tourism with professional training and education
	- Distribution of tourism employees by education
	- Percentage of tourism employees (and local people) participating in on-the-job training in a given time period
15. Local satisfaction	- Overall perception of tourism's impacts in local community
16. Tourist satisfaction	- Overall satisfaction of tourists concerning the quality and the value/price ratio of the complex tourist product
	- Percentage/change of repeat visits compared to first-time visits

THE CONCEPT OF RURAL TOURISM

Rural tourism is an old and a new phenomenon at the same time. Interest in countryside recreation started to grew already in the 19. century as a reaction to the stress of the increasing urbanisation and industrialisation. The rural scene was admired by poets and artists. The new railway companies transported more and more tourists to the countryside. However, the rural tourism of our era is different: the number of tourists involved has increased significantly and tourism has developed in all types of countryside instead of being limited to areas of exceptional scenic beauty.

Though it seems to be simple to define rural tourism as "tourism that takes place in the countryside", this definition does not include the complexity of the activity and the different forms and meanings developed in different countries. According to a broader definition, "rural tourism includes a range of activities, services and amenities provided by farmers and rural people to attract tourists to their area in order to generate extra income for their businesses" (Gannon, 1988, in te Kloeze, 1994). If this broader concept is accepted, rural tourism covers not only farm tourism or agritourism (which is generally what rural tourism means for most people), but also special interest nature holidays, touring in rural areas and residential tourism, and the services include-besides accommodation-events, festivities, outdoor recreation, production and sale of handicrafts and agricultural products, etc.

The term "rural tourism" has different meanings in different countries. In Finland, for example, it usually means renting out cottages to visitors or providing catering services in the countryside. In Hungary, a special term of "village tourism" exists, indicating that only activities and services provided in villages are included in this kind of tourism (as we will see later, village tourism typically covers low-priced accommodation, involvement in agricultural or other local activities is not common). In Slovenia, the most important form of rural tourism is tourism on family farms, where guests stay either with the farmer family or in a guest house, but visiting farms to have a meal and explore the farmyard is also popular (Verbole, 1995). In the Netherlands, the rural tourist product means especially camping on the farm, with most farm services being linked to route-bound activities as cycling, walking or horse-riding (Peters et al, 1994). In Greece, the main provision of rural tourism product is bed and breakfast with accommodation in traditionally furnished rooms and with traditional breakfasts often based on home-made products. Complementary activities-currently still on a limited scale-include restaurants and refreshment facilities or the organisation of cultural and recreational activities (Turner, 1993).

Rural tourism is one of the main priorities of tourism development in many European countries, including Hungary. The market for rural holidays is growing at the same time as the future of many rural regions is uncertain, due to changes in agricultural practice (including the effects of the Common Agricultural Policy in the EU) or the increasing attractiveness of urban living standards. Rural tourism seems to be an appropriate tool to revitalise the declining rural areas and to ensure their sustainable future by job retention or even job creation, increased job diversity, service retention, farm support, broadened cultural provision, landscape and nature conservation or the maintenance of rural arts and crafts as tourist attractions. Rural tourism often provides an incentive (and part of the necessary funding) for infrastructural development, which then contributes to the growth of other economic activities in rural areas. A specific benefit of rural tourism development can be the increasing number of opportunities for social interaction for local people who often live relatively isolated lives in agricultural communities (Swarbrooke, 1996).

RURAL TOURISM AND SUSTAINABILITY

Rural tourism is often considered to be intrinsically sustainable, for it attracts small number of visitors, there is no need for extensive infrastructural development, tourists are usually genuinely interested in the local culture and traditions. One of the main attraction of rural holidays is the personal interaction with local residents, so hosts and guests are able to share ideas and knowledge, and consequently tourism can fulfil its role as the "industry of peace", as a tool of mutual understanding.

Nevertheless, if rural tourism development is analysed on a deeper level, certain doubts arise concerning intrinsic sustainability. The most significant issue to be investigated is the economic profitability of rural tourist services, since the demand is often seasonal, the occupancy rates are low and the investment required for creating or improving facilities for tourists is often high. In most rural tourist destinations it is quite unlikely that tourism can be viable as a sole source of income. Rural tourism can usually be only one of the income-generating alternatives in a region, so its role in sustainable development is highly influenced by the performances of other economic sectors (especially agriculture).

Concerning environmental sustainability, experiences suggest that considerable investment needs to be undertaken in the environmental management of vulnerable natural assets in order to make rural tourism in any sense sustainable. Tourists are usually most attracted by the industrially least developed regions, which are particularly sensitive to human interference.

In addition, managed agricultural landscapes do not always meet the expectations of tourists based on the images of "traditional rural" landscapes represented in the tourist literature and in promotional materials.

Tourism development also influences the socio-cultural characteristics of rural destinations, both in positive and negative way (Keane & Quinn, 1990; Peters et al, 1994). As positive impacts, the following can be mentioned: rural tourism usually encourages better use of the available resources (like land, labour, capital, natural and cultural attractions), brings about socio-economic change, contributes to heritage protection and the conservation of the rural environment, provides more social contact for local people and increases their chance to learn about other cultures. As negative impacts, tourism in rural areas changes or damages the rural landscape and the natural and cultural values of a given region, rearranges social stratification (this can also be interpreted as a positive change in certain cases), puts additional pressure on the local community, changes their rhythm of life, threatens their privacy or results in the inauthentic presentation of local customs and traditions, adapted to the tourists' wishes.

Rural Tourism Development in Hungary

Rural tourism in Hungary started to develop already in the last century, and this kind of tourism became popular very soon. Before the Second World War, holidays taken in rural areas accounted for 35-45% of all holidays (Kovács, 1993). However, the rural tourism of that period entirely disappeared after 1945 and the reorganisation of the market faces significant obstacles: the lack of an institutional framework, the bad financial situation and the relative underdevelopment of those regions which possess the most attractive resources for tourism development, the little interest on behalf of professional tourist organisations (since rural tourism development promises only low profitability) and the lack of business and hospitality skills and the ageing of the local residents.

The development of rural tourism has been included (and often emphasised) in regional development plans since the

1960's, without too much success (Kõszegfalvi, 1991). Tourism development has been concentrated in a few areas of the country (mainly located at natural waters, around thermal springs and in the mountains) and traditional rural tourism was somehow "lost" in the meantime.

It has to be added that the majority of the Hungarian population living in urban areas still has relatives in the countryside, so VFR is an existing form of rural tourism, but as the motivations are different (to visit relatives, not to become familiar with farming communities' lifestyle or to learn about local crafts and customs), on their behalf a demand for an organised supply of rural tourist products is basically non-existent. So these tourists do not contribute significantly to the economic development of the visited areas, but the fact that they do pay visits to certain rural destinations limit their demand for any further holidays of this kind. In other words, their need for staying in a rural environment is mostly satisfied by their relatives without any expenses (except travel costs), so very often they are not willing to spend any additional amount of money on similar holidays in other rural areas of the country.

An other important factor to consider is that the majority of middle-class Hungarian families (i.e. the segment typically most interested in rural tourism) have their own small holiday homes somewhere in the countryside where they can spend weekends and (part of) their summer holidays. The main motivation for spending leisure time in these holiday homes is relaxation and, for most owners, very small-scale agricultural production (growing fruits and vegetables for their own consumption). Of course, this kind of residential tourism contributes to the development of infrastructure in the given areas, and also to the retention of certain services (especially retailing). On the other hand, the ownership of non-locals restricts (both physically and financially) the opportunities of local people to buy real estate, and the holiday home owners have different infrastructural and social needs than the local residents (e.g. they are not likely to support the local school, because their children go to school in their permanent residence).

New attempts to revitalise the traditional type of tourism started mainly in the 1980's, especially in the least developed areas of the country. Some small areas can present significant success, but in general the progress so far has not met the expectations. Besides the earlier presented obstacles, the domestic image of rural holidays (cheap, aimed for the least affluent, relatively boring) does not help either to attract Hungarian visitors to rural areas. In order to change this image, the Hungarian Tourism Corp. started a campaign in 1997 to promote domestic (including rural) holidays.

One of the consequences of all the above described tendencies is that most destinations developing (or planning to develop) rural tourism expect to receive mainly foreign visitors, as opposed to the general European trends. In Western Europe rural tourism is one of the growing segments of tourism, more and more Western Europeans seek to enjoy holiday experiences in the countryside (Swarbrooke, 1996). Since Eastern Europe in general is more rural than Western Europe (both considering the level of urbanisation and industrialisation, and the socio-cultural characteristics of the societies), so it is most likely to attract a growing number of visitors from the West, if the rural tourist product is appropriately developed and promoted. In Hungary at the moment, foreign tourists are mostly interested in two types of rural tourism: first, in accommodation in the vicinity of popular tourist destinations (being motivated by the much lower prices), second, in folklore programmes and horse-shows in the "puszta" (traditionally in the Great Plain in the Eastern part of the country, but nowadays horse-shows are organised also around Lake Balaton, the second most popular tourist destination of Hungary, in order to spare tourists the trouble of taking a long trip to the original "puszta"). The development of all the other types of rural tourism (including active nature holidays or participation in farm activities) is still in an early stage.

Unfortunately, the "cheap" domestic image and the low international demand are also expressed in the prices of the rural tourist services, and, consequently, in the contribution of rural tourism to the local economies. Compared to the volume of the labour invested, the profitability of rural tourism is very low in Hungary, despite the exclusivity and uniqueness of certain products (Kovács, 1993). So for those who have the necessary capital to invest in a larger-scale product, there is no real incentive to be involved in this economic activity, and the communities do not realise the profit that they expect (and that would enable them to further develop and diversify their supply in order to modify the existing "low-price-low quality" image).

Considering the further development of rural tourism in Hungary, a controversial issue is that whose interests should be prioritised. At first glance, it seems to be obvious that one of the preconditions of sustainable tourism development is the long-term consideration of local residents' interests. From this point of view, the process of modernisation, urbanisation and agricultural change should be supported also by tourists, since local residents have all the right to acquire the same level of infrastructural development and comfort as people living in urban areas. But if this argument is accepted and rural areas develop the similar way as cities, this kind of development means changes in the overall landscape, the settlements' visual image and in the way of life of local residents, and these changes are not always welcome by tourists. In Hungary we can experience that tourists are looking for the traditional village atmosphere which means for them small thatched houses with white walls, geraniums in the windows, sweep-pole well, domestic animals, etc., so they prefer the conservation of the traditional village life even against local communities' wishes for development.

Sustainability in Hungarian Rural Tourism

As we could see earlier, sustainability is a complex notion, being determined by economic, ecological and socio-cultural factors. The indicators presented in this paper might act as useful measures of those factors that together contribute to sustainable rural tourism development. In order to draw a picture of the present nature of Hungarian rural tourism, the analysis of the development process and the characteristics of the sector might be useful. There are, however, several limitations in an analysis of this kind, mainly because of the lack of accurate data. The following conclusions are mostly drawn from estimates and experiences, not from statistics, because they are simply not available. These conclusions are consequently rather subjective, though they represent the opinion of several experts and rural tourist entrepreneurs, besides that of the authors.

Analysing all the indicators, we have a relatively complex picture. The interpretation of different measures may also differ, since some indicators are of very subjective character (like local satisfaction-a person who has direct economic benefit from tourism is most likely to accept a higher number of tourists without any annoyance than someone who has to suffer all the negative consequences of tourism without benefiting) and a given quantitative value of an indicator can be evaluated in different ways by different persons. How to decide for example what percentage of an area should be protected in order to ensure the highest degree of sustainability ? If only ecological sustainability is to be achieved, then preferably the total area should be protected. But if social sustainability is considered as well, then local residents should have the opportunity to continue traditional recreational activities, e.g. fishing or angling, or the settlement should have the space to grow if the population grows, which are not always compatible with the ecological principles of protection (Ungár, 1998).

Stress-measured as the number of visitors/tourists in a given destination-is not threatening the sustainable future of Hungarian rural tourism at the moment. If we consider only those destinations which meet the definition of rural tourism presented earlier in this paper (Gannon, 1988, in te Kloeze, 1994) and do not include the well-developed holiday resorts which are actually located in the countryside, but cannot be considered as rural areas due to their high level of urbanisation, then the number of visitors/tourists is much lower than what local communities would find as appropriate. In Hungary, there are app. 2000 beds registered in rural tourism and the average occupancy rate is less than 10% (Gál, 1998). Seasonality is characteristic to the demand, but without causing any additional stress yet (in the future, if the number of tourists significantly increases, the temporal coincidence of the tourist season and the main agricultural jobs might lead to tension, but this is far from being an issue yet). Consequently, social stress is non-existent, which could be considered as a positive factor, but since it is derived from the very low level of demand (and not from the balanced distribution of visitors in space and time), it cannot be considered as a favourable indicators of sustainability.

Most of the areas of Hungary, where rural tourism is part of the general local or regional development plans, possess various natural and cultural attractions. Among these, the most important ones are the clean natural environment, the thermal springs, the hospitality of the local people, the gastronomy, the rural lifestyle, and, to a certain extent, the preserved traditions and heritage. On the other hand, the old architectural styles that made our villages so distinctive are disappearing, the construction boom in the '60s and '70s resulted in relatively similar village appearances all over the country, less and less young people know and practice the old traditions, and the general modernisation has changed the rural lifestyle. As we could see earlier in this paper, the interest of tourists looking for authentic rural experiences very often conflict with the interest of locals looking for urban comfort. Certain attractions typical of rural tourism, like the opportunity for participation in farm activities or involvement in the hosts' everyday life, are missing in the majority of destinations (though, fortunately, these latter attractions are man-made, so can be developed in the future). Altogether, the overall attractiveness of the rural areas in Hungary is acceptable, the potential for rural tourism development seems to be existing, but there is a need for a marketing approach in the development of complex tourist products, and for further diversification and development of attractions based on the needs of different tourist segments.

Local and regional plans for general development exist in all rural tourist destinations, since they are required by the law. Tourism planning is far less common, especially in those areas where rural tourism is in an early stage of development. Among the reasons for not having tourism development plans, we can find the lack of educated and experienced planners or that of a common will on behalf of the local residents, the negative previous experiences concerning tourism development plans (more plans have been written than implemented, outsider experts have often created unaccomplishable plans) or simply the lack of financial resources. The existing plans very often focus on the economic aspects of the development process, disregarding future ecological or socio-cultural consequences of the proposed actions. The necessity of a regional approach is being accepted relatively slowly: at the present low level of demand, destinations usually see each other as competitors, not as potential co-operation partners.

Protected areas of higher category have a better chance to attract visitors than others. At the moment, in the first half of 1998, Hungary has nine National Parks and countless local protected areas and further attempts are made in order to increase the territory of these areas by establishing new National Parks. The precious natural and cultural resources of these Parks (diverse flora and fauna, rare species, geological formations, typical domesticated animals, cultural landscapes, cultural heritage) serve as the basis of rural tourism development in the nearby villages (the scattered structure of the Hungarian National Park system-all but one park consist of several pieces of protected land-facilitates the involvement of these commmmunities). In general, rural tourism benefits of the existence of National Parks (lower categories of protected areas play a less significant role in the success of tourism), and the current ratio of protection can be considered as appropriate from an overall aspect of sustainability (i.e. a balance between ecological, economic and social interests seems to be achieved.

Since rural tourism development is typically low-scale and locally managed in Hungary, the involvement rate of local people is high, though it depends on how the term "local people" is defined. Especially in the smallest, least developed villages, it is quite common that the people originally living in the area have moved to bigger villages or to towns, in order to get a job or provide better education for their children. Their houses have often been bought by people from cities who looked for relaxation in natural environment or who decided to save the dying old villages. Many small-scale rural tourist businesses are managed by these people, who, by origin, are not local, but, by their commitment and their efforts made to help a settlement or a region survive, must be evaluated as locals. Their involvement, objectives and intentions are very similar to those of the local people, so their contribution must be considered as beneficial for the sustainability of rural tourism development. The ownership of non-locals (in the above mentioned sense) in Hungarian rural tourism is not common, mainly because of the low potential profitability (it is more characteristic to the established tourist resorts like the ones around Lake Balaton).

Since the demand for rural tourism is relatively low in Hungary, the number of jobs created by this activity is not high at the moment, but the diversification of the attractions and services could induce a significant growth in this field in the near future. At the moment, rural tourism mainly provides additional income for rural families (as part-time activity particularly for the female population) and contributes to the development of pluriactivity (i.e. when a family or an individual carries out more than one type of job). The supplementary income generated by rural communities can help the development of the infrastructure or social services as well, and the perceived potential of economic development (by tourism as a catalyst) can make an area more attractive, thus more viable in the long term. Since rural tourism is a relatively new phenomenon in Hungary (not considering now the period before 1945), this is more of an expectation than a fact at the moment.

Consequently, the contribution of rural tourism to the local economy is relatively low in most rural destinations, at least in terms of registered financial income. This is partly due to the presence of grey economy (facilitated by the lack of a well-established institutional framework and the informal nature of the rural tourist services). There are no reliable statistics on the actual incomes from rural tourism, and the ratio of taxes generated by tourism to the total amount of taxes does not accurately reflect the share of the industry. (This fact also affects our knowledge of the economic diversity of an area-but even without proper statistics it can be stated that in the least developed villages rural tourism is often the only economic activity with a growth potential). Besides the financial results, rural tourism development generally improves the quality of life in the destinations (by providing broader personal contacts, by motivating people to take better care of their environment or indirectly, by assuring preference to an area in national development projects).

Environmental factors, like energy sources or waste management, are usually rather neglected in rural tourism development. Even if attempts are made to provide proper sewage or waste treatment systems all over the country, these attempts are related to tourism only in the most frequented destinations with the most urgent environmental problems (like at Lake Balaton). The utilisation of renewable energy sources is generally not an issue (when it is, the reason is mostly increased environment-consciousness, not a perceived threat of a growing number of tourists exploiting the non-renewable energy sources). For most destinations, the main priority is to provide the tourists with all the comfort they need (e.g. bathrooms). Given the present low level of demand, it seems to be totally impossible that one day masses of tourists would threaten the ecological balance of any rural destination. On the other hand, the fact that rural tourism has started to develop quite recently in Hungary, provides an opportunity for the country to adopt other regions' experiences in order to avoid mistakes made elsewhere. The stricter environmental regulations of the European Union also affect the general economic development process in Hungary, which can be beneficial for the ecological balance of rural tourism as well.

In tourism development in general, training and education of the labour force is one of the necessary requirements of sustainability. Since in rural tourism many local residents without formal tourism education are involved, their education on the main issues of sustainability must form part of the overall development process. In Hungary, the failure of several rural tourism development projects could have been strongly related to the lack of market knowledge and marketing skills. Because in many cases even the basic knowledge of running a business is missing, there is typically no specific need for studying or implementing the principles of sustainable development. The issue of sustainability usually emerges only in those heavily frequented areas where the negative impacts of tourism can already be detected.

Though there are exceptions, local people in general are far from being satisfied by rural tourism development. The main factors behind this dissatisfaction are the gap between the expected and the realised profitability, the relatively slow growth of the sector, the related bureaucracy, the lack of significant support from the state. Other contributing factors were the lack of marketing and business skills of the local people, the lack of domestic demand and the overstatement of the local resources and attractions. Especially at the beginning of the development process, hopes were high, large numbers of tourists were expected to come and spend generously, but reality has not lived up to the expectations of the communities involved. Nowadays, a more cautious development phase is in stage, the co-operation between villages and regions improves, more thorough planning takes place, the people involved are eventually gathering the necessary knowledge, skills and experiences.

On the other hand, those tourists who actually take part in rural holidays in Hungary, are usually satisfied with the quality of their experiences. Both among Hungarians and foreigners, there is a relatively high proportion of repeat visitors. Their satisfaction indicates that the product itself is perceived as of good quality by that narrow segment of customers that is attracted by it.

The only problem concerning sustainability is the low level of demand: no matter how satisfied customers are, if-at least in short run-their demand cannot ensure economic sustainability for the visited areas. (In the long run, word of mouth promotion may increase interest in rural recreation and the overall image of rural holidays may be changed as well.)

CONCLUSIONS

By the general analysis of the sustainability of rural tourism development in Hungary, an attempt was made to present the complex nature of the activity. Though rural tourism has the potential to be one of the most effective tools of regional development, it has not grown up to the expectations so far, due to several interrelated reasons described earlier in the paper.

The next step in the research of this topic will be the detailed assessment of one or several rural tourist destinations in Hungary through the presented sustainability indicators. A study of this kind would serve various purposes: it would help to test the usefulness, the appropriateness and the applicability of these indicators in the analysis of the sustainability of rural tourism, and it would contribute to the understanding of what different interest groups (including local community members, tourists, ecologists or businessmen) perceive as sustainable rural tourism development. A better understanding of these perceptions would help the planning of a rural tourism that is able to satisfy the needs of most groups for now and in the future.

10

Tourism: Types and Purposes

ADVENTURE TOURISM

Adventure tourism is a type of niche tourism involving exploration or travel to remote areas, where the traveler should expect the unexpected. Adventure tourism is rapidly growing in popularity as tourists seek unusual holidays, different from the typical beach vacation.

Adventure tourism typically involves traveling into remote, inaccessible and possibly hostile areas. It may include the performance of acts that require significant effort and grit and may also involve some degree of risk.

According to the (U.S.-based) global Adventure Travel Trade Association, "adventure travel" may be any tourist activity including two of the following three components: a physical activity, a cultural exchange or interaction, and engagement with nature.

Mountaineering expeditions, trekking, bungee jumping, rafting and rock climbing are frequently cited as an examples of adventure tourism.

MOUNTAINEERING

Mountaineering is the sport, hobby or profession of walking, hiking, trekking and climbing up mountains. It is also sometimes known as alpinism, particularly in Europe. It may be said to consist of three aspects: rock-craft, snow-craft and skiing, depending on whether the route chosen is over rock, snow or ice. All require great athletic and technical ability, and experience is also a very important part of the matter.

Technique

Snow

Snowshoes can be used to walk through deep snow approaching the mountain or on lesser slopes up the mountain. Skis can be used when conditions allow, and can be a form of the sport by itself, called Ski Mountaineering. Crampons can be used on hard snow (neve) and ice.

Glaciers

When traveling over glaciers, crevasses pose a grave danger. These giant cracks in the ice are not always visible as snow can be blown and freeze over the top to make a snowbridge. At times snowbridges can be as thin as a few inches. Climbers use a system of ropes to protect themselves from such hazards. Basic gear for glacier travel includes crampons and ice axes. Teams of two to five climbers tie into a rope equally spaced. If a climber begins to fall the other members of the team perform a self-arrest to stop the fall. The other members of the team enact a crevasse rescue to pull the fallen climber from the crevasse.

Ice

Multiple methods are used to safely travel over ice. If the terrain is steep but not vertical protection in the form of pickets or ice screws can be driven into the snow or ice and attached to the rope by the lead climber. Each climber on the team must clip past the anchor, and the last climber picks up the picket. This allows for safety should the entire team be taken off their feet. This technique is known as Simul-climbing. If the terrain becomes vertical then standard ice climbing techniques are used.

Shelter

Climbers use a few different forms of shelter depending on the situation and conditions. Shelter is a very important aspect of safety for the climber as the weather in the mountains is very unpredictable. Tall mountains require many days of camping on the mountain.

Hut

Particularly the European alpine regions have a tight network of mountain huts, in most cases managed by full time, seasonal employees. These huts offer shelter, warm and cold meals, rooms or sleeping dormitories and sanitary facilities. In terms of luxury and comfort they vary by a great deal. Most huts are only open during the spring, summer and fall months to serve recreational mountaineers but also offer a self-service section to provide shelter and a cooking place for winter mountaineers. Using the hut system enables the mountaineer to travel without heavy tent, sleeping bag and cooking supplies.

Bivy

A bivy or bivouac is simply getting a sleeping bag and Bivouac sack and laying down to sleep. Many times small half sheltered areas like cracks in rocks or simply a trench dug in the snow are used to provide a basic means of shelter as well. This technique is performed by most people only in cases of emergency, however in good weather this can be pleasant. Some climbers steadfastly committed to Alpine Style climbing plan on bivying in order to save the weight of a tent when snow conditions are not suitable for a snow cave.

Tent

Tents are the most common form of shelter used on the mountain. A four season tent is required for any camp high in the mountains. Many climbers do not use tents at high altitudes unless the snow conditions do not allow for snow caving. One of the downsides to tenting is that storm winds can be very unnerving and can cause the tent to collapse, however modern mountaineering tents are usually tested for wind speeds up to 125mph. Even so, very intense flapping of the tent fabric can hinder sleep and raise doubts about the security of the shelter in windy conditions.

Snow cave

Snow caves are the preferred way for many climbers to shelter high on the mountain. Unlike tents snow caves are silent and are actually much warmer than a tent. A correctly made snow cave will hover around freezing, which relative to outside temperatures can be very warm. Igloos are used by some climbers, but are deceptively difficult to build and require specific snow conditions.

Hazards

The craft of climbing has been developed to avoid three main types of danger: the danger of things falling on the climber (objective danger), the danger of the climber falling and inclement weather. The things that may fall include rocks, ice, snow, other climbers or their gear; the mountaineer may fall from rocks, ice or snow, or into a crevasse. In all, there are eight chief dangers: falling rocks, falling ice, snow-avalanches, falls,the climber falling, falls from ice slopes, falls down snow slopes, falls into crevasses and dangers from weather. To select and follow a route using one's skills and experience to mitigate these dangers is to exercise the climber's craft.

Falling Rocks

Every rock mountain is slowly disintegrating due to erosion, the process being especially rapid above the snow-line. Rock faces are constantly swept by falling stones, which are generally possible to dodge. Falling rocks tend to form furrows in a mountain face, and these furrows (couloirs) have to be ascended with caution, their sides often being safe when the middle is stoneswept. Rocks fall more frequently on some days than on others, according to the recent weather. Ice formed during the night may temporarily bind rocks to the face but warmth of the day or direct sun exposure may easily dislodge these rocks. Local experience is a valuable help on determining typical rockfall on such routes.

The direction of the dip of rock strata often determines the degree of danger on a particular face; the character of the rock must also be considered. Where stones fall frequently debris will be found below, whilst on snow slopes falling stones cut furrows visible from a great distance. In planning an ascent of a new peak mountaineers must look for such traces. When falling stones get mixed in considerable quantity with slushy snow or water a mud avalanche is formed (common in the Himalaya). It is vital to avoid camping in their possible line of fall.

Falling Ice

The places where ice may fall can always be determined beforehand. It falls in the broken parts of glaciers (seracs) and from overhanging cornices formed on the crests of narrow ridges. Large icicles are often formed on steep rock faces, and these fall frequently in fine weather following cold and stormy days. They have to be avoided like falling stones. Seracs are slow in formation, and slow in arriving (by glacier motion) at a condition of unstable equilibrium.

They generally fall in or just after the hottest part of the day, and their debris seldom goes far. A skillful and experienced ice-man will usually devise a safe route through a most intricate ice-fall, but such places should be avoided in the afternoon of a hot day. Hanging glaciers (i.e. glaciers perched on steep slopes) often discharge themselves over steep rock-faces, the snout breaking off at intervals. They can always be detected by their debris below. Their track should be avoided.

Avalanches

The avalanche is the most underestimated danger in the mountains. People generally think that they will be able to recognize the hazards and survive being caught. The truth is a somewhat different story. Every year, 120-150 people die in small avalanches in the Alps alone. The vast majority are reasonably experienced male skiers aged 20-35 but also include ski instructors and guides.

There is always a lot of pressure to risk a snow crossing. Turning back takes a lot of extra time and effort, supreme leadership, and most importantly there seldom is an avalanche to prove the right decision was made. Making the decision to turn around is especially hard if others are crossing the slope, but any next person could become the trigger.

There are two types of avalanche:

1. *The Slab Avalanche:* This type of avalanche occurs when a plate of snow breaks loose and starts sliding down; these are the largest and most dangerous.
    1. Hard Slab Avalanche-formed by hard-packed snow in a cohesive slab. The slab will not break up easily as it slides down the hill, resulting in large blocks tumbling down the mountain.
    2. Soft Slab Avalanche-formed again by a cohesive layer of snow bonded together, the slab tends to break up more easily.
2. *The Loose Snow Avalanche:* This type of avalanche is triggered by a small amount of moving snow that accumulates into a big slide. Also known as a "wet slide or point release" avalanche. This type of avalanche is deceptively dangerous as it can still knock a climber or skier off their feet and bury them, or sweep them over a cliff into a terrain trap.

Dangerous slides are most likely to occur on the same slopes preferred by many skiers: long and wide open, few trees or large rocks, 30 to 45 degrees of angle, large load of fresh snow, soon after a big storm, on a slope 'lee to the storm'. Solar radiation can trigger slides as well. These will typically be a point release or wet slough type of avalanche. The added weight of the wet slide can trigger a slab avalanche. Ninety percent of reported victims are caught in avalanches triggered by themselves or others in their group.

When going off-piste or traveling in alpine terrain, parties have a moral responsibility to always carry:

1. avalanche beacon
2. probe
3. shovel (retrieving victims with a shovel instead of your hands is five times faster)

and to have had avalanche training! Paradoxically, expert skiers who have avalanche training make up a large percentage of avalanche fatalities; perhaps because they are the ones more likely to ski in areas prone to avalanches.

Even with proper rescue equipment and training, there is a one-in-five chance of dying if caught in a significant avalanche, and only a 50/50 chance of being found alive if buried more than a few minutes. The best solution is to learn how to avoid risky conditions.

Falls from Rocks

The skill of a rock climber is shown by one's choice of handhold and foothold, and his adhesion to those one has chosen. Much depends on a correct estimate of the firmness of the rock where weight is to be thrown upon it. Many loose rocks are quite firm enough to bear a person's weight, but experience is needed to know which can be trusted, and skill is required in transferring the weight to them without jerking. On rotten rocks the rope must be handled with special care, lest it should start loose stones on to the heads of those below. Similar care must be given to handholds and footholds, for the same reason. When a horizontal traverse has to be made across very difficult rocks, a dangerous situation may arise unless at both ends of the traverse there be firm positions. Mutual assistance on hard rocks takes all manner of forms: two, or even three, people climbing on one another's shoulders, or using an ice axe propped up by others for a foothold. The great principle is that of co-operation, all the members of the party climbing with reference to the others, and not as independent units; each when moving must know what the climber in front and the one behind are doing. After bad weather steep rocks are often found covered with a veneer of ice (verglas), which may even render them inaccessible. Crampons are useful on such occasions.

Ice Slopes

For travel on slopes consisting of ice or hard snow, crampons are a standard part of a mountaineer's equipment. While step-cutting can sometimes be used on snow slopes of moderate angle, this can be a slow and tiring process, which does not provide the higher security of crampons. However, in soft snow or powder, crampons are easily hampered by balling of snow which reduce their effectiveness. In either case, an ice axe not only assists with balance but provides the climber with the possibility of self-arrest in case of a slip or fall. On a true ice slope however, an ice axe is rarely able to effect a self-arrest. As an additional safety precaution on steep ice slopes, the climbing rope is attached to ice screws buried into the ice.

True ice slopes are rare in Europe, though common in mountains located in the tropics, where newly-fallen snow quickly thaws on the surface and becomes sodden below, so that the next night's frost turns the whole mass into a sheet of semi-solid ice.

Snow Slopes

Snow slopes are very common, and usually easy to ascend. At the foot of a snow or ice slope is generally a big crevasse, called a bergschrund, where the final slope of the mountain rises from a snow-field or glacier. Such bergschrunds are generally too wide to be stepped across, and must be crossed by a snow bridge, which needs careful testing and a painstaking use of the rope. A steep snow slope in bad condition may be dangerous, as the whole body of snow may start as an avalanche. Such slopes are less dangerous if ascended directly than obliquely, for an oblique or horizontal track cuts them across and facilitates movement of the mass.

New snow lying on ice is especially dangerous. Experience is needed for deciding on the advisability of advancing over snow in doubtful condition. Snow on rocks is usually rotten unless it is thick; snow on snow is likely to be sound. A day or two of fine weather will usually bring new snow into sound condition. Snow cannot lie at a very steep angle, though it often deceives the eye as to its slope. Snow slopes seldom exceed 40°. Ice slopes may be much steeper. Snow slopes in early morning are usually hard and safe, but the same in the afternoon are quite soft and possibly dangerous; hence the advantage of an early start.

Crevasses

Crevasses are the slits or deep chasms formed in the substance of a glacier as it passes over an uneven bed. They may be open or hidden. In the lower part of a glacier the crevasses are open. Above the snow-line they are frequently hidden by arched-over accumulations of winter snow. The detection of hidden crevasses requires care and experience.

After a fresh fall of snow they can only be detected by sounding with the pole of the ice axe, or by looking to right and left where the open extension of a partially hidden crevasse may be obvious. The safeguard against accident is the rope, and no one should ever cross a snow-covered glacier unless roped to one, or even better to two companions. Anyone venturing onto crevasses should be trained in crevasse rescue.

Weather

The primary dangers caused by bad weather centre around the changes it causes in snow and rock conditions, making movement suddenly much more arduous and hazardous than under normal circumstances.

Whiteouts make it difficult to retrace a route while rain may prevent taking the easiest line only determined as such under dry conditions. In a storm the mountaineer who uses a compass for guidance has a great advantage over a merely empirical observer. In large snow-fields it is, of course, easier to go wrong than on rocks, but intelligence and experience are the best guides in safely navigating objective hazards.

Summer thunderstorms may produce intense lightning. If a climber happens to be standing on or near the summit, they risk being struck. There are many cases where people have been struck by lightning while climbing mountains. In most mountainous regions, local storms develop by late morning and early afternoon. Many climbers will get an "alpine start"; that is before or by first light so as to be on the way down when storms are intensifying in activity and lightning and other weather hazards are a distinct threat to safety.

Altitude

Rapid ascent can lead to altitude sickness. The best treatment is to descend immediately. The climber's motto at high altitude is "climb high, sleep low", referring to the regimen of climbing higher to acclimatize but returning to lower elevation to sleep. In the South American Andes, the chewing of coca leaves has been traditionally used to treat altitude sickness symptoms.

Common symptoms of altitude sickness include severe headache, sleep problems, nausea, lack of appetite, lethargy and body ache. Mountain sickness may progress to HACE (High Altitude Cerebral Edema) and HAPE (High Altitude Pulmonary Edema), both of which can be fatal within 24 hours.

In high mountains, atmospheric pressure is lower and this means that less oxygen is available to breathe. This is the underlying cause of altitude sickness. Everyone needs to acclimatize, even exceptional mountaineers that have been to high altitude before. Generally speaking, mountaineers start using bottled oxygen when they climb above 7,000 m. Exceptional mountaineers have climbed 8000-metre peaks (including Everest) without oxygen, almost always with a carefully planned program of acclimatization.

In 2005, researcher and mountaineer John Semple established that above-average ozone concentrations on the Tibetan plateau may pose an additional risk to climbers.

Locations

Mountaineering has become a popular sport throughout the world. In Europe the sport largely originated in the Alps, and is still immensely popular there. Other notable mountain ranges frequented by climbers include the Caucasus, the Pyrenees and the Tatra mountains. In North America climbers frequent the Rockies and Sierra Nevada of California, the Cascades of Washington and the high peaks of Alaska. There has been a long tradition of climbers going on expeditions to the Greater Ranges, a term generally used for the Andes and the high peaks of Asia including the Himalaya, Pamirs and

Tien Shan. In the past this was often on exploratory trips or to make first ascents. With the advent of cheaper long-haul air travel mountaineering holidays in the Greater Ranges are now undertaken much more frequently and ascents of even Everest and Vinson Massif (the highest mountain in Antarctica) are offered as a "package holiday". Other popular mountaineering areas of more local interest include the Southern Alps of New Zealand, the Japanese Alps the Scottish Highlands and the mountains of Scandinavia.

History

- Though it is unknown whether his intention was to reach a summit, Ötzi ascended at least 3,000 m in the Alps about 5,300 years ago. His remains were found at that altitude, preserved in a glacier.
- The first recorded mountain ascent in the Common Era is Roman Emperor Hadrian's ascent of Etna (3,350 m) to see the sun rise in 121.
- Peter III of Aragon climbed Canigou in the Pyrenees in the last quarter of the 13th century.
- The first ascent of the Popocatépetl (5,426 m in Mexico) was reported in 1289 by members of a local tribe (Tecanuapas)
- Jean Buridan climbed Mont Ventoux around 1316.
- The Italian poet Petrarch wrote that on April 26, 1336 he, together with his brother and two servants, climbed to the top of Mont Ventoux (1,909 m). His account of the trip was composed later as a letter to his friend Francesco Dionigi. Subsequentlv, April 26, 1336 came to be regarded as the "birth of alpinism", and Petrarch (Petrarca alpinista) as the "father of alpinism".
- The Rochemelon (3,538 m) in the Italian Alps was climbed in 1358.
- In the late 1400s and early 1500s ascents were made of numerous high peaks in the Andes, for religious purposes by the citizens of the Inca Empire and their

subjects. They constructed platforms, houses and altars on many summits and carried out sacrifices, including human sacrifices. The highest peak they are known for certain to have climbed is Llullaillaco (6,739 m). They may also have ascended the highest peak in the Andes, Aconcagua (6,962 m) as a sacrifice victim has been found at over 5,000 m on this peak.

- In 1492 the ascent of Mont Aiguille was made by order of Charles VIII of France. The Humanists of the 16th century adopted a new attitude towards mountains, but the disturbed state of Europe nipped in the bud the nascent mountaineering of the Zurich school.
- Leonardo da Vinci climbed to a snow-field in the neighborhood of the Val Sesia and made scientific observations.
- In 1642 Darby Field made the first recorded ascent of Mount Washington, then known as Agiocochook, in New Hampshire.
- Konrad Gesner and Josias Simler of Zurich visited and described mountains, and made regular ascents. The use of ice axe and rope were locally invented at this time. No mountain expeditions of note are recorded in the 17th century.
- Richard Pococke and William Windham's historic visit to Chamonix was made in 1741, and set the trend for visiting glaciers.
- In 1744 the Titus was climbed, the first true ascent of a snow-mountain.
- The first attempt to ascend Mont Blanc was made in 1775 by a party of natives. In 1786 Dr Michel Paccard and Jacques Balmat gained the summit for the first time. Horace-Bénédict de Saussure, the initiator of the first ascent followed next year.
- The Norwegian mountain climber, Jens Esmark was the first person to ascend Snøhetta in 1798, part of the Dovrefjell range in Southern Norway. The same year he

lead the first expedition to Bitihorn, a small mountain in the southernmost outskirts of Jotunheimen, Norway. In 1810 he was the first person to ascend Mount Gaustatoppen in Telemark, Norway.

- The Jungfrau was climbed in 1811, the Finsteraarhorn in 1812, and the Breithorn in 1813. Thereafter, tourists showed a tendency to climb, and the body of Alpine guides began to come into existence as a consequence.
- Citlaltépetl (5720 m in Mexico) was first climbed in 1848 by F. Maynard & G. Reynolds.
- Systematic mountaineering, as a sport, is usually dated from Sir Alfred Wills's ascent of the Wetterhorn in 1854. The first ascent of Monte Rosa was made in 1855.
- The Alpine Club was founded in London in 1857, and was soon imitated in most European countries. Edward Whymper's ascent of the Matterhorn in 1865 marked the close of the main period of Alpine conquest-the Golden age of alpinism-during which the craft of climbing was invented and 'perfected', the body of professional guides formed and their traditions fixed.
- Passing to other ranges, the exploration of the Pyrenees was concurrent with that of the Alps. The Caucasus followed, mainly owing to the initiative of D. W. Freshfield; it was first visited by exploring climbers in 1868, and most of its great peaks were climbed by 1888.
- The Edelweiss Club Salzburg was founded in Salzburg in 1881, and had 3 members make the First Ascent on 2 Eight-thousanders, Broad Peak (1957) and Dhaulagiri (1960).
- Trained climbers turned their attention to the mountains of North America in 1888, when the Rev. W. S. Green made an expedition to the Selkirk Mountains. From that time exploration has gone on apace, and many English and American climbing parties have surveyed most of the highest peaks; Pikes Peak (14,115 ft.) having been climbed by Mr. E. James and party in 1820, and

Mt. Saint Elias (18,008 ft.) by the Duke of the Abruzzi and party in 1897. The exploration of the highest Andes was begun in 1879-1880, when Whymper climbed Chimborazo and explored the mountains of Ecuador. The Cordillera between Chile and Argentina was visited by Dr. Gussfeldt in 1883, who ascended Maipo (17,270 ft.) and attempted Aconcagua (22,841 ft.). That peak was first climbed by the Fitzgerald expedition in 1897.

- The Andes of Bolivia were first explored by Sir William Martin Conway in 1898. Chilean and Argentine expeditions revealed the structure of the southern Cordillera in the years 1885-1898. Conway visited the mountains of Tierra del Fuego.
- New Zealand's Southern Alps were first visited in 1882 by the Rev. W. S. Green, and shortly afterwards a New Zealand Alpine Club was founded, and by their activities the exploration of the range was pushed forward. In 1895, Major Edward Arthur Fitzgerald, made an important journey in this range. Tom Fyfe and party climbed Aoraki/Mount Cook on Christmas Day 1894, denying Fitzgerald the first ascent. Fitzgerald was en route from Britain with Swiss guide Matthias Zurbriggen to claim the peak. So piqued at being beaten to the top of Mount Cook, he refused to climb it and concentrated on other peaks in the area. Later in the trip Zubriggen soloed Mount Cook up a ridge that now bears his name.
- The first mountains of the arctic region explored were those of Spitzbergen by Sir W. M. Conway's expeditions in 1896 and 1897.
- Of the high African peaks, Kilimanjaro was climbed in 1889 by Dr. Hans Meyer, Mt. Kenya in 1899 by Halford John Mackinder, and a peak of Ruwenzori by H. J. Moore in 1900.
- The Asiatic mountains were initially surveyed on orders of the British Empire. In 1892 Sir William Martin Conway explored the Karakoram Himalaya, and climbed a peak of 23,000 ft. In 1895 Albert F. Mummery died

while attempting Nanga Parbat, while in 1899 D. W. Freshfield took an expedition to the snowy regions of Sikkim. In 1899, 1903, 1906 and 1908 Mrs Fannie Bullock Workman made ascents in the Himalayas, including one of the Nun Kun peaks (23,300 ft.). A number of Gurkha sepoys were trained as expert mountaineers by Major the Hon. C. G. Bruce, and a good deal of exploration was accomplished by them.

- The Rucksack Club was founded in Manchester, England in 1902.
- The American Alpine Club was founded in 1902.
- In 1902, the Eckenstein-Crowley Expedition, lead by mountaineer Oscar Eckenstein and occultist Aleister Crowley, was the first to attempt to scale Chogo Ri (now known as K2 in the west). They reached 22,000 feet before turning back due to weather and other mishaps.
- In 1905, Aleister Crowley led the first expedition to Kanchenjunga, the third highest mountain in the world. Four members of that party were killed in an avalanche. Some claims say they reached around 21,300 feet before turning back, however Crowley's autobiography claims they reached about 25,000 feet.
- The 1950s saw the first ascents of all the eight-thousanders but two, starting with Annapurna in 1950 by Maurice Herzog and Louis Lachenal. The world's highest mountain (above mean sea level), Mount Everest (8,848 m) was first climbed on May 29, 1953 by Sir Edmund Hillary and Tenzing Norgay from the south side in Nepal. Just a few months later, Hermann Buhl made the first ascent of Nanga Parbat (8,125 m), a remarkable solo climb, the only eight-thousander to be solo'd on the first ascent. K2 (8,611 m), the second highest peak in the world was first scaled in 1954. In 1964, the final eight-thousander to be climbed was Shishapangma (8,013 m), the lowest of all the 8,000 metre peaks.

OUTDOOR EDUCATION

Outdoor education usually refers to organized learning that takes place in the outdoors. Outdoor education programs often involve residential or journey-based experiences in which students participate in a variety of adventurous challenges such as hiking, climbing, canoeing, ropes courses, and group games. Outdoor education draws upon the philosophy and theory of experiential education and on environmental education.

Terminology

Outdoor education is closely related to terms such as adventure education, challenge education, experiential education, and environmental education. These terms, however, all represent slightly different emphases in philosophy and method. Adventure education, for example, focuses on participating in activities with perceived risks and does not necessarily occur outdoors. Consensus about the meaning of these terms is somewhat loose and varies between cultures.

Aims

Some typical aims of outdoor education are:

- to learn how to overcome adversity
- to learn alongside others
- to develop a deeper relationship with nature.

Outdoor education spans the three domains of self, others, and the natural world. The relative emphasis of these three domains varies from one program to another. An outdoor education program can, for example, emphasize one (or more) of these aims:

- to reduce recidivism
- to enhance teamwork
- to teach outdoor survival skills
- to promote spirituality
- to understand natural environments
- to develop leadership skills
- to improve problem solving skills

HISTORY

Modern outdoor education owes its beginnings to a number of separate initiatives. Organized camping was in evidence in the late nineteenth century and early twentieth century in Europe, the UK, the USA, Australia and New Zealand. The Scouting movement, established in 1907 by Robert Baden-Powell, employs non-formal education with an emphasis on practical outdoor activities. The first Outward Bound centre at Aberdovey in Wales was established during the second world war. The Forest Schools of Denmark are examples of programs with similar aims and objectives. A key outdoor education pioneer was Kurt Hahn, a German educator who founded schools such as the Schule Schloss Salem in Germany, Gordonstoun School in Scotland, and Atlantic College in Wales, the United World Colleges movement, the Duke of Edinburgh Award scheme (which emphasizes community service, craftsmanship skills, physical skill, and outdoor expeditions) and the Outward Bound movement.

The second half of the twentieth century saw rapid growth of outdoor education in all sectors (state, voluntary and commercial) with an ever-widening range of client groups and applications. In this period Outward Bound spread to over 40 countries around the world, including the USA in the 1960s. This, in turn, spawned many offshoot programs, including Project Adventure and the National Outdoor Leadership School. (Further 'North America' developments are described in the 'Around the World' section below.) Other fields that are related to (or part of) 'outdoor education' include: adventure therapy, adventure recreation, adventure tourism, and ropes courses. A history of outdoor education in the UK has been documented by Lynn Cook (1999) and a history of outdoor education in New Zealand has been published in Pip Lynch's 'Camping in the Curriculum' (2007).

Philosophy

People are at their rawest level when outdoors. We remember that we are part of a greater ecosystem and are not as bound by social customs and norms. In essence we are more true to ourselves and it is easier to see people as people regardless of race, class, religion etc. Outdoor education also helps instill the basic elements of teamwork because we are forced to work together and rely on others. For many people a high ropes course or an outdoor activity may stretch their comfort zone and cause them to challenge themselves physically which in turn can lead to challenging oneself mentally.

Theory

A wide range of social science and specific outdoor education theories and models have been applied in an effort to better understand outdoor education. Amongst the key theoretical models or concepts are:

- Group development theories
- the Outward Bound Process Model
- Stress, optimal arousal, and psychological flow theories
- Psychoevolutionary theory and the Biophilia hypothesis

AROUND THE WORLD

Outdoor education occurs, in one form or another, in most if not all countries of the world. However, it can be implemented very differently, depending on the cultural context. Some countries, for example, view outdoor education as synonymous with environmental education, whilst other countries treat outdoor education and environmental education as distinct. Modern forms of outdoor education are most prevalent in UK, USA, Australia, New Zealand, Europe and to some extent Asia and Africa. A map is available of locations of outdoor education organisations, facilities, and people.

United Kingdom

After the second world war many local authorities in the UK emulated the Outward Bound principles and set up their own outdoor education centres for school children. Visits to these outdoor centres were often subsidised, allowing many children from the towns and cities their first real experience of the outdoor world.

By the late 1980s most UK local education authorities had an outdoor education centre, and there was a growing private sector offering similar experiences. Government moves to offer more autonomy to schools have badly affected this provision. Under regulations for the local management of schools that took effect in England and Wales from 1992 onwards, the majority of the money spent on education in the UK now goes direct to the school, and local authorities often find it difficult to subsidise their outdoor education centres. As a result many have closed.

One of the most significant changes in outdoor education in Great Britain came as a result of the Lyme Bay kayaking tragedy in March, 1993. This tragedy accelerated governmental discussions until, in January 1995, the Activity Centres (Young Persons' Safety) Act 1995 was passed through Parliament in January 1995 and an independent licensing authority, the Adventure Activities Licensing Authority (AALA) was formed.

Overall, the AALA appears to have succeeded in its mission, but it has also created debate regarding whether it is possible for young people to experience adventure in an 'educational way' within tight regulations. Some people view AALA regulations as tight and thus, restricting their opportunity to provide what they believe to be meaningful outdoor education.

One further area worthy of note is the Campaign for Adventure (Campaign for Adventure, 2000a). This campaign started in 2000 following a one day conference titled "A Question of Balance." Since then the campaign has concentrated on lobbying political individuals and parties to support risk taking and to acknowledge and work against the increasing trends indicated by a "culture of fear." This phrase is the title of Furedi's (1997) book, which is heavily cited in recent UK outdoor education literature. As with most political campaigns it is difficult to assess progress but the work of those involved in the campaign can be followed on line (Campaign for Adventure, 2000a). Consistent with this position, a recent report from the Office of Standards in Education, which covers England and Wales, concluded that outdoor education is uniquely placed to offer structured opportunities for students to identify hazards, calculate the related risks and decide the significance of a risk in order to determine and implement the precautions necessary to eliminate and minimise risk. Students' involvement in risk management makes them aware of potential harm and contributes towards their being able to take greater responsibility for their own and others' safety. (Ofsted, 2004, p. 13)

While on the surface Ofsted may appear to be consistent with the Campaign for Adventure there are some significant inconsistencies here worthy of brief explanation. It appears that Ofsted is suggesting that the very idea of risk taking is to be avoided and the role of outdoor education could be to enable students to assess risk and then 'eliminate or minimise' it. A contrary position is taken by the Campaign for Adventure based on adventure and risk as, at least an educational value, and perhaps even as central to life and a way of being, which is threatened by a culture of fear. The Campaign for Adventure believe that life is best approached with a spirit of adventure and that absolute safety is unachievable.

Recently there has been concern expressed about the decline in the number and quality of school trips in the UK. In 2005 the Parliamentary select committee on Education published a report on 'Education outside the classroom' which called on the UK government to do more to protect and promote outdoor education. In response the government promised to issue a manifesto for outdoor education, setting out what schools ought to offer their pupils.

North America

The origin of outdoor education in the USA is difficult to pinpoint. North American culture, particularly since European colonization in the 17th century, has embraced a pioneering spirit. This contributed to the extensive development of organized camping programs during the 20th century, Outward Bound programs since the 1960s, as well as many related off-shoot programs including Project Adventure, the National Outdoor Leadership School, the ropes course industry, and many other applications including wilderness orientation programs within colleges and universities and adventure therapy. In the 1970's, the Association for Experiential Education was also formed, along with the Journal of Experiential Education which continues to have a strong focus on adventure education scholarship and practice.

India

Outdoor Education in India

Outdoor education is relatively new to schools in India, though it is quite well established abroad. Acceptance is slowly increasing with a few schools advocating outbound adventure based programmes among students, to enhance personal growth through experiential learning and increase awareness about various subjects like the environment, ecology, wildlife, history, archaeology, geography and adventure sports. Some organisations that currently offer such programmes for schools are OETS and Wide Aware in Mumbai.Youreka& Ozonewho offer open summer programs based out of Delhi in north and Bangalore in South.

Germany

The term 'outdoor education' doesn't seem to have an exact equivalent in the German language although Kurt Hahn, one of key figures in the development of outdoor education in the twentieth century was German. In general, outdoor or adventure education is not as widespread in Germany as in other developed regions, such as North America, Australia, and the UK. However, a closely related educational approach called experiential education (In German: "Erlebnispädagogik") is commonly applied.

Most organisations and companies offering programs and activities based on experiential education for children and youth also offer similar programs for adults and especially corporate teams which are then mostly referred to as 'outdoor trainings'.

Judging from the kind of outdoor training programs available in an internet search, the main clientele of German outdoor training providers seem to be corporate teams and organisations seeking team building and personal development. There is also a wide range of organisations offering outdoor programs based on experiential education for children, adolescents, families and school classes with or without disabilities. German schools have seemingly started to make increased use of outdoor and experiential possibilities when planning their school trips but the experiential approach is rarely implemented in the normal school system and it is by no means as common for school students to experience outdoor education trips as it is other countries.

A more detailed summary of German outdoor education and experiential educational providers and networks is available.

Critical Views

Loynes (1998) has suggested that outdoor education is increasingly an entertainment park consumption experience.

In a controversial paper critiquing the algorithmic paradigm Loynes (2002) has also called for an increase in "creativity, spontaneity and vitality" (p. 124). These dialogues indicate a need for those working in outdoor education to examine assumptions to ensure that their work is educational (Hovelynck & Peeters, 2003).

Effects

There is much anecdotal evidence about benefits of outdoor education experiences; teachers, for example, often speak of the improvement they have in relationships with students following a trip. However, hard evidence showing that outdoor education has a demonstrable long-term effect on behaviour or educational achievement is harder to identify; this may be in part because of the difficulty involved in conducting studies which separate out the effects of outdoor education on meaningful outcomes.

A major meta-analysis of 97 empirical outcome studies indicated a moderately positive overall effect of adventure education programs on outcomes such as self-concept, leadership, and communication skills. Interestingly, this study also indicated that there appeared to be ongoing positive effects, unless most educational interventions whose effects tend to fade.

RAFTING

Rafting or whitewater rafting is a recreational activity utilizing a raft to navigate a river or other bodies of water. This is usually done on whitewater or different degrees of rough water, in order to thrill and excite the raft passengers. The development of this activity as a leisure sport has become popular since the mid 1970s.

History

Rafting is one of the earliest means of transportation, used as a means for shipping people, hunting, and transferring food.

In 1842, Lieutenant John Fremont of the U.S. Army first journalized his rafting expedition on the Platte River. Horace H. Day designed the equipment he used in rafting. Day's rafts were constructed from four independent rubber cloth tubes and wrap-around floor.

In 1960s, rafting was then recognized and paths like Grand Canyon were routed and whitewater rafting companies were established.

In 1970s, rafting marked its major development as a leisure sport when it was then included in the Munich Olympic Games.

In 1980s, as rafting continued to gain its popularity, a lot of rivers were opened for rafting activities. Rivers in South America and Africa were just a few of them.

In 1990s, rafting was included in major game events like the Barcelona Games in 1992, Atlanta Games in 1996, and the whitewater events of the Summer Olympic Games hosted by Ocoee River in Tennessee Valley. In addition, the International Federation of Rafting was instituted in 1997 and in 1999 the first Official International Championship was held. Nowadays, river rafting is still gaining popularity among extreme water sports in order to thrill and excite the raft passengers.

Whitewater Rafts

Rafts were originally the simplest form of man's transportation in water and were then made of several logs, planks or reeds which were fastened together. Nowadays, inflatable boat were used as rafts which were later adopted by the military for beach assaults. It consists of very durable, multi-layered rubberized or vinyl fabrics with several independent air chambers. Its length varies between 3.5 m (11 ft) and 6 m (20 ft), the width between 1.8 m (6 ft) and 2.5 m (8 ft). The exception to this size rule is usually the packraft, which is designed as a portable single-person raft and may be as small as 1.5m long and weigh as little as 4 lbs.

Rafts come in a few different forms. In Europe the most common is the symmetrical raft steered with a paddle at the stern. Other types are the asymmetrical, rudder-controlled raft and the symmetrical raft with central helm (oars). Rafts are usually propelled with ordinary paddles and typically hold 4 to 12 persons. In Russia, rafts are often hand made and are often a catamaran style with two inflatable tubes attached to a frame. Pairs of paddlers navigate these rafts. Catamaran style rafts have become popular in the western United States as well, but are typically rowed instead of paddled.

Classes of Whitewater:

Class 1: Very small rough areas, requires no manuevering. (Skill Level: None)

Class 2: Some rough water, maybe some rocks, might require manuevering.(Skill Level: Basic Paddling Skil)

Class 3: Whitewater, small waves, maybe a small drop, but no considerable danger. May require significant manuevering.(Skill Level: Experienced paddling skills)

Class 4: Whitewater, medium waves, maybe rocks, maybe a considerable drop, sharp manuevers may be needed. (Skill Level: Whitewater Experience)

Class 5: Whitewater, large waves, maybe large rocks and hazards, maybe a large drop, precise maneuvering (Skill Level: Advanced Whitewater Experience)

Class 6: Whitewater, huge waves, huge rocks and hazards, maybe huge drops. Attempting a Class 6 will most likely end in serious injury or death. If someone navigates a 6 without harm, luck can be given most of the credit. (Skill Level: Expert)

Safety

Whitewater rafting can be a dangerous sport, especially if basic safety precautions are not observed. In the past there have been many accidents; both commercial trips and private trips have seen their share of injuries and fatalities, though private travel has stereotypically been associated with greater risk. Depending on the area, legislated safety measures now exist for rafting operators, ranging from certification of outfitters, rafts, and raft leaders, to more stringent regulations about equipment and procedures.

It is generally advisable to discuss safety measures with a rafting operator before signing on for a trip. The equipment used and the qualifications of the company and raft guides are essential information to be considered.

Like most outdoor sports, rafting in general has become safer over the years. Expertise in the sport has increased, and equipment has become more specialized and increased in quality. This is no doubt as a result of the difficulty rating of most river runs has changed.

A classic example would be the Colorado River in the Grand Canyon, which has swallowed whole expeditions in the past, leaving only fragments of boats but is now run safely by commercial outfitters hundreds of times each year, with relatively untrained passengers.

Risks in whitewater rafting stem from both environmental dangers and from improper behavior. Certain features on rivers are inherently unsafe and have remained consistently so despite the passage of time. These would include "keeper hydraulics", "strainers" (e.g. fallen trees), dams (especially low-head dams, which tend to produce river-wide keeper hydraulics), undercut rocks, and of course dangerously high waterfalls. Rafting with experienced guides are the safest way to avoid such features.

Even in safe areas, however, moving water can always present risks--such as when a swimmer attempts to stand up on a rocky riverbed in strong current, risking foot entrapment. Irresponsible behavior along the lines of rafting while intoxicated has also contributed to many accidents.

To combat the illusion that rafting is akin to an amusement park ride, and to underscore the personal responsibility each rafter faces on a trip, rafting outfitters generally require customers to sign waiver forms indicating understanding and acceptance of the risks. Rafting trips often begin with safety presentations to educate customers about problems that may arise.

Having said all this, the overall risk level on a rafting trip with experienced guides using proper precautions is low. Thousands of people safely enjoy raft trips every year.

Issues with Rafting

Like all wilderness sports, rafting has to balance the conflict between nature protection and nature use. Because of frequent problems in the past, some rivers now have regulations restricting or specifying the annual and daily operating times.

Conflicts have also arisen with environmentalists when rafting operators, often in co-operation with municipalities and tourism associations, alter the riverbed by dredging and/or blasting in order to eliminate safety risks or create more interesting whitewater features in the river. Incongruously these measures usually are only temporary, since a riverbed is subject to permanent changes.

On the other hand, rafting contributes to the economy of many alpine regions which in turn may contribute to the protection of rivers from hydroelectric power generation and other development. Additionally, white water rafting trips can promote environmentalism. By experiencing first hand the beauty of a given river, individuals who would otherwise be indifferent to the environmental concerns of an area may gain a strong desire to protect and preserve that area because of a positive outdoors experience.

POPULAR RAFTING LOCATIONS

Africa

- Bujagali Falls on the Nile
- Omo River
- Tana River
- Zambezi River

Asia and Oceania

- Tully River in Queensland, Australia
- Kelani River at Kitulgala in Sri Lanka
- Ganga (Ganges River) and its tributaries in India
- Zanskar River in India
- Yoshino River in Japan
- Bhote Koshi river in Nepal
- Kali Gandaki river in Nepal
- Karnali river in Nepal
- Kawarau River in New Zealand
- Shotover River in New Zealand
- Whataroa River, New Zealand
- Hokitika River, New Zealand
- Chico River, Kalinga, Philippines
- Cagayan de Oro, Philippines
- Jeram Besu, Pahang, Malaysia
- Padas River, Sabah, Malaysia Image:Padasraft c.jpg
- Kiulu River, Sabah, Malaysia

Carribean

- Rio Yaque del Norte near Jarabacoa, Dominican Republic

Europe

- River Findhorn near Aviemore in Scotland, United Kingdom

- Afon Tryweryn near Bala in Wales, United Kingdom
- Tiroler Oberland in the Landeck and Imst Region in Tirol, Austria
- Enns River in Austria
- Tara River (Montenegro), Montenegro
- Una River, Bosnia and Herzegovina
- Neretva River, Bosnia and Herzegovina
- Drina River in Bosnia and Hercegovina
- Soca River in Slovenia
- Sjoa River in Norway
- Lim river in Serbia

Middle East

- Al Assi in North East Lebanon, Northern Bekaa Valley
- Al Litani in East Lebanon, in the Bekaa Valley
- Nahr Al Kalb in West Lebanon

North America

Eastern

- Black River in Watertown, New York
- Chattooga River near Clayton, Georgia in South Carolina
- Cheat River in Albright, West Virginia
- Cheoah River near Robbinsville, North Carolina
- Delaware River, along the border of New Jersey and Pennsylvania
- Deerfield River in northwest Massachusetts
- Nolichucky River flowing into Erwin, Tennessee (northeast Tennessee)
- Gauley River and New River "Grand Canyon of the East" in West Virginia
- Hudson River near Lake George, New York

- James River in Virginia (particularly in Richmond)
- Kennebec River, Dead River, and Penobscot River in Maine
- Lachine Rapids in Montreal, Quebec
- Lehigh River in Pennsylvania
- Moose River near Old Forge, New York
- Nantahala River in Bryson City, North Carolina
- Ocoee River and Appalachian Mountains in the southeastern United States
- Ocoee River flowing into Copperhill, Tennessee (southeast Tennessee)
- Ottawa River at Calumet Island in the Whitewater Region, Ontario
- Pigeon River flowing into Hartford, Tennessee (east Tennessee)
- U.S. National Whitewater Center in Charlotte, North Carolina
- Watauga River flowing into Elizabethton, Tennessee (northeast Tennessee)
- Youghiogheny River in Ohiopyle, Pennsylvania

Western

- American River near Coloma, California in the USA
- Arkansas River near the Royal Gorge in Colorado
- Colorado River, especially through the Grand Canyon starting at Lee's Ferry, Arizona
- Denali National Park and Preserve, starting at the Denali Lodge
- Deschutes River in central Oregon
- Kern River in California
- Kicking Horse River in Golden, British Columbia, Canada

- Lochsa River in Idaho
- Methow River near Methow, Washington
- Rogue River near Grants Pass, Oregon
- Salmon River and its tributaries in Idaho
- Skagit River near Marblemount, Washington
- Skykomish River near Gold Bar, Washington
- Snake River near Jackson Hole, Wyoming
- Tieton River near Naches, Washington
- Truckee River near Lake Tahoe, California starting at Lake Tahoe Dam
- Tuolomne River near Groveland, California
- Wenatchee River near Leavenworth, Washington
- White Salmon River near Husum, Washington

Central America

- Cahabon River in Guatemala
- Nahualate River in Guatemala
- Pacuare River in Costa Rica

South America

- Futaleufu River in Chile, South America

RIVER TREKKING

River trekking or river tracing is a form of hiking or outdoor adventure activity, particularly popular in Hong Kong and Taiwan, and, in some ways, similar to canyoning or canyoneering.

River trekking is a combination of trekking and climbing and sometimes swimming along the river. It involves particular techniques like rock climbing, climbing on wet surfaces, understanding the geographical features of river and valleys, knotting, dealing with sudden bad weather and find out possible exits from the river.

RIVER TREKKING IN DIFFERENT COUNTRIES

Hong Kong

River trekking has developed in Hong Kong since mid-20th century. Currently, there are numerous hiking groups organize regular trekking activities in Hong Kong. However, river trekking is a bit underground. There are no formal schools, formal coaches, formal sites, official recognition or qualifications on river trekking, even though it involves particular skills and certain level of risks. In Hong Kong, any natural rivers can be found in the country side, there would be the possible sites for river trekking.

Attractions and Popularity

River trekking is especially popular in Hong Kong because it is totally a surprise that in this highly developed region are preserved a number of excellent geographical features in its rivers in the countryside. Through river trekking, it is possible to access numerous waterfalls, large ponds, pot holes, other special geographical features as well as special species of animals and plants. Also, it is a very cheap activity in comparison with other challenging outdoor activities like rock climbing, rowling and wind-surfing. No training courses are needed because there is no one in Hong Kong who would provide training for river trekking. However, river trekking has long been one of the most popular outdoor activities in Hong Kong, even though most of the river trekking routes or sites are indicated as "danger" or "no entry" by the government. There is a trend that more and more foreigners and even tourists are taking part in this activity.

The Nine Big Rivers

The Nine Big Rivers are the nine rivers that are most popular among river trekkers in Hong Kong. The Nine Big Rivers include:

- Tai Shing River, located in Tsuen Wan
- Wan Chung River, located in Tai Po
- Ng Tung River, located in Tai Po

- Wong Lung River, located on Lantau Island near Tung Chung
- Sheng Luk River, located in Sai Kung
- Man Cheng Po, located in the west of Lantau Island
- Lotus River, located in Tai Lam Country Park
- Ngon Sam River, located on Lantau Island near Great Buddha
- Ping Nam River, located close to the border between Hong Kong and mainland China

Taiwan

This sport is popular throughout Taiwan, where it is generally called river tracing (??).

Rating of Difficuties

As river trekking has a certain level of risk, experienced river trekkers or hiking groups have developed rating systems about difficuties on different rivers. The ratings usually are various from 1 to 5 stars, even though a few rivers can be more than 5 stars because of their extreme difficulties. Such ratings are largely subjective, depends largely on river trekker's own experience. Therefore, different people or hiking groups would give different number of stars on the same river. According to Hong Kong Adverntruer, an English Website about hiking and river trekking in Hong Kong, difficult scale of different rivers as:

- 1 star: can be handled by normal healthy persons
- 2 stars: not too easy
- 3 stars: fairly difficult
- 4 stars: difficult, absolutely not for beginners
- 5 stars: very difficult, very demanding in term of strength and skill

Risk and Danger

River trekking has certain level of risk. There are occasional accidents in river trekking, including falls from steep cliffs or waterfalls, drownings, exhaustion, or getting lost. Risks that should be prepared for include the following:

First, sudden changes in weather, like rainstorms, can cause rapid rises in water levels and speed in the river. Also, the number of viable paths and climbing areas inside the river valley would be reduced suddenly in a very short period. Besides this, bad or misty weather would also cause low visibility. Low visibility may come in to quickly for trekkers to adapt to. Therefore, a torch (flashlight), preferably a head-mounted one, is a must for river trekking.

Second, steep cliffs inside river valleys require a certain level of rock climbing skills. However, because of the moisturing environment inside the river valley, some rock surfaces can be very wet and some rocks can be very loose despite appearing solid. To deal with such wet climbing conditions, a pair of professional river-trekking boots are strongly advised.

Damage to Stream Systems Caused by River Trekking

Due to the increasing popularity of river trekking, the activity has resulted in some damage to certain streams. The most noticeable kinds of damage are:

- Rubbish left by river trekking groups
- Use of aerosol spraypaints to mark route directions on rocks and trees
- Discarded climbing equipment and unnecessary bolting
- Damage to trees and other flora when used as leverage by trekkers
- Graffiti written in paint, ink and correction fluid

Such damage is, unfortunately, quite common in Hong Kong and goes against the philosophy of leave no trace, which most outdoor adventure sports adhere to.

CANYONING

Canyoning (also known as canyoneering) is traveling in canyons using a variety of techniques that may include walking, scrambling, climbing, jumping, abseiling, and/or swimming. Although hiking down a canyon that is non-technical (canyon hiking) is often referred to as canyoneering, the terms canyoning and canyoneering are more often associated with technical descents-those that require rappels (abseils) and ropework, technical climbing or down-climbing, technical jumps, and/or technical swims.

Canyoning is frequently done in remote and rugged settings and often requires navigational, route-finding and other skills and preparation needed for wilderness travel.

Canyons that are ideal for canyoning are often cut into the bedrock stone, forming narrow gorges with numerous drops, beautifully sculpted walls, and sometimes spectacular waterfalls. Most canyons are cut into limestone, granite or sandstone, though other rock types are found. Canyons can be very easy or extremely difficult, though emphasis in the sport is usually on aesthetics and fun rather than pure difficulty. A wide variety of canyoning routes are found throughout the world, and canyoning is enjoyed by people of all ages and skill levels.

Canyoning gear includes climbing hardware, static ropes, helmets, wetsuits, and specially designed shoes, packs, and rope bags. While canyoners have used and adapted climbing, hiking, and river running gear for years, more and more specialized gear is invented and manufactured as canyoning popularity increases.

Canyoning Around the World

In most parts of the world canyoning is done in mountain canyons with flowing water. Countries with established canyoning include: Australia, New Zealand, Spain, France, Ecuador, Japan, Italy, Switzerland, Germany, Austria, Reunion Island, Greece (Crete), Jordan, Canada, Mexico, Brazil, Croatia, Turkey, Israel, Mauritius and the United States. In South Africa, canyons that involve lots of jumping are common, and it is called Kloofing. Even in Hong Kong, where there are numerous stream gorges, a similar activity called stream or river trekking is popular. In Japan and Taiwan it's called river tracing and typically involves traveling upstream. In the United States, descending mountain canyons with flowing water is often referred to as canyoning, and descending non-flowing (though often wet) desert canyons is referred to as canyoneering. Most canyoneering in the United States occurs in the many slot canyons carved in the sandstone found throughout the Colorado Plateau. Outside of the Colorado Plateau, numerous canyoning opportunities are found in the San Gabriel, Sierra Nevada, Cascade, and Rocky Mountain ranges.

Hazards

Canyoning can be dangerous. Escape out the sides of a canyon is often impossible, and completion of the descent is the only possibility. Due to the remoteness and inaccessibility of many canyons, rescue can be impossible for several hours or several days.

High Water Flow / hydraulics

Canyons with significant water flow may be treacherous and require special ropework techniques for safe travel. Hydraulics, undercurrents, and sieves (or strainers) occur in flowing canyons and can trap or pin and drown a canyoner. A 1993 accident in Zion National Park, Utah, USA, in which two leaders of a youth group drowned in powerful canyon hydraulics (and the lawsuit which followed) brought notoriety to the sport.

Flash Floods

A potential danger of many canyoning trips is a flash flood. A canyon "flashes" when a large amount of precipitation falls in the drainage, and water levels in the canyon rise quickly as the runoff rushes down the canyon. In canyons that drain large areas, the rainfall could be many kilometers away from the canyoners, completely unbeknown to them. A calm or even dry canyon can quickly become a violent torrent due to a severe thunderstorm in the vicinity. Fatalities have occurred as a result of flash floods; in one widely-publicized 1999 incident, 21 tourists on a commercial canyoning adventure trip drowned in Saxetenbach Gorge, Switzerland.

Hypothermia and Hyperthermia

Temperature related illnesses are also canyoning hazards. In arid desert canyons, heat exhaustion can occur if proper hydration levels are not maintained and adequate steps are not taken to avoid the intense rays of the sun. Hypothermia can be a serious danger in any canyon that contains water, during anytime of the year. Wetsuits and drysuits can mitigate this danger to a large degree, but when people miscalculate the amount of water protection they will need, dangerous and sometimes fatal situations can occur. Hypothermia due to inadequate cold water prctection is cited as a cause of a 2005 incident in which two college students drowned in a remote Utah canyon.

Keeper Potholes

Some canyoneering, especially in sandstone slots, involves escaping from large potholes. Also called "keeper potholes," these features, carved out by falling water at the bottom of a drop in the watercourse, are circular pits that often contain water that is too deep to stand up in and whose walls are too smooth to easily climb out of. Canyoneers use several unique and creative devices to escape potholes, including hooks used for aid climbing attached to long poles and specialized weighted bags that are attached to ropes and tossed over the lip of a pothole.

Very Narrow Slots

Narrow slot canyons, especially those narrower than humans, present difficult obstacles for canyoners. At times a canyoner is forced to climb up (using chimneying or off-width climbing techniques) to a height where one can comfortably maneuver laterally with pressure on both walls of the canyon. This tends to be strenuous and can require climbing high above the canyon floor, unprotected, for long periods of time. Failure to complete the required moves could result in being trapped in a canyon where rescue is extremely difficult.

Narrow sandstone slot canyons tend have abrasive walls which act as sandpaper as a canyoner moves or slides along them. This abrasion tends to rip clothing and gear, and can cause painful skin abrasion.

HIKING

Hiking is a form of walking, undertaken with the specific purpose of exploring and enjoying the scenery. It usually takes place on trails in rural or wilderness areas.

The word 'hiking' is understood in all English-speaking countries, but there are differences in usage. In some places, off-trail hiking is called 'cross-country hiking', 'bushwhacking', or 'bush-bashing'. In the United Kingdom, hiking is a slightly old-fashioned word, with a flavor more of heartiness and exercise than of enjoying the outdoors; the activity described here would be called 'hillwalking' or simply 'walking'. Australians use the term 'bushwalking' for both on-and off-trail hiking. New Zealanders use 'tramping' (particularly for overnight and longer trips), 'walking' or 'bushwalking'. Hiking in the mountainous regions of Nepal and India is sometimes called 'trekking'. Overnight hiking is called 'backpacking' in some parts of the world. Hiking a long-distance trail from end to end is referred to as 'thru-hiking' in some places.

Hiking is one of the fundamental outdoor activities on which many others are based. Many beautiful places can only be reached overland by hiking, and enthusiasts regard hiking as the best way to see nature. It is seen as better than a tour in a vehicle of any kind (or on an animal; see horseback riding) because the hiker's senses are not intruded upon by distractions such as windows, engine noise, airborne dust and fellow passengers. Hiking over long distances or over difficult terrain does require some degree of physical ability and knowledge.

Ecological Impact of Hiking

Hikers often seek beautiful environments in which to hike. Ironically, these environments are often fragile: hikers may accidentally destroy the environment that they enjoy. The action of an individual may not strongly affect the environment. However, the mass effect of a large number of hikers can degrade the environment. For example, gathering wood in an alpine area to start a fire may be harmless once (except for wildfire risk). Years of gathering wood, however, can strip an alpine area of valuable nutrients. Generally, protected areas such as parks have regulations in place to protect the environment. If hikers follow such regulations, their impact can be minimized. Such regulations include forbidding wood fires, restricting camping to established camp sites, disposing or packing out fecal matter, imposing a quota on the number of hikers per day.

Many hikers espouse the philosophy of Leave No Trace: hiking in a way such that future hikers cannot detect the presence of previous hikers. Practitioners of this philosophy obey its strictures, even in the absence of area regulations.

Human waste is often a major source of environmental impact from hiking. These wastes can contaminate the watershed and make other hikers ill. Bacterial contamination can be avoided by digging catholes 10 to 25 cm deep (4 to 10 inches, depending on local soil composition) and covering after use. If these catholes are dug at least 60 m (200 feet) away from water sources and trails, the risk of contamination is minimized. Many hikers warn other hikers about the location of their catholes by marking them with sticks stuck into the ground.

Sometimes, hikers enjoy viewing rare or endangered species. However, some species (such as martens or bighorn sheep) are very sensitive to the presence of humans, especially around mating season. Hikers should learn the habits and habitats of the endangered species, in order to avoid adverse impact. There is one situation where an individual hiker can make a large impact on an ecosystem: inadvertently starting a wildfire. For example, in 2005, a Czech backpacker burned 7% of Torres del Paine National Park in Chile by knocking over an illegal gas portable stove. Obeying area regulations and setting up cooking devices on bare ground will reduce the risk of wildfire.

Etiquette of Hiking

Because hiking is a recreational experience, hikers expect it to be pleasant. Sometimes hikers can interfere with each others' enjoyment, or that of other users of the land, but they can minimize this interference by following good etiquette. For example:

- When two groups of hikers meet on a steep trail, there may be contention for use of the trail. To avoid conflict, a custom has developed in some areas whereby the group moving uphill has the right-of-way. In other situations, the larger of the two groups will usually yield to the smaller.
- Being forced to hike much faster or slower than one's natural pace can be annoying, and difficult to maintain consistently. More seriously, walking unnaturally fast dramatically increases fatigue and exhaustion, and may cause injury. If a group splits between fast and slow hikers, the slow hikers may be left behind or become lost. A common custom is to encourage the slowest hiker to hike in the lead and have everyone match that speed. Another custom is to have an experienced hiker sweep up the rear, to ensure that everyone in the group is safe and nobody straggles.
- Hikers often enjoy the silence and solitude of their surroundings. Loud sounds, such as shouting or loud conversation, disrupt this enjoyment. Some hikers purposely avoid loud sounds, out of deference to other hikers. Staying quiet will also increase the likelihood of encountering wildlife. (This is a hazard if dangerous animals are present; see "Personal safety hazards".)
- Hikers sometimes trespass onto private property from public land or rights of way (easements). Such trespass can alienate the property owners and (in countries where rights of way are not protected by law) close down hiking rights-of-way. To maximize hiking opportunities for everyone, most hikers will either stay on public land and easements, or solicit permission from property owners. Staying on well-marked trails avoids the possibility of trespass.
- Tree branches or other vegetation often hang low across trails. A passing hiker may cause a tree branch to snap

back in the face of a hiker behind. While it is courteous to warn following hikers if a branch is likely to snap back, it is every hiker's responsibility to allow enough space between himself and the hiker ahead to avoid the hazard.

- When two groups of hikers meet, it is considered a common courtesy to exchange greetings (either verbal or physical (e.g. smiles and friendly nods)). To pass another group without such acknowledgement is seen as rude.

Personal Safety Hazards

Hiking may produce threats to personal safety. These threats can be dangerous circumstances while hiking and/or specific accidents or ailments. Dangerous hiking circumstances include losing the way, inclement weather, hazardous terrain, or exacerbation of pre-existing medical conditions.

Specific accidents include metabolic imbalances (such as dehydration or hypothermia), topical injuries (such as frostbite or sunburn), attacks by animals, or internal injuries (such as ankle sprain).

Hikers often propose a set of behavioral prescriptions to minimize these threats. A well-known example of such a set of prescription is the Ten Essentials.

Kinds of hiking:

- Hiking
- Backpacking, also known as trekking, a multi-day, often arduous hike especially in mountainous regions
- Thru-hiking, hiking a trail from end to end
- Hillwalking
- Dog hiking, hiking with dogs
- Naked hiking
- Waterfalling, aka waterfall hunting and waterfall hiking. Hiking with the purpose of finding and enjoying waterfalls.

URBAN EXPLORATION

Urban exploration (often shortened as urbex or UE) is the examination of the normally unseen or off-limits parts of human civilization. Urban exploration is also commonly referred to as infiltration, although some people consider infiltration to be more closely associated with the exploration of active or inhabited sites. In the USA, it may also be referred to as "draining" (when exploring drains) "urban spelunking", and "urban caving", "vadding", "building hacking", "Reality hacking" or "roof and tunnel hacking".

Targets of Exploration

Abandonments

Ventures into abandoned structures are perhaps the most common example of urban exploration. Abandoned sites are generally entered first by locals, and often sport large amounts of graffiti and acts of vandalism. Explorers face various risks in abandoned structures including collapsing roofs and floors, broken glass, guard dogs, the presence of chemicals, other harmful substances, most notably asbestos, hostile squatters and sometimes motion detectors. Some explorers wear respirators to protect their airways.

Exploration targets vary from one country to another, but some of the more popular or high-profile abandonments include amusement parks, grain elevators, factories, missile silos, hospitals, asylums, and sanatoriums.

Many explorers of abandonments find the decay of uninhabited spaces to be beautiful; many of these explorers are also photographers. Some abandonments are heavily guarded with motion sensors and active security. Others are more easily accessible and carry less risk of discovery. Abandonments are also popular among history buffs, 'urban archaeologists,' 'ghost hunters' and fans of graffiti art.

Active Buildings

Another aspect of urban exploration is the practice of exploring active or in use buildings. This includes seeing secured or "member-only" areas, mechanical rooms, roofs, elevator rooms, abandoned floors and other normally unseen parts of such buildings. The term 'infiltration' is often associated with the exploration of active structures.

Catacombs

Catacombs such as those found in Paris, Rome and Naples have been investigated by urban explorers. The catacombs under Paris, for instance, have been considered the "Holy Grail" by some due to their extensive nature and history.

Sewers and Storm Drains

Entry into storm drains, or draining, is another common form of UE. Groups devoted to the task have arisen, such as the Cave Clan in Australia. Draining has a specialized set of guidelines, the foremost of which is "When it rains, no drains!"

A small subset of explorers enter sanitary sewers. Sometimes they are the only connection to caves or other subterranean feature. Sewers are among the most dangerous locations to explore owing to extremely high risks of poisoning by build up of toxic gases naturally found in all sewers (commonly methane and hydrogen sulphide). There have been large numbers of fatalities from around the world through being overcome by toxic gases from sewers and the only safe way to enter a sewer is if the atmosphere has been tested by a working monitoring device and other confined space entry procedures followed.

Transit Tunnels

The subset of urban exploration deals with exploring active and abandoned subway and underground railway tunnels and bores. Since these are in major cities, they carry stiff penalties if one should be caught while trespassing in these, especially after the September 11, 2001 attacks. As a result, this type of exploration is rarely publicized. Although they exist worldwide, those who partake in this often reside near New York City, Toronto, London, Sydney and Moscow, along with many other major cities throughout the world.

Utility Tunnels

Universities and other large institutions, such as hospitals, often distribute steam for heating buildings from a central heating plant. These steam ducts are generally run through utility tunnels, which are often accessible solely for the purposes of maintenance. Many of these steam tunnels, such as those on college campuses, often also have a tradition of exploration by students. This was once called vadding at MIT, though students there now refer to it as roof and tunnel hacking.

Steam tunnels in general have been getting more secure in recent years, due to their use for carrying network backbones and perceived risk of their use in terrorist activities, safety and liability.

Some steam tunnels have dirt floors, no lighting and can have temperatures upwards of 115 degrees Fahrenheit (46° C). Others have concrete floors, bright light, and can even be quite nice and feature a cool temperature. Most steam tunnels have large intake fans to bring in fresh air, and push all of the hot air out the back.

Ethics

Most urban explorers understand the risks they face if caught while trespassing or breaking and entering. The crime is generally seen as a means to an end, however, rather than being the focal point of the hobby. There are some urban explorers that tend to stick to a basic set of "ethical practices" out of respect for the locations that they visit, as well as for any other explorers who may want to visit later. The hobby, however, is still ultimately an unstructured one, and there are rarely two explorers who share the same views on ethics. As such, there are many exceptions to these "practices".

To some, the idea behind these "ethical practices" is to leave buildings in the same state that they were in before they were visited. The common, but not always entirely accurate catchphrase for this ethical standpoint is the Sierra Club's motto: "take nothing but pictures, leave nothing but footprints." Some try and adhere to this motto which frowns heavily upon theft, vandalism, tagging, graffiti, and any other crime except for trespassing.

Some explorers, though, remove items from abandoned sites to preserve them or to keep as souvenirs. More often than not, these explorers save these items from further decay or destruction when a location has become a target of vandalism or is being demolished.

Another counterpoint to the "leave no trace" ethic is tagging. Graffiti in drains is sometimes condoned or encouraged as long as speleothems and other features aren't damaged. Drainers may use it to indicate how far down the drain a given explorer has been. Similarly, tags may be left in very inaccessible places such as inside false ceilings, at the tops of elevator shafts, and so on.

Some locations contain a small area reserved for leaving tags, known as a guest book. These vary from actual books to blackboards to pieces of scrap metal or wood, or even the dust on an old piece of machinery. Rarely, employee guest books will be found, made before the business in question closed. Tags, especially those left in guest books, are sometimes referred to as "sign-ins", and the process of leaving them is "signing in". In marked contrast to the values of mainstream U.S. urban graffiti, tags are generally made to be unobtrusive, being written in conventional or slightly enlarged handwriting with pens or markers rather than larger markings made with paint.

As with many other cases of ethical principles, it is primarily up to the individual to make their own decisions based on their viewpoints and their current situation.

Popularity

The rise in the popularity of urban exploration can be attributed to its increased media attention. Recent television shows, such as "Urban Explorers" on the Discovery Channel, MTV's Fear, and the ghost hunting exploits of The Atlantic Paranormal Society have packaged the hobby for a popular audience; Talks and exhibits on urban exploration have appeared at the 5th and 6th Hackers on Planet Earth Conference, complementing numerous newspaper articles and interviews. With the advent rise in the relative popularity of the hobby due to this increased focus, there has been increasing discussion on whether the extra attention has been beneficial to urban exploration as a whole.

The growing popularity of the activity has resulted not just in increased attention from explorers, but also from vandals and law enforcement. The illicit aspects of urban exploring, which may include trespassing and breaking and entering, have brought along with them critical articles in mainstream newspapers. In one recent article, web-postings and photographs from the web-site Urban Exploration Resource were cited as evidence that explorers were trespassing in a closed prison in Northern Virginia. Users had posted specific details on entry points and how "easy" it was to gain entry to the disused facility.

In that regard, some explorers have become wary of posting information and photographs on UE-related websites for fear of being prosecuted for trespassing. Recently there has been a conflict of interest between explorers about this issue. Additionally, arguments focus on whether online listings of explorable structures undermine the "underground" aspect of urban exploration.

Along with the rise in the popularity of urban exploring, numerous events have been hosted throughout the world. These organized meetings have included campouts, barbeques, day-long explorations, and tours of active and abandoned sites. While most of these are illegal in the sense that they involve trespassing or breaking and entering, a handful of meets, such as a recent event held at the West Virginia State Penitentiary, involve tours or lock-ins. Others include UE-related gatherings, such as a meet held by an urban explorer who calls himself Shiroi in which stunts were performed in an abandoned structure. This has received mixed criticism from the urban exploration community.

11

BACKPACKING (WILDERNESS)

INTRODUCTION

Backpacking (also tramping or trekking or bushwalking in some countries) combines hiking and camping in a single trip. A backpacker hikes into the backcountry to spend one or more nights there, and carries supplies and equipment to satisfy sleeping and eating needs.

What is Backpacking?

A backpacker packs all of his or her gear into a backpack. This gear must include food, water, and shelter, or the means to obtain them, but very little else, and often in a more compact and simpler form than one would use for stationary camping.

A backpacking trip must include at least one overnight stay in the wilderness (otherwise it is a day hike). Many backpacking trips last just a weekend (one or two nights), but long-distance expeditions may last weeks or months, sometimes aided by planned food and supply drops.

Backpacking camps are more spartan than ordinary camps. In areas that experience a regular traffic of backpackers, a hike-in camp might have a fire ring and a small wooden bulletin board with a map and some warning or information signs. Many hike-in camps are no more than level patches of ground without scrub or underbrush. In very remote areas, established camps do not exist at all, and travelers must choose appropriate camps themselves.

In some places, backpackers have access to lodging that are more substantial than a tent. In the more remote parts of Great Britain, bothies exist to provide simple (free) accommodation for backpackers. Another example is the High Sierra Camps in Yosemite National Park.

Mountain huts provide similar accommodation in other countries, so being a member of a mountain hut organization is advantageous (perhaps required) to make use of their facilities. On other trails (e.g. the Appalachian Trail) there are somewhat more established shelters of a sort that offer a place for weary hikers to spend the night without needing to set up a tent.

Most backpackers purposely try to avoid impacting on the land through which they travel. This includes following established trails as much as possible, not removing anything, and not leaving residue in the backcountry. The Leave No Trace movement offers a set of guidelines for low-impact backpacking ("Leave nothing but footprints. Take nothing but photos. Kill nothing but time.").

PROFESSIONAL BACKPACKING

In the military a framed backpack is referred to as a "rucksack" or simply a "ruck". Soldiers who serve in the militaries of most nation-states usually receive at least some rudimentary backpacking training while infantrymen are often trained to a more advanced backpacking skill level.

They share many common attributes with amateur backpackers: being self-contained, use of land-navigation skills and actively minimizing their environmental foot-print. Although there are also a few differences such as the need to carry an assault rifle, other weapons, ammunition and communication equipment as well as at times maintaining "noise and light discipline", which means remaining silent and in darkness to avoid detection.

Other professional backpackers may be scientific and academic researchers, professional guides, photographers, park-rangers and "search & rescue" personnel.

Motivation

People are drawn to backpacking primarily for recreation, to explore places that they consider beautiful and fascinating, many of which cannot be accessed in any other way. A backpacker can travel deeper into remote areas, away from people and their effects, than a day-hiker can. However, backpacking presents more advantages besides distance of travel. Many weekend trips cover routes that could be hiked in a single day, but people choose to backpack them anyway, for the experience of staying overnight.

These possibilities come with disadvantages. The weight of a pack, laden with supplies and gear, forces backpackers to travel more slowly than day-hikers would, and it can become a nuisance and a distraction from enjoying the scenery. In addition, camp chores (such as pitching camp, breaking camp, and cooking) can easily consume several hours every day.

Backpackers face many risks, including adverse weather, difficult terrain, treacherous river crossings, and hungry or unpredictable animals (although the perceived danger from wild animals usually greatly exceeds the true risk). They are subject to illnesses, which run the gamut from simple dehydration to heat exhaustion, hypothermia, altitude sickness, and physical injury. The remoteness of backpacking locations exacerbates any mishap. However, these hazards do not deter backpackers who are properly prepared. Some simply accept danger as a risk that they must endure if they want to backpack; for others, the potential dangers actually enhance the allure of the wilderness.

Equipment

Almost all backpackers seek to minimize the weight and bulk of gear carried. A lighter pack causes less fatigue, injury and soreness, and allows the backpacker to travel longer distances. Every piece of equipment is evaluated for a balance of utility versus weight. Significant reductions in weight can usually be achieved with little sacrifice in equipment utility, though very lightweight equipment is usually significantly more costly. A large industry has developed to provide lightweight gear and food for backpackers. The gear includes the backpacks themselves, as well as ordinary camping equipment modified to reduce the weight, by either reducing the size, reducing the durability, or using lighter materials such as special plastics, alloys of aluminium, titanium, composite materials, impregnanted fabrics and carbon fiber. Designers of portable stoves and tents have been particularly ingenious. Homemade gear is common too, such as the beverage-can stove.

Some backpackers use lighter and more compact gear than do others. The most radical measures taken in this regard are sometimes called ultralight backpacking.

Due to the emphasis on weight reduction, a practical joke common in some circles is to secretly pack a small but relatively heavy luxury item, such as a soft drink, into another backpacker's pack. Then, once the group stops for a rest, the perpetrator retrieves the item, thanks the bearer for carrying it, and consumes it.

Water

Backpackers always carry some water from the trailhead, to drink while walking. For short trips, they may carry enough to last the whole trip, but for long trips this is not practical. A backpacker needs anywhere from two to eight liters or more per day, depending on conditions, making a water supply for more than a few days prohibitively heavy. Backpackers typically carry two to four liters of water depending on conditions and availability. Although some backpacking camps in heavily-used areas provide potable water, it must usually be obtained from lakes and streams. Drinking and cooking water nearly always needs treatment with a filter or purifier to protect against bacteria and protozoa (see Potability of backcountry water and Portable water purification). If water is unavailable, or if the only water available is irreparably filthy, backpackers may need to carry large amounts of water for long distances.

Water may be stored in bottles or in soft, collapsible hydration packs (bladders). Some backpackers store water in ordinary plastic beverage bottles, while others use special Lexan bottles or metal canteens. For accessibility they may be carried by a shoulder strap or attached to the outside of a pack. Bladders are typically made of plastic, rubber, and/or fabric. They are light, easily stored and collapsible. They may be equipped with drinking hoses for easy access while hiking. In spite of this convenience, bladders are more prone to leaking than bottles, particularly at the hose connections. Hoses also allow the hiker to lose track of the water supply in the bladder and to deplete it prematurely.

Food

Some backpackers enjoy cooking elaborate meals with fresh ingredients, particularly on short trips, and others carry the gear and take the time to catch fish or hunt small game for food. However, especially for long expeditions, most backpackers' food criteria are roughly the same: high energy content (particularly protein), with long shelf life and low mass and volume. An additional concern is weight; while Dutch oven and campfire cookery are historically popular, small liquid-fuel campstoves and ultralight cooking pots made of aluminum or titanium are more common in modern usage due to weight limitations and fire restrictions in many locales.

Ordinary household foods used on backpacking trips include cheese, bread, sausage, fruit, peanut butter, and pasta. Popular snack foods include trail mix, easily prepared at home; convenient and nutritious energy bars; and chocolate and other forms of candy, which provide quick energy and flavor. Traditional outdoor food includes dried foodstuffs such as jerky or pemmican, and also products like oatmeal (which can also be consumed raw in emergency situations).

Most backpackers avoid canned food, except for meats or small delicacies. Metal cans and their contents are usually heavy, and, like all trash, the empties must be carried back out.

For dinners, many hikers use specially manufactured, pre-cooked food that can be eaten hot. It is often sold in large, stiff bags that double as eating vessels. One common variety of special backpacking food is freeze-dried food, which can be quickly reconstituted by adding hot water. One can also purchase a commercial food dehydrator which removes the majority of water from a pre-cooked meal. To eat, water is mixed in with the meal several hours before eating and allowed to rehyrdate before heating. Some various distributors of this are Backpackers Pantry and Mountain Outfitters. Another kind of special backpacking food is UHT-packaged without dehydration, and can be reheated with a special, water-activated chemical heater. This technology originated with the U.S. military's Meal Ready-to-Eat ("MRE"), but is now produced also for the commercial market. The small chemical heater obviates the need for a portable stove and fuel, but the meals and packaging weigh so much that, for more than a few meals, there is no weight advantage. On the other hand, MRE's were developed with many more factors than mere weight in mind, and they still make excellent backpacking food for several reasons, such as a) they do not need to be rehydrated nor heated or cooked in any manner, b) they are very durably packaged, c) a single MRE contains a full meal, complete with snack and desert, d) they offer a great deal of variety in each meal, including condiments such as Tabasco sauce, e) they are individually packaged inside the "brown plastic wrapper", so that you can place individual components in various pockets and "eat on the move". As more and more "big box" retail stores carry pre-packaged dehydrated foods (such as Mountain House Brand) however, it is becoming increasingly easier to buy packaged meals retail versus mail order, whereas MRE's are rarely carried in retail stores.

There is a genre of cookbooks specializing in trailside food and the special challenges inherent in backcountry cooking. Most such cookbooks espouse one of two philosophies; the first, generally used on short trips, involves planning out meals and preparing many ingredients in one's home kitchen before departure. The second method, bulk rationing, simply supplies the hiker with ingredients, allowing on-trail cooking with minimal prior planning, and is sometimes used for extended outings. A third form of the genre deals in Dutch oven cookery, which has considerable historical cachet (especially in countries such as the United States with a long pioneer tradition), but is dependent on suitable location, for a campfire.

WINTER BACKPACKING

Although backpacking in the winter is rewarding, it can be dangerous and generally requires more gear. Backpackers may need skis or snowshoes to traverse deep snow, or crampons to cross ice. Cotton clothing, which absorbs moisture and chills the body, is particularly dangerous in cold weather, so backpackers stick to synthetic materials or materials that won't hold moisture. Special low-temperature sleeping bags and tents can be expensive, but will be more comfortable than many layers of warm clothing. However when hiking in cold weather it is always better to hike with varying layers of clothing so that as the body heats up layers can be taken off without causing the wearer to sweat or become very chilled.

SKILLS AND SAFETY

- Survival skills are handy for peace of mind: In case the weather, terrain or environment is more challenging than prepared for, or for dealing with shortcomings in
- Navigation and orienteering are useful to find the trailhead, then find and follow a route to a desired sequence of destinations, and then an exit. In case of disorientation, orienteering skills are important to determine where you are and formulate a route to somewhere more desirable. At their most basic, navigation skills allow you to choose the correct sequence of trails to follow.
- First Aid: effectively dealing with minor injuries (splinters, punctures, sprains) is considered by many a fundamental backcountry skill. More subtle, but maybe even more important, is recognizing and promptly treating hypothermia, heat stroke, dehydration and hypoxia, as these are rarely encountered in daily life.

- Leave No Trace is the backpacker's version of the golden rule: To have beautiful and pristine places to enjoy, help make them. At a minimum, don't make them worse.
- Distress signaling is a skill of last resort.

RELATED ACTIVITIES

- Hiking may or may not use backpacks.
- Canoe camping is similar to backpacking, but uses canoes or other boats for transportation.
- Ski touring and snowshoeing are alternative forms of hiking (overnight or otherwise) that can be engaged in when the ground is buried deeply in snow.
- In self-contained bicycle touring, cyclists carry their equipment in panniers or in trailers during multi-day excursions, either on pavement, or on back-country fire roads and trails.
- In animal packing ("horse packing", "mule packing", etc.), the hikers use pack animals (usually horses, mules or llamas) to carry their equipment, and sometimes they will even ride the animals. Porters are sometimes hired for the same purpose.
- Backpacking (travel) focuses on cultural attractions, rather than natural ones, though it may also include wilderness side trips.
- Adventure tourism is travel in a region or environment that is, for one reason or another, highly unpredictable or hazardous.
- Thru-hiking is traversing a long-distance trail in a single, continuous journey by starting at one end of the trail with a backpack and hiking essentially unaided to the other end.
- Ultralight backpacking is a form of backpacking focused on minimizing the weight of the gear carried. It is often employed by long distance hikers.

12

Expanding Realm of Tourism

AGRITOURISM

Agritourism is a style of vacation in which hospitality is offered on farms. This may include the opportunity to assist with farming tasks during the visit. Agritourism is often practiced in wine growing regions, as in Italy, France and Spain. In America, Agritourism is wide-spread and includes any farm open to the public at least part of the year. Tourists can pick fruits and vegetables, ride horses, taste honey, learn about wine, shop in gift shops and farm stands for local and regional produce or hand-crafted gifts, and much more. Agritourism is being developed as a valuable component of a business model to support many agricultural entities when the farm products they produce are no longer economically competitive otherwise. To help promote the single agritourism operations, some farms get together to form festivals, tours or other events.

People are more interested in how their food is produced and want to meet the producers and talk with them about what goes into food production. Children who visit the farms often have not seen a live duck, or goat, and have not picked an apple right off the tree. This form of expanded agri-tourism has given birth to what are often called "entertainment farms." These farms cater to the pick-your-own crowd, offering not only regular farm products, but also food, mazes, open-pen animals, train rides, picnic facilities and pick-your-own produce. Dude ranches offer tourists the chance to work on cattle ranches and sometimes include cattle drives.

ARCHAEOLOGICAL TOURISM

Archaeotourism or Archaeological tourism is an alternative form of cultural tourism, which aims to promote the passion for historical-archaeology and the conservation of historical sites.

Establishment

Investigator Georgeos Diaz-Montexano, who initiated a series of publications in 1995 about ArchaeoTourism, such as "Arqueología y Enigmas de la Historia", "Arqueología Sin Fronteras", "La Esfinge. Revista de Egiptologia" and "ArqueoHistoria", brought awareness to the concept of archaeological tourism. Shortly after writing these publications, he founded the first specialized society on Archaeotourism, ArqueoTour (2000). For these efforts, he is considered by some to be the founder of archaeotourism.

Like Ecological tourism (or Ecotourism), Archaeological tourism is promoted to encourage the development of cultural associations, and companies and cooperatives can be found that dedicate themselves to offer this type of service.

The best definition of archaeotourism can be found in the words of its founders:

The passion by the past is something inherent to the human being. As it says well: "Town that does not know from where town comes that does not know to where it goes".

The Archaeotourism or archaeological tourism is ideal for which they look for a higher knowledge and sublimates, tie to the meditation and the relaxation, in perfect syntcny with the surroundings or ecosystem that is, integration with the Mother Nature, but always in old places, next to the ruins of the "enigmatic missing civilizations".

Sites and places magician-monks or asylums. From the most remote prehistoric times. From the era of the dinosaurios to the Medieval Age. In order to develop his activities it has a nourished group of authentic experts in each one of the matters.

Therefore, archaeologists, paleontologists, anthropologists, historians and specialists in trips will unite their knowledge under a same objective: to offer to the traveller a wonderful and unforgettable experience, an intensive course and of introduction to each one of these manifestations of the human knowledge. This way the visitor will not be a simple traveller, will be in addition an apprentice in sciences to the past.

Some times will feel a paleontologist discovering tracks of dinosaurious and others will feel like Indiana Jones in the Damn Temple, mainly when penetrating in the mysterious caverns and artificial caves that long ago served from temples our ancestors. Enigmatic places loaded of an atmosphere of magic and mystery that, sometimes, surpass to all fiction created by the cinema...

Other Definitions

Archaeological tourism can include all products associated with public archaeological promotion, including visits to archaeological sites, museums, interpretation centers, reinactment of historical occurrences, the rediscovery of native products, festivals, or theater.

Although archaeological tourism is quite recent, many international institutions and governments have already begun to contemplate viable alternative activity for the sustainable economic-social development. Several countries have for years had programs resembling the main points of Archaeological tourism for economic income, including Egypt, Mexico and Peru.

BOOKSTORE TOURISM

Bookstore tourism is a type of cultural tourism that promotes independent bookstores as a group travel destination. It started as a grassroots effort to support locally owned and operated bookshops, many of which have struggled to compete with large bookstore chains and online retailers.

The project was initiated in 2003 by Larry Portzline, a writer and college instructor in Harrisburg, Pennsylvania who led "bookstore road trips" to other cities and recognized its potential as a group travel niche and marketing tool. He promoted the concept with a how-to book and a web site, and groups around the U.S. soon began offering similar excursions, usually via a chartered bus, and often incorporating book signings, author home tours, and historical sites. In 2005-06, the Southern California Booksellers Association and Northern California Independent Booksellers Association embraced bookstore tourism, offering trips to independent bookstores in Los Angeles, San Diego and San Francisco.

The Bookstore Tourism movement encourages schools, libraries, reading groups, and organizations of all sizes to create day-trips and literary outings to cities and towns with a concentration of independent bookstores. It also encourages local booksellers to attract bibliophiles to their communities by employing bookstore tourism as an economic development tool. Others benefiting include local retailers, restaurants, bus companies, and travel professionals.

The effort also provides organizations with an outreach opportunity to support reading and literacy.

Portzline has traveled across the country to promote the concept. In Fall 2006 he launched the National Council on Bookstore Tourism (NCBT), a nonprofit organization and trade association that will partner with booksellers, libraries, educators, literary festivals, the travel industry and economic development agencies at the national, state and local levels. In 2006 he created a promotional video featuring group "bookstore road trips" in New York City's Greenwich Village and in Los Angeles area "beach towns" and posted it on the NCBT website.

CULTURAL TOURISM

'Cultural tourism' (or culture tourism) is the subset of tourism concerned with a country or region's culture, especially its arts. It generally focuses on traditional communities who has diverse customs, unique form of art and distinct social practices, which basically distinguishes it from other types/ forms of culture. Cultural tourism includes tourism in urban areas, particularly historic or large cities and their cultural facilities such as museums and theatres. It can also include tourism in rural areas showcasing the traditions of indigenous cultural communities (i.e. festivals, rituals), and their values and lifestyle. It is generally agreed that cultural tourists spend substantially more than standard tourists do. This form of tourism is also becoming generally more popular throughout Europe.

Destination

Definition

By definition, the term destination refers broadly to any given area where tourism is a relatively important activity, like for instance having an economy significantly influenced by tourism revenues. However, it is complicated by the fact that a single, recognizable destination may include several cities, towns or municipalities, provinces, or other government entities- in island archipelago it may be the entire country.

Types

Living Cultural Areas

Due to globalization, technology and the onset of cultural tourism and ecotourism, the number of living cultural areas is continually declining. For an indigenous culture that has stayed largely separated from the surrounding majority, tourism can present both advantages and problems. On the positive side are the unique cultural practices and arts that attract the curiosity of tourists and provide opportunities for tourism and economic development. On the negative side is the issue of how to control tourism so that those same cultural amenities are not destroyed and the people do not feel violated.

Prominent Examples

Chiloé, Chile

Chiloé is Chile's largest island, located at the midway point between the capital, Santiago, and the country's extreme south at Tierra del Fuego. Chiloé is the site of the Chiloé Model

Forest, member of the same network as the Calakmul and Eastern Ontario Model Forests. Having evolved for centuries isolated from mainland Chile, the "Chilotes" developed a strong, self-reliant culture, rich in folklore, mythology and tradition. This very identity is what constitutes the island's major attraction for domestic tourists in Chile and increasingly, for international tourists.

As in the Calakmul case above, tourism to Chiloé is very strongly based on the island's cultural heritage, predominantly consisting of crafts markets, appreciation of cultural landscapes, museum exhibitions, seafood cuisine and architectural heritage (Chiloé's old churches). However, the average tourist to the island will have little opportunity to see Chilotes involved in their living cultural activities, such as the elaborate preparation of the islands famous "curanto" meal, rich in shellfish, meat and potatoes, the management practices of their farm and forest lands, boat building and more.

In order to overcome the cultural and organizational barriers that keep suppliers of living cultural heritage and tour operators apart, the Chiloé diocese of Ancud established a private foundation called "Fundación con Todos" (One for All Foundation). Among other activities, the Foundation has played a key role in helping a number of Chilote households organize themselves into an "agrotourism" network. The Foundation helped Chilote households make the preparation required to accommodate tourists (including training in sanitation and maintenance of facilities, the provision of basic infrastructure) and complemented this effort with a professional marketing campaign. These works were undertaken with the financial support of other agencies.

Again, in cooperation with the EOMF and the Chiloé Model Forest, a cultural and natural heritage tour was organized to Argentina and Chile, including a three-day visit to Chiloé, permitting some of the Chilote households to host a group of cultural heritage tourists for the first time. The visits were very successful and should be the first of more to come, helping establish the credibility of Chiloé's agrotourism network among other tour operators.

Orrissa Tribes

Nestling on the eastern coast of India, Orissa is one of the most exquisite regions dominated by exotic sandy beaches, plenteous wild life, and holy temples famous for their architectural splendor and primitive lifestyle. The charm of the city is still well-nigh chaste and unrevealed by the visitors, up to its full extent. The other lure of the city lies in its tribal population dotted with more than 62 tribal communities. The tribal communities of Orissa constitute about 23% of its total population. Orissa is inhabited by tribes like Saora or Sabar that had a respectable mentioning in the epic of Mahabharata.

Mostly the Orissa tribes are high land habitats with opulent ethnic trait, cultures and customs dominated by varying languages. The culture conscious tribes are able to preserve their social customs and dignified values. The most primitive tribes are Bondas, Gadabas, Koyas, Kondhas and Sauras.

The culture of tribal Orissa is affluent with their own folk songs and dances, their tattoos. Tribal culture of Orissa is well depicted in its modern city in form of poems, art and craft or music.

The tribes have adapted the Hindu traditions and culture from centuries, which is mixed with their own culture giving a distinct zest to the entire racial. Songs and dances are the essence of the tribal culture of Orissa. The traditions and the ceremonies for wedding, birth and death all are represented by singing songs, rural dances along with feasts.

The Tribal Folk Orissan tribes are strong, assiduous and simple hospitable tribes, normally like to be reserved and maintain distance from the people of other communities, as they are too shy. The major occupation of these tribes is agriculture and fishing and hunting. Men usually wear loin attire and women rap long stretch of cloth around them. Women are adorned with ornaments like bangles, armlets, bracelets, necklaces, rings, hairpins etc usually made of silvers, aluminum, and brass. The practice of tattooing is prevalent among women folk. Girls above 5 years are found with tattoo mark on their faces and hands.

Festival Celebration Numbers of deities are worshiped by the tribes for their happy life. Many festivals are also celebrated with much of enthusiasm and excitement. The ceremony rituals are observed through out the year in order to appease their deities and ascendant.

The most significant festival of the year are the chaita parab and push parab-this day all able men of the village go on a hunting expedition. The tribes with their cultural dance, song and music all distinguish custom of their artistic life, which demarcate them from the other non tribal groups.

Orissa acquire every thing Orissa is a state, embellished with hilly terrain of the Eastern Ghats, where primitive tribes dwell and a beautiful stretch of the Indo-Aryans coast where modern life persists. A blend of 2 discrete civilization with contrast cultures, beautiful landscapes, beaches, rich wildlife, offers the best of India to its visitors.

Historical Sites

Modern Urban District

Theme Parks and Country Clubs

Coastal or Island Ecosystems

Inland Natural Area

Key Principles

Destination Planning

As the issue of globalization takes place to this modern time, the challenge of preserving the few remaining cultural community around the world is becoming hard. In a tribal based community, reaching economic advancement with minimal negative impacts is an essential objective to any destination planner.

Since they are using the culture of the region as the main attraction, sustainable destination development of the area is vital for them to prevent the negative impacts (i.e. destroying the authentic identity of the tribal community) due to tourism.

Management Issues

Certainly, the principle of "one size fits all" doesn't apply to destination planning. The needs, expectations, and anticipated benefits from tourism vary greatly from one destination to another. This is clearly exemplified as local communities living in regions with tourism potential (destinations) develop a vision for what kind of tourism they want to facilitate, depending on issues and concerns they want to be settled or satisfied.

Destination Planning Resources

Planning Guides

It is important that the destination planner takes into account the diverse definition of culture as the term is subjective. Satisfying tourists' interests such as landscapes, seascapes, art, nature, traditions, ways of life and other products associated to them-which may be categorized cultural in the broadest sense of the word, is a prime consideration as it marks the initial phase of the development of a cultural destination.

The quality of service and destination, which doesn't solely depend on the cultural heritage but more importantly to the cultural environment, can further be developed by setting controls and policies which shall govern the community and its stakeholders. It is therefore safe to say that the planner should be on the ball with the varying meaning of culture itself as this fuels the formulation of development policies that shall entail efficient planning and monitored growth (e.g. strict policy on the protection and preservation of the community).

Local community, tourists, the destination and sustainable tourism.

While satisfying tourists' interests and demands may be a top priority, it is also imperative to ruminate the subsystems of the destination's (residents). Development pressures should be anticipated and set to their minimum level so as to conserve the area's resources and prevent a saturation of the destination as to not abuse the product and the residents correspondingly. The plan should incorporate the locals to its gain by training and employing them and in the process encourage them to participate to the travel business. Keep in mind that the plan should make travellers not only aware about the destination but also concern on how to help it sustain its character while broadening their travelling experience.

Planning Tools

Sources of Data

The core of a planner's job is to design an appropriate planning process and facilitate community decision. Ample information which is a crucial requirement is contributed through various technical researches and analyzes. Here are some of the helpful tools commonly used by planners to aid them:

1. Key Informant Interviews
2. Libraries, Internet, and Survey Research
3. Census and Statistical Analysis
4. Spatial Analysis with Geographical Information System (GIS) and Global Positioning System (GPS) technologies

Key Institutions

Participating structures are primarily led by the government's local authorities and the official tourism board or council, with the involvement of various NGOs, community and indigenous representatives, development organizations, and the academe.

Case Studies

Cultural and Ecotourism in the Mountainous Regions of Central Asia and in the Himalayas

Tourism is coming to the previously isolated but spectacular mountainous regions of Central Asia, the Hindu Kush and the Himalayas. Closed for so many years to visitors from abroad, it now attracts a growing number of foreign tourists by its unique culture and splendid natural beauty. However, while this influx of tourists is bringing economic opportunities and employment to local populations, helping to promote these little-known regions of the world, it has also brought challenges along with it: to ensure that it is well-managed and that its benefits are shared by all.

As a response to this concern, the Norwegian Government, as well as the UNESCO, organized an interdisciplinary project called the Development of Cultural and Eco-tourism in the Mountainous Regions of Central Asia and the Himalayas project. It aims to establish links and promote cooperation between local communities, national and international NGOs, and tour agencies in order to heighten the role of the local community and involve them fully in the employment opportunities and income-generating activities that tourism can bring. Project activities include training local tour guides, producing high-quality craft items and promoting home-stays and bed-and-breakfast type accommodation. As of now, the project is drawing on the expertise of international NGOs and tourism professionals in the seven participating countries, making a practical and positive contribution to alleviating poverty by helping local communities to draw the maximum benefit from their region's tourism potential, while protecting the environmental and cultural heritage of the region concerned.

DARK TOURISM

Dark tourism or Grief tourism is tourism involving travel to sites associated with death and suffering. Thanatourism, derived from the Ancient Greek word thanatos for the personification of death, is associated with dark tourism but refers more specifically to violent death; it is used in fewer contexts than the terms dark tourism and grief tourism.

This includes sites of pilgrimage such the site of St Peter's death in Rome; castles and battlefields such as Culloden near Inverness, Scotland; sites of disaster, either natural or man made such as Ground Zero in New York; prisons now open to the public such as Beaumaris Prison in Anglesey, Wales; and purpose built centers such as the London Dungeon.

One of the most notorious destinations for dark tourism is the Nazi extermination camp at Auschwitz in Poland.

DISASTER TOURISM

Disaster tourism is the act of traveling to a disaster area as a matter of curiosity. The behavior can be a nuisance if it hinders rescue, relief, and recovery operations.

Hurricane Katrina

Disaster tourism took hold in the Greater New Orleans Area in the aftermath of Hurricane Katrina. There are now guided bus tours to neighborhoods that were severely damaged by storm-related flooding. Some local residents have criticized these tours as unethical, because the tour companies are profiting from the misery of their communities and families. The Army Corp of Engineers has noted that traffic from tour buses and other tourist vehicles have interfered with the movement of trucks and other cleanup equipment on single-lane residential roads.

Furthermore, during the first six months after the storm, most of these neighborhoods lacked electricity, phone access, street signs, or access to emergency medical or police assistance. Simply traveling to these neighborhoods was hazardous. For these reasons, organized disaster tours are now banned from two of the most severely damaged areas in the city, the Lower 9th and St. Bernard Parish near the Industrial Canal.

On the other hand, such communities as Gentilly and Lakeview, along the 17th Street Canal, have welcomed organized tour groups as a means to publicize the scale of the destruction and attract more aid to the city. Much of the recovery effort in the New Orleans relies on out-of-state volunteers and donations.

Numerous non-profit organization, including Habitat for Humanity International and Catholic Charities, have converged on the city to gut and rebuild homes. There is also a movement by local residents to bring congressmen and other national leaders to the city and view the damage in person, since recovery efforts have been hampered by the failure of many homeowners and businesses to receive claims from their insurance providers.

DRUG TOURISM

Drug tourism is travel for the purpose of obtaining or using drugs for personal use that are unavailable or illegal in one's home jurisdiction. This would include crossing a national border to obtain drugs over the counter that are not sold in one's own country, or traveling to another country in order to obtain or use narcotics that are illegal in one's own country, or even traveling from one U.S. state to another in order to buy alcohol or tobacco more easily (although this last situation is often considered too trivial to qualify as drug tourism).

Drug tourism has many legal implications, and persons engaging in it sometimes risk prosecution for drug smuggling or other drug-related charges in their home jurisdictions or in the jurisdictions they are visiting, especially if they bring their purchases home rather than using them abroad. The act of traveling for the purpose of buying or using drugs is itself a criminal offense in some jurisdictions.

Amsterdam is a popular destinations for drug tourists, due to the Dutch government's acceptance of marijuana use and possession. Another Dutch city which is visited frequently by drug tourists is Maastricht because of its position close to the borders of Germany and Belgium. Other popular destinations include Southeast Asia and South America. Drug tourism thrives because legislation controlling the sale, possession, and use of drugs varies dramatically from one jurisdiction to another.

ECOTOURISM

Ecotourism, also known as ecological tourism, is a form of tourism which appeals to the ecologically and socially conscious. Generally speaking, ecotourism focuses on local culture, wilderness adventures, volunteering, personal growth, and learning new ways to live on the planet; typically involving travel to destinations where flora, fauna, and cultural heritage are the primary attractions.

Responsible ecotourism includes programs that minimize the negative aspects of conventional tourism on the environment, and enhance the cultural integrity of local people. Therefore, in addition to evaluating environmental and cultural factors, an integral part of ecotourism is in the promotion of recycling, energy efficiency, water conservation, and creation of economic opportunities for the local communities.

Many global environmental organizations and aid agencies believe that ecotourism has great potential for sustainable development.

Ideally, ecotourism should satisfy several criteria, such as:

- conservation of biological diversity and cultural diversity, through ecosystem protection
- promotion of sustainable use of biodiversity, by providing jobs to local populations
- sharing of socio-economic benefits with local communities and indigenous people by having their informed consent and participation in the management of ecotourism enterprises.
- increase of environmental & cultural knowledge
- minimization of tourism's own environmental impact
- affordability and lack of waste in the form of luxury
- local culture, flora and fauna being the main attractions

For many countries, ecotourism is not simply a marginal activity to finance protection of the environment but as a major industry of the national economy. For example, in places such as Costa Rica, Ecuador, Nepal, Kenya, Madagascar, and Antarctica, ecotourism represents a significant portion of the gross domestic product and economic activity.

The concept of ecotourism is widely misunderstood, and in practice is often used as a marketing tool to promote tourism that is related to nature. Critics claim that ecotourism as practiced and abused often consists of placing a hotel in a splendid landscape, to the detriment of the ecosystem. According to them, ecotourism must above all sensitize people with the beauty and the fragility of nature. They condemn some operators as "greenwashing" their operations; using the label of "ecotourism" and "green-friendly", while behaving in environmentally irresponsible ways. Although academics disagree about who can be classified as an ecotourist and there is precious little statistical data, some estimate that more than five million ecotourists-the majority of the ecotourist population-come from the United States, with others from Western Europe, Canada, and Australia.

Currently there are various moves to create national and international ecotourism accrediation programs, although the process is also controversial. Ecotourism certificates have been put in place at Costa Rica, although some critics have dismissed these programs as greenwashing.

History

Ecotourism, responsible tourism, and sustainable development have become prevalent concepts since the late 1980s, and ecotourism has experienced arguably the fastest growth of all sub-sectors in the tourism industry. The popularity represents a change in tourist perceptions, increased environmental awareness, and a desire to explore natural environments. Such changes have become a statement affirming one's social identity, educational sophistication, and disposable income as it has about preserving the Amazon rainforest or the Caribbean reef for posterity.

With its great potential for environmental protection, the United Nations celebrated the "International Year of Ecotourism" in 2002.

Criticisms

Definitional Problems and Greenwashing

To approach an understanding of the problem, a clear definition must delineate what is, and is not, ecotourism. Ideally, ecotourism satisfies several general criteria, including the conservation of biological diversity and cultural, diversity through ecosystem protection, promotion of sustainable use of biodiversity, share of socio-economic benefits with local communities through informed consent and participation, increase in environmental and cultural knowledge, affordability and reduced waste, and minimization of its own environmental impact. In such ways, it contributes to the long term benefits to both the environment and local communities.

However, in the continuum of tourism activities that stretch from conventional tourism to ecotourism proper, there has been a lot of contention to the limit at which biodiversity preservation, local socio-economic benefits, and environmental impact can be considered "ecotourism". For this reason, environmentalists, special interest groups, and governments define ecotourism differently. Environmental organizations have generally insisted that ecotourism is nature-based, sustainably managed, conservation supporting, and environmentally educated. The tourist industry and governments, however, focus more on the product aspect, treating ecotourism as equivalent to any sort of tourism based in nature. As a further complication, many terms are used under the rubric of ecotourism. Nature tourism, low impact tourism, green tourism, bio-tourism, ecologically responsible tourism, and others have been used in literature and marketing, although they are not necessary synonymous with ecotourism.

The problems associated with defining ecotourism have led to confusion among tourists and academics alike. Definitional problems are also subject of considerable public controversy and concern because of greenwashing, a trend towards the commercialization of tourism schemes disguised as sustainable, nature based, and environmentally friendly ecotourism. According to McLaren, these schemes are environmentally destructive, economically exploitative, and culturally insensitive at its worst. They are also morally disconcerting because they mislead tourists and manipulate their concerns for the environment. Despite objections, greenwashing continues to grow unabated. The Nature's Sacred Paradise, a theme park in Quintana Roo, Mexico, is responsible for displacing local Mayan communities and illegally keeping endangered species in captivity to attract visitors. The development and success of such large scale, energy intensive, and ecologically unsustainable schemes are a testament to the tremendous profits associated with being labeled as ecotourism.

The Negative Psycho-social Impact of Ecotourism

Ecotourism is the trend towards the commercialization of tourism throughout the nation. This trend has become one of the fastest growing sectors of the tourism industry growing annual 10-15% worldwide (Kamuaro, 2007). Ecotourism was first introduced in Africa in the 1950's with the legalization of hunting (Kamuaro, 2007). This need for recreational hunting zones lead to the creation of protected areas, national parks, and game reserves. Today these areas have become important revenue-earning venues with the establishment of lodges and tourist campsites.

One definition of ecotourism is "the practice of low-impact, educational, ecologically and culturally sensitive travel that benefits local communities and host countries" (Honey, 1999). Many of the ecotourism projects are not meeting these standards. Even if some of the guidelines are being executed, the local communities are still facing other negative impacts. South Africa is one of the countries that are reaping significant economic benefits from ecotourism, but negative effects including, physical displacement of persons, gross violation of fundamental rights, and environmental hazards far out weigh the medium-term economic benefits (Kamuaro, 2007). A tremendous amount of money is being spent and human resources continue to be used for ecotourism despite the lack of success stories, and even more money is put into public relation campaigns to dilute the effects of the criticism. Ecotourism channels resources away from other projects that could contribute more sustainable and realistic solutions to pressing social and environmental problems. "The money tourism can generate often ties parks and managements to eco-tourism" (Walpole et al. 2001).

But there is a tension in this relationship because eco-tourism often causes conflict and changes in land-use rights, fails to deliver promises of community-level benefits, damages environments, and has plenty of other social impacts. Indeed many argue repeatedly that eco-tourism is neither ecologically nor socially beneficial, yet it persists as a strategy for conservation and development (West, 2006). While several studies are being done on ways to improve the ecotourism structure, these examples provide reason that it should just stop all together.

The ecotourism system exercises tremendous financial and political influence. The evidence above shows that at the very least a strong case exists for restraining such activities. Funding could be used for field studies aimed at finding alternative solutions to tourism and the diverse problems Africa faces in result of urbanization, industrialization, and over exploitation of agriculture (Kamuaro, 2007). At the local level ecotourism has become a source of conflict over control of land, resources, and tourism profits. There are many problems with the idea of ecotourism. Environmental, the effects on the local people, and conflicts over profit distribution are only a few of the negative effects of ecotourism. In a perfect world more efforts would be made towards educating tourists of the environmental and social effects of their travels. Very few regulations or laws stand in place as boundaries for the investors in ecotourism. These should be implemented to prohibit the promotion of unsustainable ecotourism projects and materials which project false images of destinations, demeaning local and indigenous cultures.

Direct Environmental Impacts

Ecotourism operations typically fail to live up to conservation ideals. It is often overlooked that ecotourism is a highly consumer-centered activity, and that environmental conservation is only a means to further economic growth.

Although ecotourism is intended for small groups, even a modest increase in population, however temporary, puts extra pressure on the local environment and necessitates the development of additional infrastructure and amenities. The construction of water treatment plants, sanitation facilities, and lodges come with the exploitation of non-renewable energy sources and the utilization of already limited local resources. The conversion of natural land to such tourist infrastructure is implicated in deforestation and habitat deterioration of butterflies in Mexico and squirrel monkeys in Costa Rica. In other cases, the environment suffers because local communities are unable to meet the infrastructure demands of ecotourism. The lack of adequate sanitation facilities in many East African parks results in the disposal of campsite sewage in rivers, contaminating the wildlife, livestock, and people who draw drinking water from it.

Aside from environmental degradation with tourist infrastructure, population pressures from ecotourism also leaves behind garbage and pollution associated with the Western lifestyle. Although ecotourists claim to be educationally sophisticated and environmentally concerned, they rarely understand the ecological consequences of their visits and how their day-to-day activities append physical impacts on the environment.

As one scientist observes, they "rarely acknowledge how the meals they eat, the toilets they flush, the water they drink, and so on, are all part of broader regional economic and ecological systems they are helping to reconfigure with their very activities." Nor do ecotourists recognize the great consumption of non-renewable energy required to arrive at their destination, which is typically more remote than conventional tourism destinations. For instance, an exotic journey to a place 10,000 kilometers away consumes about 700 liters of fuel per person.

Ecotourism activities are, in of itself, issues in environmental impact because they disturb fauna and flora. Ecotourists believe that because they are only taking pictures and leaving footprints, they keep ecotourism sites pristine, but even harmless sounding activities such as a nature hike can be ecologically destructive.

In the Annapurna Circuit in Nepal, ecotourists have worn down the marked trails and created alternate routes, contributing to soil impaction, erosion, and plant damage. Where the ecotourism activity involves wildlife viewing, it can scare away animals, disrupt their feeding and nesting sites, or acclimate them to the presence of people. In Kenya, disruption of wildlife observers drive cheetahs off their reserves, increasing the risk of inbreeding and further endangering the species.

Environmental Hazards

We already understand that biodiversity and environmentally intact lands form the basis of ecological stability. Unfortunately, industrialization, urbanization, and unsustainable agriculture practices have all had serious effects on the environment. Ecotourism is now also playing a role in this depletion. While the term ecotourism may sound relatively benign, one of its most serious impacts is its consumption of virgin territories (Kamuaro, 2007). These invasions often include deforestation, disruption of ecological life systems and various forms of pollution, all of which contribute to environmental degradation. The number of motor vehicles crossing the park increases as tour drivers search for rare species. The number of roads has disrupted the grass cover which has serious effects on plant and animal species. These areas also have a higher rate of disturbances and invasive species because of all the traffic moving off the beaten path into new undiscovered areas (Kamuaro, 2007). Ecotourism also has an affect on species through the value placed on them. "Certain species have gone from being little known or valued by local people to being highly valued commodities. The commodification of plants may erase their social value and lead to overproduction within protected areas. Local people and their images can also be turned into commodities" (West, 2006). Kamuaro brings up a relatively obvious contradiction, any commercial venture into unspoiled, pristine land with or without the "eco" prefix as a contradiction in terms. To generate revenue you have to have a high number of traffic, tourists, which inevitably means a higher pressure on the environment.

Local Peoples

Most forms of ecotourism are owned by foreign investors and corporations that provide few benefits to local communities. An overwhelming majority of profits are put into the pockets of investors instead of reinvestment into the local economy or environmental protection. The limited numbers of local people who are employed in the economy enter at its lowest level, and are unable to live in tourist areas because of meager wages and a two market system. In some cases, the resentment by local people results in environmental degradation. As a highly publicized case, the Maasai nomads in Kenya killed wildlife in national parks to show aversion to unfair compensation terms and displacement from traditional lands. The lack of economic opportunities for local people also constrains them to degrade the environment as a means of sustenance. The presence of affluent ecotourists encourage the development of destructive markets in wildlife souvenirs, such as the sale of coral trinkets on tropical islands and animal products in Asia, contributing to illegal harvesting and poaching from the environment. In Surinam, sea turtle reserves use a large portion of their budget to guard against these activities.

Displacement of People

One of the most powerful examples of communities being moved in order to create a park is the story of the Masai. About 70% of national parks and game reserves in East Africa are on Masai land (Kamuaro, 2007). The first undesirable impact of tourism was that of the extent of land lost from the Masai culture. Local and national governments took advantage of the Masai's ignorance on the situation and robbed them of huge chunks of grazing land, putting to risk their only socioeconomic livelihood. In Kenya the Masai also have not gained any economic benefits. Despite lose of their land, employment favors better educated workers. Further more the investors in this area are not local and have not put profits back into local economy. In some cases game reserves can be created without informing or consulting local people, who come to find out about the situation when an eviction notice is delivered (Kamuaro, 2007).

Another source of resentment is the manipulation of the local people by their government. "Eco-tourism works to create simplistic images of local people and their uses and understandings of their surroundings. Through the lens of these simplified images, officials direct policies and projects towards the local people and the local people are blamed if the projects fail" (West, 2006). Clearly tourism as a trade is not empowering the local people who make it rich and satisfying. Instead ecotourism exploits and depletes, particularly in African Masai tribes. It has to be reoriented to serve useful to local communities and to become sustainable.

Threats to Indigenous Cultures

Ecotourism often claims that it preserves and "enhances" local cultures. However, evidence shows that with the establishment of protected areas local people have illegally lost their homes, and most often with no compensation (Kamuaro, 2007). What about pushing people onto marginal lands with harsh climates, poor soils, lack of water, and infested with livestock and disease is "enhancing"? The establishment of parks does nothing but create harsh survival realities and deprives the people of their traditional use of land and natural resources. Ethnic groups are increasingly being seen as a "backdrop" to the scenery and wildlife. The local people struggle for cultural survival and freedom of cultural expression while being "observed" by tourists. Local indigenous people also have strong resentment towards the change, "Tourism has been allowed to develop with virtually no controls. Too many lodges have been built, too much firewood is being used and no limits are being placed on tourism vehicles. They regularly drive off-track and harass the wildlife. Their vehicle tracks crisscross the entire Masai Mara. Inevitably the bush is becoming eroded and degraded" (Kamuaro, 2007).

Mismanagement of Ecotourism Sites

While governments are typically entrusted with the administration and enforcement of environmental protection, they often lack the commitment or capability to manage ecotourism sites effectively. The regulations for environmental protection may be vaguely defined, costly to implement, hard to enforce, and uncertain in effectiveness. Government regulatory agencies, as political bodies, are susceptible to making decisions that spend budget on politically beneficial but environmentally unproductive projects. Because of prestige and conspicuousness, the construction of an attractive visitor's center at an ecotourism site may take precedence over more pressing environmental concerns like acquiring habitat, protecting endemic species, and removing invasive ones. Finally, influential groups can pressure and sway the interests of the government to their favor. The government and its regulators can become vested in the benefits of the ecotourism industry which they are supposed to regulate, causing restrictive environmental regulations and enforcement to become more lenient.

Management of ecotourism sites by private ecotourism companies offers an alternative to the cost of regulation and deficiency of government agencies. It is believed that these companies have a self interest in limited environmental degradation, because tourists will pay more for pristine environments, which translates to higher profit. However, theory indicates that this practice is not economically feasible and will fail to manage the environment.

The model of monopolistic competition states that distinctiveness will entail profits, but profits will promote imitation. A company that protects its ecotourism sites is able to charge a premium for the novel experience and pristine environment. But when other companies view the success of this approach, they also enter the market with similar practices, increasing competition and reducing demand. Eventually, the demand will be reduced until the economic profit is zero. A cost-benefit analysis shows that the company bears the cost of environmental protection without receiving the gains. Without economic incentive, the whole premise of self interest through environmental protection is quashed; instead, ecotourism companies will minimize environment related expenses and maximize tourism demand.

The tragedy of the commons offers another model for economic unsustainability from environmental protection, in ecotourism sites utilized by many companies. Although there is a communal incentive to protect the environment, maximizing the benefits in the long run, a company will conclude that it is in their best interest to utilize the ecotourism site beyond its sustainable level. By increasing the number of ecotourists, for instance, a company gains all the economic benefit while paying only a part of the environmental cost. In the same way, a company recognizes that there is no incentive to actively protect the environment; they bear all the costs, while the benefits are shared by all other companies. The result, again, is mismanagement.

Taken together, the mobility of foreign investment and lack of economic incentive for environmental protection means that ecotourism companies are disposed to establishing themselves in new sites once their existing one is sufficiently degraded.

Improving Sustainability

Regulation and Accreditation

Because the regulation of ecotourism is poorly implemented or nonexistent, ecologically destructive greenwashed operations like underwater hotels, helicopter tours, and wildlife theme parks are categorized as ecotourism along with canoeing, camping, photography, and wildlife observation. The failure to acknowledge responsible, low impact ecotourism puts these companies at a competitive disadvantage.

Many environmentalists have argued for a global standard of accreditation, differentiating ecotourism companies based on their level of environmental commitment. A national or international regulatory board would enforce accreditation procedures, with representation from various groups including governments, hotels, tour operators, travel agents, guides, airlines, local authorities, conservation organizations, and non-governmental organizations. The decisions of the board would be sanctioned by governments, so that non-compliant companies would be legally required to disassociate themselves from the use of the ecotourism brand.

Crinion suggests a Green Stars System based on criteria including a management plan, benefit for the local community, small group interaction, education value, and staff training. Ecotourists who consider their choices would be confident of a genuine ecotourism experience when they see the higher star rating.

In addition, environmental impact assessments could be used as a form of accreditation. Feasibility is evaluated from a scientific basis, and recommendations could be made to optimally plan infrastructure, set tourist capacity, and manage the ecology. This form of accreditation is more sensitive to site specific conditions.

Guidelines and Education for Ecotourists

An environmental protection strategy must address the issue of ecotourists removed from the cause-and-effect of their actions on the environment. More initiatives should be carried out to improve their awareness, sensitize them to environmental issues, and care about the places they visit.

Tour guides are an obvious and direct medium to communicate awareness. With the confidence of ecotourists and intimate knowledge of the environment, they can actively discuss conservation issues. A tour guide training program in Costa Rica's Tortuguero National Park has helped mitigate negative environmental impacts by providing information and regulating tourists on the parks' beaches used by nesting endangered sea turtles.

Small Scale, Slow Growth, Locally based Ecotourism

The underdevelopment theory of tourism describes a new form of imperialism by multinational corporations that control ecotourism resources. These corporations finance and profit from the development of large scale ecotourism that causes excessive environmental degradation, loss of traditional culture and way of life, and exploitation of local labor. In Zimbabwe and Nepal's Annapurna region, where underdevelopment is taking place, more than 90 percent of ecotourism revenues are expatriated to the parent countries, and less than 5 percent go into local communities.

The lack of sustainability highlights the need for small scale, slow growth, and locally based ecotourism. Local peoples have a vested interest in the well being of their community, and are therefore more accountable to environmental protection than multinational corporations. The lack of control, westernization, adverse impacts to the environment, loss of culture and traditions outweigh the benefits of establishing large scale ecotourism.

The increased contributions of communities to locally managed ecotourism create viable economic opportunities, including high level management positions, and reduce environmental issues associated with poverty and unemployment. Because the ecotourism experience is marketed to a different lifestyle from large scale ecotourism, the development of facilities and infrastructure does not need to conform to corporate Western tourism standards, and can be much simpler and less expensive. There is a greater multiplier effect on the economy, because local products, materials, and labor are used. Profits accrue locally, and import leakages are reduced. However, even this form of tourism may require foreign investment for promotion or start up. When such investments are required, it is cruical for communities for find a company or non-governmental organization that reflects the philosophy of ecotourism; sensitive to their concerns and willing to cooperate at the expense of profit.

The basic assumption of the multiplier effect is that the economy starts off with unused resources, for example, that many workers are cyclically unemployed and much of industrial capacity is sitting idle or incompletely utilized. By increasing demand in the economy it is then possible to boost production. If the economy was already at full employment, with only structural, frictional, or other supply-side types of unemployment, any attempt to boost demand would only lead to inflation. For various laissez-faire schools of economics which embrace Say's Law and deny the possibility of Keynesian inefficiency and under-employment of resources, therefore, the multiplier concept is irrelevant or wrong-headed.

As an example, consider the government increasing its expenditure on roads by $1 million, without a corresponding increase in taxation. This sum would go to the road builders, who would hire more workers and distribute the money as wages and profits. The households receiving these incomes will save part of the money and spend the rest on consumer goods. These expenditures in turn will generate more jobs, wages, and profits, and so on with the income and spending circulating around the economy.

The multiplier effect arises because of the induced increases in consumer spending which occur due to the increased incomes--and because of the feedback into increasing business revenues, jobs, and income again. This process does not lead to an economic explosion not only because of the supply-side barriers at potential output (full employment) but because at each "round", the increase in consumer spending is less than the increase in consumer incomes. That is, the marginal propensity to consume (mpc) is less than one, so that each round some extra income goes into saving, leaking out of the cumulative process. Each increase in spending is thus smaller than that of the previous round, preventing an explosion.

EXTREME TOURISM

Extreme tourism or shock tourism is a type of niche tourism involving travel to dangerous places (mountains, jungles, deserts, caves, etc.) or participation in dangerous events. Extreme tourism overlaps with extreme sport. The two share the main attraction, "adrenaline rush" caused by an element of risk, and differing mostly in the degree of engagement and professionalism.

Extreme tourism is a growing business in the countries of the former Soviet Union (Russia, Ukraine, Armenia, etc.) and in South American countries like Peru, Chile and Argentina. The mountainous and rugged terrain of Northern Pakistan has also developed into a popular extreme tourism location.

While traditional tourism requires significant investments in hotels, roads, etc., extreme tourism requires much less to jump-start a business. In addition to traditional travel-based tourism destinations, various exotic attractions are suggested, such as flyovers in MiGs at 2.5 Mach, ice diving in the White Sea, or travelling across the Chernobyl zone.

FEMALE SEX TOURISM

Female sex tourism is travel by women, partially or fully for the purpose of having sex.

Overview

Female sex tourism differs from male sex tourism in that women do not use bars, sex shows and formal tours to meet foreign men. There are "de facto" tours, however, such as airplanes bound to the Gambia in West Africa full of British and Scandinavian women seeking affairs with beach boys.

Often such trips are referred to by women as "romance tourism."

Women usually give clothes, meals, cash and gifts to their male prostitutes. In some destinations, there are "going rates" for male companionship, ranging from $50 to $200. In few destinations, especially in Southern Europe, Turkey, Bali and the French Caribbean, men do not expect to be compensated.

Destinations

While men tend to go to Asia for sex tourism, women tend to head to the Caribbean, Southern Europe, and Africa. The patterns have been explored by Michel Houellebecq in Platform and in the non-fiction work Romance on the Road, and are important in that they support the idea that sex tourism by both men and women reflects serious problems in the tourists' home countries, including a dating war, or profound conflict between the sexes.

Thailand, the Dominican Republic and Cuba are exceptional in that both male and female sex tourists find these places all-purpose sexual emporia.

The primary destinations for female sex tourism are Southern Europe (mainly Italy, Greece, Turkey, Croatia and Spain), the Caribbean (led by Jamaica, Barbados and the Dominican Republic), Ghana and Kenya in Africa, Bali in Indonesia and Phuketin Thailand. Lesser destinations include Nepal, Morocco, Fiji, Ecuador and Costa Rica.

Lesbian sex tourism is nascent but evident in Lesbos (Mytilini) in Greece; Bangkok and Pattaya in Thailand, and on Bali in Indonesia.

Terms used for Female Sex Tourists

Tourist women are called Shirley Valentines (if British), longtails (in Bermuda), yellow cabs (Japan) and, in Jamaica, milk bottles if newly arrived or Stellas if black. Female sex tourism in Barbados has been dubbed "Canadian secretary syndrome."

The men who chase tourist women are kamakia ("fishing harpoons," Greece),galebovi ("seagulls,"Croatia), sharks (Costa Rica), rent-a-dreads, rent-a-rastas, rent-a-gents and the Foreign Service (Caribbean), Kuta Cowboys or pemburu-bule ("whitey hunters," Bali), Marlboro men (Jordan), bomsas or bumsters (the Gambia), sanky pankies (Dominican Republic), "gringa hunter" in Ecuador and "brichero" in Peru.

History

Barring some isolated cases of women traveling for sex among North American Indian tribes and within Turkey, female travel sex (involving American and English women) began in Rome in the late 1840s, at the same time as feminism's first wave, which encouraged independence and travel.

Affairs and intrigues, particularly between American heiresses and down-on their luck European aristocrats, continued steadily until World War I and inspired Henry James's Daisy Miller, Joaquin Miller's The One Fair Woman, and much of the early output of E.M. Forster.

Female sex travel declined from the time of the Depression until the 1960s, with the exception of India, Nepal and Thailand, where intrepid women from England, France, Czechoslovakia, the United States and elsewhere continued to attract the attention of maharajas and other Asian royals, despite the uproar of World War II.

Coincident with the explosion of leisure travel in the 1960s and feminism's second wave, sex tourism by women re-ignited, first via French Canadian women traveling to Barbados and Swedish and Northern European women to Spain, Greece, Yugoslavia and the Gambia. Female sex travel became ubiquitous throughout the Caribbean, from the tiniest islands through the big destinations of Jamaica, the Dominican Republic and Barbados.

In the 1990s, women from Japan and Taiwan began to appear on the beaches of Bali and Phuket in Thailand.

Today, many other destinations are popular, including Morocco, Nepal, Thailand, Ecuador, Costa Rica, Mexico--everywhere with beaches (or in Nepal's case, mountains) and a surplus of underemployed men.

Reasons

Female sex tourism's first and second waves coincided not only with feminism but with Victorian-era man shortages that began in England and later cropped in continental Europe and the United States.

Other societal reasons for women seeking intimate companionship abroad include the dating war, as typified by extreme competition between the sexes in schools, the workplace, while dating, in marriages, and even in contentious divorces. The dating war appears to especially drive sex tourism by Australian and Japanese women, and to a lesser extent, German and Scandinavian female tourists.

Another factor in women engaging in holiday romance is identity loss. Many women behave while traveling in a way at odds to how they behave at home, where fear of the "slut" label curbs the kind of hedonistic behavior seen on holiday. Traveling and expatriate women often try on a new, more experimental identity when away from family and friends.

Additional reasons include:

- sexual connoisseurship--an interest in experiencing a variety of men
- a search for healing after a divorce or breakup (see Michelle Thomas, in Major academic publications, below)

- prolonged involuntary celibacy
- the commodification of sex, whereby affection is now something that can be purchased by women, as well as men, as well as the globalization of sex and affection markets
- interest in fulfilling sexual fantasies

Depictions

Non-fiction books include Anne Cumming's The Love Habit and The Love Quest, Fiona Pitt-Kethley's The Pan Principle and Journeys to the Underworld, Cleo Odzer's Patpong Sisters and Lucretia Stewart's The Weather Prophet.

Female sex tourists have been notoriously difficult to find and interview on the record (see de Albuquerque, 1998, in "Major academic publications" subheading, below). Thus some observers have turned to film and fiction to examine the motivations of women who travel for sex, love and affection. Movies include Heading South (Vers le Sud), with Charlotte Rampling which depicts three Western tourists in Haiti in the 1970s, taking their pleasure with local men. Earlier film depictions include How Stella Got Her Groove Back and Shirley Valentine. Stella led to a quantifiable increase in trips by women to Jamaica, according to Michele Faul's Associated Press article, 12/6/1998, " 'Stella' the Movie Attracting Single Women to Jamaica."

Important works of fiction include, in addition to Michel Houellebecq's Platform, Erica Jong's Fear of Flying.

SEX TOURISM

Sex tourism is travel to engage in sexual intercourse or sexual activity with prostitutes, and is typically undertaken internationally by tourists from wealthier countries whose payment for services may then be rendered either in cash or in kind.

The World Tourism Organization, a specialized agency of the United Nations, defines sex tourism as "trips organized from within the tourism sector, or from outside this sector but using its structures and networks, with the primary purpose of effecting a commercial sexual relationship by the tourist with residents at the destination". The U.N. opposes sex tourism citing health, social and cultural consequences for both tourist home countries and destination countries, especially in situations exploiting gender, age, social and economic inequalities in sex tourism destinations.

Attractions for sex tourists can include reduced costs for services in the destination country, along with either legal prostitution or indifferent law enforcement and access to child prostitution.

Destinations

National destinations for sex tourists include Thailand, Brazil, Dominican Republic, Costa Rica, and Cuba.

An individual city or region can have a particular reputation as a sex tourist destination. Many of these coincide with major red-light districts, and include Amsterdam in the Netherlands; Zona Norte in Tijuana, Mexico; Bangkok, Pattaya and Phuket in Thailand; Vladivostok in Russian Far East, destination for Japanese sex tourists, and Angeles City, the site of a former United States military base in the province of Pampanga, Philippines.

In the United States, prostitution is largely illegal, with the exception of rural areas of the state of Nevada; these have become a sex tourist destination for some Americans. To a lesser extent, several other large cities in the U.S. are also domestic sex tourist destinations despite legal sanctions on prostitution.

Conversely, prostitution is a legal activity in a growing list of other nations worldwide including in many of these destinations.

Female Sex Tourism Destinations

The primary destinations for female sex tourism are Southern Europe (mainly Italy, former Yugoslavia, Turkey,

Greece and Spain), the Caribbean (led by Jamaica, Barbados and the Dominican Republic), parts of Africa, Pattaya or Phuket in Thailand. Lesser destinations include Nepal, Morocco, Fiji, Ecuador and Costa Rica. Female sex tourism differs from male sex tourism, in that women do not usually go to specific bars. Women usually give clothes, meals, cash and gifts to their prostitutes, but not all (especially in Southern Europe) expect compensation.

Criminality and Controversy

Tourism Involving Sex with Minors

Child Wise defines child sex tourism as "the commercial sexual exploitation of children by foreigners", usually referring to:

- travel to other countries to engage in sexual acts with children, or
- foreigners engaging in sexual activity with children while overseas

While most sex tourists only engage in this activity with other adults, some actively look for child prostitutes, while others are not very selective either way regarding age. The WTO makes a distinction between "sex tourism" and "child sex tourism." A tourist who has sex with a child prostitute offends the spirit of the international Convention on the Rights of the Child and the Optional protocol on the sale of children, child prostitution and child pornography, and, in addition to breaking the law in the host country, might well also be doing so in the country the tourist is a national of. A growing number of countries are enacting laws with extra-territorial reach in order to meet their obligations under the covenants above, and consequently punishing citizens who engage in sex with minors whilst overseas. But being difficult to police and enforce these crimes continue nonetheless.

The term "child" is often used as defined by the international conventions above and refers to any person below the age of consent. Many countries have signed the Worst Forms of Child Labour Convention, 1999 and implemented domestic law making having sex with child prostitutes a criminal offence for their nationals or inhabitants including when practised abroad regardless of whether it is forbidden by the laws of the destination country. Singapore has been criticized for having no such law, in spite of being adjacent to the sex tourism destination of Batam in Indonesia, which has many underage sex workers, many of whom have been forced into prostitution.

In 2004 Canada started to prosecute individuals under the sex tourism law. The first individual charged in Canada under this law was Donald Bakker. Australia has long done so: with a conviction in 1996 after enactment of legislation in 1994. Its Government has, for example, caused an international political incident in pressing for the extradition of suspended Solomon Islands Attorney-General Julian Moti, an Australian citizen, to face possible charges over alleged offences dating back to 1997.

According to the Cambodia minister for Woman's Affairs, it is not tourists who are the prime culprits of pedophilia in her country, but the locals.

Legal Issues in the United States

Federal law (see PROTECT Act of 2003) prohibits United States citizens or permanent residents to engage in international travel with the purpose or effect of having commercial sex with a person under the age of 18, or any sex with a person under the age of 16; facilitating such travel is also illegal. Arrests by Immigration and Customs Enforcement are becoming common, however prosecutions under this law are still very rare.

As of 2005, there has been one effort to prosecute a sex tour operator: Big Apple Oriental Tours of New York was prosecuted for "promotion of prostitution" by the New York State Attorney General after lobbying by feminist human rights groups, however the case has been thrown out twice.

HR 972, the Trafficking Victims Protection Reauthorization Act of 2005 reauthorizes the 2000 law, but it also gives U.S. law enforcement better tools to study human trafficking within the United States and to prosecute those who purchase sex acts. The measure authorizes $50 million for grants to state and local law enforcement to investigate and prosecute persons who engage in the purchase of commercial sex acts.

Scandals

In 2005 it was reported that Philippe Servaty, a newspaper columnist for Le Soir, traveled to Morocco where he persuaded women to engage in sexual activity by promising to marry and bring them to Belgium. He then posted photos online to boast of his conquests, but when his explicit materials were circulated back to Morocco many of the women were arrested, had their lives ruined, committed suicide or disappeared.

Academic Study

University of Leicester sociologists studied this subject as part of a research project for the Economic and Social Research Council and End Child Prostitution and Trafficking campaign. The study included interviews with over 250 Caribbean sex tourists. Among their findings:

- Preconceptions about race and gender influenced their opinions.
- Economically underdeveloped tourist-receiving countries are promoted as being culturally different so that (in the Western tourist's understanding) prostitution and traditional male domination of women have less stigma than similar practices might have in their home countries.

Documentaries

Canadian film makers have been active at reporting on sex tourism. Documentary titles include:

- Falang: Behind Bangkok's Smile by Jordon Clark (2005) (this title at the Internet Movie Database), set in Thailand
- the CBC series, the Lens episode "Selling Sex in Heaven" (2005) (this title at the Internet Movie Database), set in the Philippines.

- Channel 4 Cutting Edge episode "The Child Sex Trade" (2003), set in Romania, Italy

Depictions in Fiction and Popular Culture

- The 2005 film Heading South describes the experiences of a group of middle-aged women in the late 1970s, who travel to Haiti for the purposes of sexual tourism.
- In the animated TV series South Park the character Chef joins the Super Adventure Club which travels the world having sex with children.
- Sex tourism is a major theme of Platform, a novel by Michel Houellebecq.
- In the 2005 film Hostel, directed by Eli Roth, depicts sex tourism in Slovakia
- The film Macho Dancer deals with male sex workers in Manila. It includes characters who are female prostitutes.

Trafficking in Human Beings

Trafficking of human beings is the recruitment, transportation, transfer, harbouring or receipt of people for the purpose of exploitation. Trafficking involves a process of using illicit means such as threat, use of force, or other forms of coercion, of abduction, of fraud, of deception, of the abuse of power or of a position of vulnerability.

Exploitation includes forcing people into prostitution or other forms of sexual exploitation, forced labour or services, slavery or practices similar to slavery, servitude or the removal of organs. For children exploitation may include also, illicit international adoption, trafficking for early marriage, recruitment as child soldiers, for begging or for sports (such as child camel jockeys or football players), or for recruitment for religious cults.

Overview

Human trafficking differs from people smuggling. In the latter, people voluntarily request smuggler's service for fees and there may be no deception involved in the (illegal) agreement. On arrival at their destination, the smuggled person is usually free. On the other hand, the trafficking victim is enslaved, or the terms of their debt bondage are fraudulent or highly exploitative. The trafficker takes away the basic human rights of the victim. Victims are sometimes tricked and lured by false promises or physically forced. Some traffickers use coercive and manipulative tactics including deception, intimidation, feigned love, isolation, threat and use of physical force, debt bondage, other abuse, or even force-feeding with drugs to control their victims.

In the case of children, such practices are considered child trafficking even if none of the illicit means previously described are used.

Trafficked people usually come from the poorer regions of the world, where opportunities are limited, and are often from the most vulnerable in society, such as runaways, refugees, or other displaced persons, (though they may come from any social background, class or race. People who are seeking entry to other countries may be picked up by traffickers, and-typically-misled into thinking that they will be free after being smuggled across the border. In some cases, they are captured through slave raiding, although this is increasingly rare.

Trafficking of children often involves exploitation of the parents' extreme poverty. The latter may sell children to traffickers in order to pay off debts or gain income or they may be deceived concerning the prospects of training and a better life for their children. In West Africa, trafficked children have often lost one or both parents to the African AIDS crisis.

Women, who form over 80% of trafficking victims, are particularly at risk to become involved in sex trafficking. Potential kidnappers exploit lack of opportunities, promise good jobs or opportunities for study, and then force the victims to become prostitutes, participate in pornography or escort services. Through agents and brokers who arrange the travel and job placements, women are escorted to their destinations and delivered to the employers. Upon reaching their destinations, some women learn that they have been deceived about the nature of the work they will do; most have been lied to about the financial arrangements and conditions of their employment; and all find themselves in coercive and abusive situations from which escape is both difficult and dangerous.

The main motive of a woman (in some cases an underage girl) to accept an offer from a trafficker is better financial opportunities for herself or her family. In many cases traffickers initially offer 'legitimate' work or the promise of an opportunity to study. The main types of work offered are in the catering and hotel industry, in bars and clubs, modeling contracts, or au pair work. Offers of marriage are sometimes used by traffickers as well as threats, intimidation and kidnapping. In the majority of cases, the women end up in prostitution. Also some (migrating) prostitutes become victims of human trafficking. Some women know they will be working as prostitutes, but they have a too-rosy picture of the circumstances and the conditions of the work in the country of destination.

Men are also at risk of being trafficked for unskilled work predominantly involving hard labor. Other forms of trafficking include bonded and sweatshop labor, forced marriage, and domestic servitude. Children are also trafficked for both labor exploitation and sexual exploitation. On a related issue, children are forced to be child soldiers.

Many women are forced into the sex trade after answering false advertisements, and others are simply kidnapped. Thousands of children from Asia, Africa, and South America are sold into the global sex trade every year. Often they are kidnapped or orphaned, and sometimes they are actually sold by their own families.

Extent

United States State Department data "estimated 600,000 to 820,000 men, women, and children [are] trafficked across international borders each year, approximately 80 percent are women and girls and up to 50 percent are minors. The data also illustrate that the majority of transnational victims are trafficked into commercial sexual exploitation." Due to the illegal nature of trafficking and differences in methodology, the exact extent is unknown.

An estimated 14,000 people are trafficked into the United States each year, although again because trafficking is illegal, accurate statistics are difficult. According to the Massachusetts based Trafficking Victims Outreach and Services Networkin Massachusetts alone, there were 55 documented cases of human trafficking in 2005 and the first half of 2006 in Massachusetts. In 2004, the Royal Canadian Mounted Police (RCMP) estimated that 600-800 persons are trafficked into Canada annually and that additional 1,500-2,200 persons are trafficked through Canada into the United States.

In the United Kingdom, 71 women were known to have been trafficked into prostitution in 1998 and the Home Office recognized that the scale is likely greater as the problem is hidden and research estimates that the actual figure could be up to 1,420 women trafficked into the UK during the same period. Trafficking in people is increasing in Africa, South Asia and into North America.

Russia is a major source of women trafficked globally for the purpose of sexual exploitation. Annually, thousands of Russian women end up as prostitutes in China, Japan or South Korea. Russia is also a significant destination and transit country for persons trafficked for sexual and labor exploitation from regional and neighboring countries into Russia, and on to the Gulf states, Europe, Asia, and North America. The ILO estimates that 20 percent of the five million illegal immigrants in Russia are victims of forced labor, which is a form of trafficking. There were reports of trafficking of children and of child sex tourism in Russia. The Government of Russia has made some effort to combat trafficking but has also been criticized for not complying with the minimum standards for the elimination of trafficking.

The majority of child trafficking cases are in Asia, although it is a global problem. In Thailand, non-governmental organisations (NGO) have estimated that up to a third of prostitutes are children under 18, many trafficked from outside

Thailand. In Ukraine, a survey conducted by the NGO "La Strada-Ukraine" in 2001-2003, based on a sample of 106 women being trafficked out of Ukraine found that 3% were under 18, and the US State Department reported in 2004 that incidents of minors being trafficked was increasing.

In Asia, Japan is the major destination country for trafficked women, especially from the Philippines and Thailand. The US State Department has rated Japan as either a 'Tier 2' or a 'Tier 2 Watchlist' country every year since 2001 in its annual Trafficking in Persons reports. Both these ratings implied that Japan was (to a greater or lesser extent) not fully compliant with minimum standards for the elimination of human trafficking trade.

In Ukraine, a survey conducted by the NGO "La Strada-Ukraine" in 2001-2003, based on a sample of 106 women being trafficked out of Ukraine found that 3% were under 18, and the US State Department reported in 2004 that incidents of minors being trafficked was increasing.

In the United Kingdom, Vietnamese human trafficking have been discovered in the past few years. Many Vietnamese people are trafficked to work in illegal Vietnamese cannabis factories throughout the country, as the recent police Operation Keymer showed. Another recent police Operation Pentameter discovered illegal Vietnamese are also smuggled in to work in Vietnamese nail salons. Recently the UK authority planned to deport over 500 children back to Vietnam who had been smuggled into the country.

Reporters have witnessed a rapid increase in prostitution in Cambodia, Bosnia, and Kosovo after UN and, in the case of the latter two, NATO peacekeeping forces moved in. Peacekeeping forces have been linked to trafficking and forced prostitution. Proponents of peacekeeping argue that the actions of a few should not incriminate the many participants in the mission, yet NATO and the UN have come under criticism for not taking the issue of forced prostitution linked to peacekeeping missions seriously enough. In the western world, Canada in particular has a major problem with modern-day sexual slavery.

In a 2006 report the Future Group, a Canadian humanitarian organization dedicated to ending human trafficking, ranked eight industrialized nations and gave Canada an F for its "abysmal" record treating victims. The report, titled "Falling Short of the Mark: An International Study on the Treatment of Human Trafficking Victims", concluded that Canada "is an international embarrassment" when it comes to combatting this form of slavery.

The report's principal author Benjamin Perrin wrote, "Canada has ignored calls for reform and continues to re-traumatize trafficking victims, with few exceptions, by subjecting them to routine deportation and fails to provide even basic support services."

In the report, the only other country to flunk was the United Kingdom, which received a D, while the United States received a B+ and Australia, Norway, Sweden, Germany and Italy all received grades of B or B-. The report criticizes former Liberal Party of Canada cabinet ministers Irwin Cotler, Joe Volpe and Pierre Pettigrew for "passing the buck" on the issue.

Commenting on the report, the then Minister of Citizenship and Immigration, Monte Solberg told Sun Media Corporation, "It's very damning, and if there are obvious legislative or regulatory fixes that need to be done, those have to become priorities, given especially that we're talking about very vulnerable people."

Cause of Trafficking

Some causes of trafficking include:

- poverty
- perceived higher standards of life elsewhere
- lack of employement opportunities
- organised crime and presence of organised criminal gangs
- regional imbalances
- economic disparities

- social discrimination
- corruption in governement
- political instability
- armed conflict
- uprooting of communities because of mega projects without proper Resttlement and Rehabilitation packages.
- Profitability
- Growing deprivation and marginalization of the poor
- Insufficient penalties against traffickers
- According to the UN a major factor that has allowed the growth of sexual trafficking is "Governments and human rights organizations alike have simply judged the woman guilty of prostitution and minimized the trafficker's role."
- Driven by demand; demand is high for prostitutes and other forms of labor in host countries; therefore there is a very profitable market available to those who wish to become handlers.

Trafficking in people has been facilitated by porous borders and advanced communication technologies, it has become increasingly transnational in scope and highly lucrative. Unlike drugs or arms, people can be "sold" many times. The opening up of Asian markets, porous borders, the end of the Soviet Union and the collapse of the former Yugoslavia have contributed to this globalization.

Government Action against Human Trafficking

A human trafficking awareness poster from the Canadian Department of Justice

Actions taken to combat human trafficking vary from government to government. Some have introduced legislation specifically aimed at making human trafficking illegal. Governments can also develop systems of co-operation between different nation's law enforcement agencies and with non-government organisations (NGOs).

Other actions governments could take is raise awareness. This can take on three forms. Firstly in raising awareness amongst potential victims, in particular in countries where human traffickers are active. Secondly, raising awareness amongst police, social welfare workers and immigration officers. And in countries where prostitution is legal or semi-legal, raising awareness amongst the clients of prostitution, to look out for signs of a human trafficking victim.

Laws against trafficking in the United States are prosecuted at the federal level. The overwhelming majority of states do not have laws against human trafficking. For example, in Maryland it is a felony to have sex with a minor, but only a misdemeanor for making it available to those who wish to have sex with a minor. Raising awareness can take on different forms. One method is through the use of awareness films or through posters.

Criticism of Bangladesh on Human Trafficking

In June 2006, the government of Bangladesh issued a restraining order preventing Sigma Huda, U.N. special reporter on trafficking in persons, from leaving the country to deliver a key report on trafficking before the Human Rights Council in Geneva on June 11, 2007. U.N. High Commissioner for Human Rights Louise Arbour has asked Bangladesh to clarify corruption charges against a U.N. human rights investigator, which will prevent her from addressing the main U.N. rights body. The Coalition Against Trafficking in Women issued a statement calling this "an outrage and a violation of her right to freedom of movement and freedom of speech."

International Law

In 2000 the United Nations adopted the Convention against Transnational Organized Crime, also called the Palermo Convention and two Palermo protocols thereto:

- Protocol to Prevent, Suppress and Punish Trafficking in Persons, especially Women and Children; and
- Protocol against the Smuggling of Migrants by Land, Sea and Air.

All of these instruments contain elements of the current international law on trafficking in human beings.

Council of Europe

The Council of Europe Convention on Action against Trafficking in Human Beings was adopted by the Council of Europe on 16 May 2005. The aim of the convention is to prevent and combat the trafficking in human beings. Of the 46 members of the Council of Europe, so far 31 have signed the convention and 1 has ratified it.(29 June 2006).

United States Federal Law

The United States federal government has taken a firm stance against human trafficking both within its borders and beyond. Domestically, human trafficking is prosecuted through the Civil Rights Division, Criminal Section of the United States Department of Justice. Older statutes used to protect 13th Amendment rights within United States borders are Title 18 U.S.C., Sections 1581 and 1584. Section 1584 makes it a crime to force a person to work against his will. This compulsion can be effected by use of force, threat of force, threat of legal coercion or by "a climate of fear", that is, an environment wherein individuals believe they may be harmed by leaving or refusing to work. Section 1581 similarly makes it illegal to force a person to work through "debt servitude".

New laws were passed under the Victims of Trafficking and Violence Protection Act of 2000. The new laws responded to a changing face of trafficking in the United States. It allowed for greater statutory maximum sentences for traffickers, provided resources for protection of and assistance for victims of trafficking and created avenues for inter-agency cooperation in the field of human trafficking. It also allows many trafficking victims to remain in the United States and apply for permanent residency. This law also attempted to encourage efforts to prevent human trafficking internationally, by creating annual country reports on trafficking, as well as by tying financial non-humanitarian assistance to foreign countries to real efforts in addressing human trafficking.

International NPOs, such as Human Rights Watch and Amnesty International, have called on the United States to improve its measures aimed at reducing trafficking. They recommend that the United States more fully implement the "United Nations Protocol to Prevent, Suppress and Punish Trafficking in Persons, Especially Women and Children" and the "United Nations Convention against Transnational Organized Crime" and for immigration officers to improve their awareness of trafficking and support the victims of trafficking.

United States State Law on Trafficking Several states have also written laws to address human trafficking in their borders. Florida has written trafficking statutes criminalizing forced labor, sex trafficking, and document servitude. Florida also provides for mandatory law enforcement trainings and victim services.

On May 8, 2006, Connecticut passed an act addressing human trafficking that criminalized coerced work, and made trafficking a violation of the Connecticut RICO Act.

Human Trafficking in Popular Culture

Lilya 4-ever, a film based loosely on the real life of Dangoule Rasalaite, portrays a young woman from the former Soviet Union who is deceived into being trafficked for exploitation in Sweden. Human trafficking has also been portrayed in the Canadian/UK TV drama Sex Traffic. Based on true events, Svetlana's Journey by Michael Cory Davis depicts the trials of a 13-year-old who loses her family and is sold to human traffickers by her adoptive family. Drugged, raped, and forced to endure continuous abuse by her 'clients' and traffickers, she finally commits suicide.

The 2007 film Trade deals with human trafficking out of Mexico and a brother's attempt to rescue his kidnapped and trafficked young sister. It is based on Peter Landesman's article about sex slaves, which was featured as the cover story in the January 24, 2004 issue of New York Times Magazine.

The film The Transporter deals with the hero, Frank Martin, played by Jason Statham, trying to stop a container full of men and women being illegally transported. Human Trafficking (2005) (TV) by Christian Duguay stars Mira Sorvino, Donald Sutherland, and Richard Carlyle. A sixteen-year-old girl from the Ukraine, a single mother from Russia, an orphaned seventeen-year-old girl from Romania, and a twelve-year-old American tourist become the victims of international sex slave traffickers. Sorvino and Sutherland are the Immigration and Customs Enforcement (ICE) agents who struggle to save them.

FREE INDEPENDENT TRAVELER/TOURIST (FIT)

With world travel market having undergone significant changes over the last few years a new type of tourist has emerged known as the Free Independent Traveler or Tourist (FIT). The definition is broad but tends to refer to people over 35, often, though not necessarily, of above average income who like to travel in small groups, usually couples. They eschew mass tourism and the holiday package concept promoted by Travel operators, in favour of a more individualistic approach to travel.

There are two implications to the idea of the Free Independent Traveler. One is important in the context of a marketing niche with a distinct economic behaviour whilst the other concentrates more on the philosophy of travel. This distinction can be summarised in how they are described. For the economic importance of tourism and for marketing purposes they are Free Independent Travelers (Upper case as they are an identifiable group within the market) whilst the people themselves are perhaps more attracted to the possibilities and lack of limitations in the concept of being a free, independent traveler.

Free Independent Travelers as an Alternative Movement

They tend to be environmentally aware, enjoy experiencing new ways of life and are enthusiastic, off the beaten track explorers practising for travel what the Slow Food Movement does for eating. They enjoy good food, architecture, and the heritage of local cultures. They tend to reject the traditional Package holiday model and even the Dynamic packaging system of doing things. People may garner information from a wide variety of sources or tips. The Guardian Newspaper's ivebeenthere site or Lonely Planet's forum are all examples and represent the fundamental difference between the FIT and other types of travel that this is about sharing and passing on of ideas and knowledge in accordance with the much talked about Web 2.0. The FIT vacation is a custom built cocktail then with suggestions from friends, forums, speciality providers or others creating the idea around which the vacation is built. The FITs themselves are responsible for adding components in place of the traditional package operators. The rise of low cost airlines in the US and Europe has also increased the supply of alternative and lower cost short haul destinations fueling demand for these newly available markets. Southwest Airlines in the US, Ryanair and easyJet in Europe and later Spanish, German and nationally orientated airlines grew up adding destinations and creating an internationally networked portfolio of air-routes delivering people to destinations that were not previously available at a commercial, international level.

The internet is fundamental to the rise of the FIT, offering them the suggestions, for example, of a good meal out in Rome from a fellow FIT, across the globe, who ate there last week.

Free Independent Travelers as an Economic Phenomenon

Here they are an important and growing sector in the market. Governments, regional tourist boards and other public sectors responsible for tourism development try to attract them. Why? The basic principle is economics. FITs spread their money around in a more efficient fashion. Fifteen FITs will eat, sleep, snack, take a coffee, go to theatres/art shows/opera festivals/ football games/rural villages in fifteen different locations and introduce their money in hundreds of different channels harnessing the power of Keynes' multiplier effect in a much more efficient manner. Contrast this with a group tour of another 15 people run by Tour Operator 1 based in and delivering share-holder profit to Country A. Their tour to Country B is less efficient from an economic development point of view as the Tour Operator controls so many of the components in the chain. Also those 15 sleep in the same hotel and eat in the same restaurants ensuring that though their money stimulates the local economy it tends to do so in a less than optimally efficient manner.

GARDEN TOURISM

Garden tourism is a type of niche tourism involving visits or travel to botanical gardens and places which are significant in the history of gardening. Garden tourists often travel individually in countries with which they are familiar but often prefer to join organized garden tours in countries where they might experience difficulties with language, travel or finding accommodation in the vicinity of the garden.

The list of famous gardens which attract garden tourists from afar includes: Sissinghurst Castle Garden and Stourhead in England, Versailles and Giverny in France, Keukenhof in Holland, Villa d'Este and Villa Lante in Italy, Alhambra in Spain, Longwood Gardens and Filoli in the USA, Taj Mahal in India, Ryoan-ji in Japan. In the year 2000 the Alhambra and the Taj Mahal both received over 2 million visitors. This poses problems for the landscape manager.

Michel de Montaigne was one of the earliest garden tourists to record his impressions of gardens (c1580). John Evelyn also recorded his visits to gardens in France and Italy, as did Fynes Moryson. At the start of the twenty-first century Britain had the largest number of gardens open to the public for tourist visits: over 3,500 gardens are listed in Gardens of England and Wales Open for Charity (the 'Yellow Book').

GUEST RANCH

"Dude ranch" redirects here. For the blink-182 album, see Dude Ranch (album).

The guest ranch, also known as a dude ranch, is a type of ranch oriented towards visitors or tourism. It is a phenomenon of the romanticization of the American West after the official closing of the United States frontier in the late 19th century.

The Western adventures of hardy aristocrats like Theodore Roosevelt were made available to paying guests from cities or the East, called "tenderfeet," "greenhorns," or "dudes" in the West. After World War I, the transcontinental railroad network brought these paying visitors to the local depot, where a wagon would be waiting for them. Some guest ranch visitors expected a somewhat edited version of the "cowboy life," while others were more tolerant of the odors and timetable of a working ranch. Guest ranches have also become a feature of the Australian Outback.

In the United States, guest ranches are a long-established tradition and continue to be a popular vacation destination. Depending on the climate, some guest ranches are open only in the summer or winter, others offer "year-round" service in all four seasons. College students are often recruited to work at guest ranches during the summer months. Common jobs offered to college students include: housekeeping, wrangler, dining staff, and office staff or babysitters.

Hunting Ranches

Some guest ranches cater to hunters. Some feature native wildlife such as whitetail deer, mule deer, bison or elk. Others feature exotic species imported from other nations such as Africa and India. Both types of ranches are highly controversial. While many traditional ranches allow hunters and outfitters on their land to hunt native game, the act of confining game to guarantee a kill is considered unsporting by some people.

The introduction of non-native species on ranches is even more controversial because of concerns that these "exotics" may escape and contaminate the gene pool of native species or spread previously unknown disease. The advocates of hunting ranches argue in turn that they help protect native herds from over-hunting and the stocking of exotic species actually increases their numbers and may help save them from extinction.

HERITAGE TOURISM

Cultural heritage tourism (or just heritage tourism) is a branch of tourism oriented towards the cultural heritage of the location where tourism is occurring. Culture has always been a major object of travel, as the development of the Grand Tour from the 16th century onwards attests. In the 20th century, some people have claimed, culture ceased to be the objective of tourism: tourism is now culture. Cultural attractions play an important role in tourism at all levels, from the global highlights of world culture to attractions that underpin local identities. (Richards, 1996)

According to the Weiler and Hall, culture, heritage and the arts have long contributed to appeal of tourist destination. However, in recent years 'culture' has been rediscovered as an important marketing tool to attract those travellers with special interests in heritage and arts. According to the Hollinshead, cultural heritage tourism defines as cultural heritage tourism is the fastest growing segment of the tourism industry because there is a trend toward an increase specialization among tourist. This trend is evident in the rise in the volume of tourists who seek adventure, culture, history, archaeology and interaction with local people.

Cultural heritage tourism is important for various reasons; it has a positive economic and social impact, it establishes and reinforces identity, it helps preserve the cultural heritage, with culture as an instrument it facilitates harmony and understanding among people, it supports culture and helps renew tourism (Richards, 1996).

Cultural heritage tourism has a number of objectives that must be met within the context of sustainable development such as; the conservation of cultural resources, accurate interpretation of resources, authentic visitors experience, and the stimulation of the earned revenues of cultural resources. We can see therefore, that cultural heritage tourism is not only concerned with identification, management and protection of the heritage values but it must also be involved in understanding the impact of tourism on communities and regions, achieving economic and social benefits, providing financial resources for protection, as well as marketing and promotion. (J. M. Fladmark, 1994)

Heritage tourism involves visiting historical or industrial sites that may include old canals, railways, battlegrounds, etc. The overall purpose is to gain an appreciation of the past. It also refers to the marketing of a location to members of a diaspora who have distant family roots there.

Decolonization and immigration form the major background of much contemporary heritage tourism. Falling travel costs have also made heritage tourism possible for more people.

Another possible form involves religious travel or pilgrimages. Many Catholics from around the world come to the Vatican and other sites such as Lourdes or Fátima. Large numbers of Jews have both visited Israel and emigrated there. Many have also gone to Holocaust sites and memorials. Islam commands its followers to take the hajj to Mecca, thus differentiating it somewhat from tourism in the usual sense, though the trip can also be a culturally important event for the pilgrim.

Heritage Tourism can also be attributed to historical events that have been dramatised to make them more entertaining. For example a historical tour of a town or city using a theme such as ghosts or vikings.

LITERARY TOURISM

Literary Tourism is a type of cultural tourism that deals with places and events from fictional texts as well as the lives of their authors. This could include following the route a fictional character charts in a novel, visiting particular settings from a story or tracking down the haunts of a novelist.

Literary tourists are specifically interested in how places have influenced writing and at the same time how writing has created place. In order to become a literary tourist you only need a novel and an inquisitive mind-set, however there are literary guides, literary maps and literary tours to help you on your way.

In addition to visiting author and book sites, literary tourists often engage in bookstore tourism, browsing local bookshops for titles specifically related to the sites as well as other regional books and authors.

Literary Tourism in KwaZulu-Natal

'Literary Tourism in KwaZulu-Natal' is a National Research Foundation funded project that is working on a Literary Map that connects authors whose lives or work is tied in some significant way to specific places in KwaZulu-Natal, South Africa. Each author entry contains a short biography, a selected bibliography and an excerpt from the author's work that relates to the place identified in the map. The map can be viewed here:

MUSIC TOURISM

Music tourism is the act of visiting a city or town in order to see a gig or festival. With the presence of the tourist, money is spent and the local economy benefits. This sort of tourism is particularly important to small villages such as Glastonbury, as well as large cities like Glasgow.

NAKED HIKING

Naked walking, naked hiking, or Freehiking is a sub-set of the modern form of social nudity. For some people, naked hiking may appear to be some form of energetic sport; however, for most it is simply a pleasant recreational pastime, with no social agenda.

Context

Naturism has traditionally been an activity engaged in a private space or landed club environment. Modern naturism is moving towards a public space, as well including a more active component. Although naturists have always been interested in health and fitness, indeed this was a prerequisite to many early gatherings, and most clubs have volleyball nets and table tennis tables, there has always been a slight reluctance to walk, run or cycle naked. One reason for this has been the secluded nature of the early clubs, private from prying eyes and textiles, and the limited area in which the early pioneers had to work with.

Modern naturism in nude-tolerant societies is moving out of the private enclosure and towards the arena of public nudity, where it is deemed ok to be not only naked in public, but where it is also ok to be active (from a stroll to action sports) in the nude. The point about being active is that many people appear to find static nudity acceptable, for example in the media (porn magazines or page 3 girls in newspapers), and theatre (non-moving Greek-statue-like nudity), but moving nudity, in contrast, seems to generate heated feeling.

Attention and Opinion

Naked outdoor activity is a subject expounded clearly in the publications of the Nacktiv site. People simply go about their normal day to day business, or recreational activities, naked. The more naked bodies people see in a public setting the more likely they are to question the advertising and media industries' onesided linking of sex with nudity. Public active nudists go out of their way to be discreet, and are to be seen walking in remote mountain areas, through quiet forests and woods, across distant fields and scrubland, and not in densely populated areas, often not meeting anyone else at all.

In the United Kingdom, Steve Gough, known as The Naked Rambler, received much media coverage for walking naked from Land's End to John o' Groats in 2003-2004 and again in 2005-2006. He was arrested and imprisoned several times during both his walks. In both 2005 and 2006 the European Alps were crossed naked during a one week hiking (tour), there was little media coverage and no-one was arrested or troubled.

Special Considerations

Although extremists might insist that naked hiking should be all-naked, and nothing but naked, as in all things one should remain practical and sensible about such activities.

Sensible footwear might mean bare feet on the beach, but wearing mountain boots in the mountains. Sunstroke or sunburn is a danger by any activity, naked or not, but naked hiking in the high mountains exposes the body to an increased level of sunshine not found at sea level, so sunscreen and a sun hat are essential items. Bugs, such as mosquitoes and midges, can be particularly troublesome, especially in sensitive areas, so anti-bug formulas are often needed by participants in this activity. Walking through a bunch of stinging nettles, or a field full of high thistles, can be an interesting experience (even with shorts on). Naturally, extra care must be taken.

NEO TOURISM

Neo Tourism is a term coined by the Korea tourism organization that comprehensively describes the newly changing trend of the tourism.

Definition of Neo Tourism

Following the changes in the economic, social and cultural paradigm of the last century, the form of tourism is changing as well. "Neo Tourism" is a term that comprehensively describes the new aspects of such changes and diversification of the tourism. The "Neo Tourism" incorporates concepts such as 'Sustainable tourism' which puts emphasis on the environmental sustainability and 'Special Interest Tourism (SIT)' which reflects postmodern social phenomenon.

The Origin of Neo Tourism

Initially the term "Neo Tourism" was generated to explain a form of tourism which has not existed before, to say, "New Tourism". However, with continuous advents of various types of tourism, it has become necessary to categorize those concepts in further details and eventually the "Neo Tourism" has taken more concrete meaning as such including the essential key words in the category. Those essential key words are as follows.

- Postmodernism
- Sustainability
- Digitalization

Application of Neo Tourism

The term of "Neo Tourism" can explain the following types of tourism.

- Tourism that satisfies individual interests and purposes appearing with post-modern social change
- Tourism that avoids the environmental destruction and ensure experiencing the untouched nature
- Tourism that manages various matters such as gathering information and making reservation through Internet.

The term "Neo Tourism" can be used from the suppliers' point of view as well as the customers' in the following concepts.

- Creating a new type of tourism product by connecting tourism industry with other industries. (ex. Medical tourism, Edu Tourism)
- Developing environmentally and socially sustainable tourist attractions
- Utilizing IT technology such as internet and ubiquitous systems to promote and sale the tourism products

POP-CULTURE TOURISM

Pop-culture tourism is the act of traveling to locations featured in literature, film, music, or any other form of popular entertainment.

Popular destinations have included:

- Los Angeles, California film studios.
- the Iowa cornfields featured in Field of Dreams
- New Zealand after The Lord of the Rings was filmed there
- The Louvre in which the book and movie The Da Vinci Code takes place
- Tom's Restaurant which is known to many as Monk's from Seinfeld
- Prince Edward Island, in which the Canadian novel Anne of Green Gables takes place, is a popular attraction for tourists, notably from Japan.
- South Korea because of the recent Hallyu phenomenon in East Asia.

- Japan for japanophiles or lovers of Japanese pop-culture.
- North Bend, Washington and in particular Twede's Cafe where much of the television show Twin Peaks was shot.
- Roslyn, Washington, which stood in for Cicely Alaska in the television show Northern Exposure.
- Tunisia, location of the filming of the Star Wars movies.

Pop-culture tourism is in some respects akin to pilgrimage, with its modern equivalents of places of pilgrimage, such as Elvis Presley's Graceland and the grave of Jim Morrison in Père Lachaise Cemetery. Another pop-culture tourism destination is Vulcan, Alberta Canada. In the early 1990s this small rural community began to explore ways it could capitalize on the coincidence of the Town's name being the same as popular Star Trek Character, Mr. Spock's home planet: Vulcan, to develop its local tourism industry.

PERPETUAL TRAVELER

The term perpetual traveler (PT, permanent tourist or prior taxpayer) refers to both a lifestyle and a philosophy.

Background

In practical terms, perpetual travelers are people who live in such a way that they are not considered a legal resident of any of the countries in which they spend time. In this way, they seek to avoid the legal obligations which may accompany residency, such as taxes, jury duty, and military service. For example, while PT's may hold citizenship in one or more countries that impose taxes based solely on residency, their legal residence will most likely be in a tax haven. They may spend the majority of their time in other countries, never staying long enough to be considered a resident.

Tax Avoidance

It is possible to live for several months, and in some cases even own property, in many countries without paying income tax. For example, one can spend up to 122 days each year in the United States without being considered a resident or being required to file a US tax return.

Some PT's are wealthy individuals whose primary motivation is tax avoidance. By exploiting the rules in place for tourists and travelers, individuals may be able to legally reduce or eliminate their tax burden. However other PT's, such as itinerants, may adopt this lifestyle for purely self-ownership reasons, just to be free from government authority, interference and "The System".

Five Flag Theory

Many perpetual travelers attempt to organize their affairs around the "Five Flags" theory, arranging for different facets of their lives to fall under the jurisdiction of separate countries, or flags. This is an extension of W.G. Hill's original "Three Flags" approach.

Whether to minimize governmental interference (via taxes or otherwise), or to maximize privacy, the theory proposes that you arrange for each of the following to be in a separate country:

1. Passport and Citizenship-in a country that does not tax money earned outside the country
2. Legal Residence-in a tax haven
3. Business Base-where you earn your money
4. Asset Haven-where you keep your money
5. Playgrounds-where you spend your money

Philosophy

On the surface, perpetual tourists have some things in common with world citizens, in that they see themselves as untethered to any one nation. However, PT's generally seem to eschew the humanistic and utopian overtones of world citizenship. Many PT's align themselves closely with the libertarian school of thought, which advocates individual sovereignty-sovereignty vested in the individual rather than in nation-states.

PILGRIMAGE

In religion and spirituality, a pilgrimage is a long journey or search of great moral significance. Sometimes, it is a journey to a sacred place or shrine of importance to a person's beliefs and faith. Members of every major religion participate in pilgrimages. A person who makes such a journey is called a pilgrim.

Buddhism offers four sites of pilgrimage: the Buddha's birthplace at Kapilavastu, the site where he attained Enlightenment Bodh Gaya, where he first preached at Benares, and where he achieved Parinirvana at Kusinagara.

In the kingdoms of Israel and Judah the visitation of certain ancient cult-centers was repressed in the 7th century BC, when the worship was restricted to Jahweh at the temple in Jerusalem. In Syria, the shrine of Astarte at the headwater spring of the river Adonis survived until it was destroyed by order of Emperor Constantine in the 4th century AD.

In mainland Greece, a stream of individuals made their way to Delphi or the oracle of Zeus at Dodona, and once every four years, at the period of the Olympic games, the temple of Zeus at Olympia formed the goal of swarms of pilgrims from every part of the Hellenic world. When Alexander the Great reached Egypt, he put his whole vast enterprise on hold, while he made his way with a small band deep into the Libyan desert, to consult the oracle of Ammun. During the imperium of his Ptolemaic heirs, the shrine of Isis at Philae received many votive inscriptions from Greeks on behalf of their kindred far away at home.

Although a pilgrimage is normally viewed in the context of religion, the personality cults cultivated by communist leaders ironically gave birth to pilgrimages of their own. Prior to the demise of the USSR in 1991, a visit to Lenin's Mausoleum in Red Square, Moscow can be said to have had all the characteristics exhibiting a pilgrimage-for Communists. This type of pilgrimage to a personality cult is still evident today on people who pay visits of homage to Mao Tse Tung, Kim Il Sung, and Ho Chi Minh.

Effects on Trade

Pilgrims contributed an important element to long-distance trade before the modern era, and brought prosperity to successful pilgrimage sites, an economic phenomenon unequalled until the tourist trade of the 20th century. Encouraging pilgrims was a motivation for assembling (and sometimes fabricating) relics and for writing hagiographies of local saints, filled with inspiring accounts of miracle cures. Lourdes and other modern pilgrimage sites keep this spirit alive.

Modern Pilgrimage

Pilgrimages are still made throughout the world: modern-day pilgrimages include the Way of St. James, the Hajj, and the pilgrimage to Mount Kailash. In modern usage, the terms pilgrim and pilgrimage can also have a somewhat devalued meaning as they are often applied in a secular context. For example, fans of Elvis Presley may choose to visit his home, Graceland, in Memphis, Tennessee. Similarly one may refer to a cultural center such as Venice as a "tourists' Mecca".

Pilgrimage Centres in Various Times and Cultures

Antiquity

Many ancient religions had holy sites, temples and groves, where pilgrimages were made.

- Karnak, Egypt.
- Thebes, Egypt.
- Kurukshetra, India
- Delphi, Greece. Oracle.
- Dodona, Epirus, Greece. Oracle.
- Ephesus Temple of Diana.
- Baalbek Lebanon.

Bahá'í Faith

A Bahá'í pilgrimage currently consists of visiting the holy places in Haifa, Akká, and Bahjí in Northwest Israel. Bahá'ís do not have access to other places designated as sites for pilgrimage.

Bahá'u'lláh decreed pilgrimage in His Motherbook (Kitáb-i-Aqdas) to two places: the House of Bahá'u'lláh in Baghdad, Iraq, and the House of the Báb in Shiraz, Iran. In two separate Tablets, known as Suriy-i-Hajj, He prescribed specific rites for each of these pilgrimages (lifting the injunction regarding the shaving of one's head for pilgrimage in the Kitáb-i-Aqdas). It is obligatory to make the pilgrimage, "if one can afford it and is able to do so, and if no obstacle stands in one's way". Bahá'ís are free to choose between the two Houses, as either has been deemed sufficient. And although women are not bound to perform pilgrimage, they are certainly not prohibited to do so.

Later, `Abdu'l-Bahá designated the Shrine of Bahá'u'lláh at Bahji (the Qiblih) as a site of visitation. No rites have been prescribed for this.

Buddhism

Gautama Buddha spoke of the four sites most worthy of pilgrimage for his followers to visit:

- Lumbini: birth place (in Nepal)
- Bodh Gaya: place of Enlightenment
- Sarnath: (formally Isipathana) where he delivered his first teaching
- Kusinara: (now Kusinagar, India) where he attained mahaparinirvana (passed away).

Other pilgrimage places in India and Nepal connected to the life of Gautama Buddha are: Savatthi, Pataliputta, Nalanda, Gaya, Vesali, Sankasia, Kapilavastu, Kosambi, Rajagaha, Varanasi.

Other famous places for buddhist pilgrimage in various countries include:

- India: Sanchi, Ellora, Ajanta.
- Thailand: Sukhothai, Ayutthaya, Wat Phra Kaew, Wat Doi Suthep.

- Tibet: Lhasa (traditional home of the Dalai Lama), Mount Kailash, Lake Nam-tso.
- Cambodia: Angkor Wat, Silver Pagoda.
- Sri Lanka: Polonnaruwa, Temple of the Tooth (Kandy), Anuradhapura.
- Laos: Luang Prabang.
- Myanmar: Bagan, Sagaing Hill.
- Nepal: Bodhnath, Swayambhunath.
- Indonesia: Borobudur.
- China: Yung-kang, Lung-men caves.
- Japan: Kyoto, Nara.

Communism

- USSR: Moscow, Mausoleum of Lenin in Red Square.
- China: Peking, Mausoleum of Mao Tse Tung in Tiananmen Square.
- Germany: Trier, Birthplace of Karl Marx in Trier

Christianity

Pilgrimages were first made to sites connected with the birth, life, crucifixion and resurrection of Jesus. Surviving descriptions of Christian pilgrimages to the Holy Land date from the 4th century, when pilgrimage was encouraged by church fathers like Saint Jerome. Pilgrimages also began to be made to Rome and other sites associated with the Apostles, Saints and Christian martyrs, as well as to places where there have been apparitions of the Virgin Mary. The crusades to the holy land are also considered to be mass armed pilgrimages.

The second largest single pilgrimage in the history of Christendom was to the Funeral of Pope John Paul II after his death on April 2, 2005. An estimated four million people travelled to Vatican City, in addition to the almost three million people already living in Rome, to see the body of Pope John Paul II lie in state.

World Youth Day is a major Catholic Pilgrimage, specifically for people aged 16-35. It is held internationally every 2-3 years. In 2005, young Catholics visited Cologne, Germany. In 1995, the largest gathering of all time was to World Youth Day in Manila, Philippines, where four million people from all over the world attended.

The major Christian pilgrimages are to:

- Jerusalem. Site of the crucifixion and resurrection of Jesus.
- Rome on roads such as the Via Francigena. Site of the deaths of Saint Peter, Saint Paul and other early martyrs. Location of sacred relics of various saints, relics of the Passion, important churches and headquarters of the Catholic Church.
- Constantinople (today Istanbul, Turkey). Former capital of the Byzantine Empire and the see of one of the five ancient Patriarchates and spiritual see of the Eastern Orthodox Church. Hagia Sophia, former cathedral and burial place of many Ecumenical Patriarchs.
- Lourdes, France. Apparition of the Virgin Mary. The second most visited Christian pilgrimage site after Rome.
- Santiago de Compostela in Spain on the Way of St James (Spanish: El Camino de Santiago). This famous medieval pilgrimage to the shrine of Saint James is still popular today.

Other important Christian pilgrimage sites include:

- Assisi, Italy, St. Francis of Assisi and St Clare, relics
- Ávila, Spain, St Theresa of Avila, relics
- Bethlehem, in Israel, Birthplace of Jesus and King David.
- Canterbury Cathedral associated with Saint Thomas Becket.
- Cap-de-la-Madeleine, Quebec, Canada in honour of Our Lady of the Cape.
- Cathedral of Chartres, France.

- Miercurea Ciuc, Transylvania, Romania. Whit Sunday gathering of (mostly ethnic Hungarian) Catholics.
- Croagh Patrick, Ireland. Saint Patrick.
- Conques, France
- Cologne, Germany. Relics of the Three Magi.
- Czestochowa, Poland.Black Madonna of Czestochowa is housed pernamently in theJasna Góra Monastery
- Glastonbury, England. St Joseph of Arimathea.
- Goa, India. St. Francis Xavier
- Hill of Crosses, Lithuania
- House of the Virgin Mary, Turkey. Pope John-Paul II declared the Shrine of Virgin Mary as a pilgrimage place for Christians.
- Issoudun, France. Notre-Dame du Sacré-Coeur
- Kapel in 't Zand, Limburg
- Kevelaer, Germany
- Knock, Ireland
- Lichen, Sanctuary of Our Lady of Lichen
- Lisieux, France. Saint Therese of Lisieux, burial place.
- Lourdes, France. Apparition of the Virgin Mary. Place of healing.
- Mariazell, Austria. Marian Shrine to Austria and Hungary
- Medugorje, Bosnia-Herzegovina. Apparitions of the Virgin Mary at the present.
- Mount Athos, Greece. Orthodox monastic centre.
- Mount Nebo, Jordan. Traditional site of the death of Moses.
- Mount Sinai, Egypt, holy mountain to the ancient Hebrews, traditional site has been commemorated since time of Constantine
- Nazareth, Israel, hometown of Jesus

- Fatima, Portugal. Apparition of the Virgin Mary.
- Padua, Italy, St Anthony, relics
- Paris (Sacred-Heart Basilica Basilica of the Sacré Cœur; and Saint Catherine Labouré)
- Rosslyn Chapel, Scotland
- Sacri Monti, Italy. The Sacred Mountains of Piedmont and Lombardy.
- San Giovanni Rotondo, Italy, St Pio from Pietrelcina
- Guadalupe, Spain
- Sea of Galilee, Israel, site of Jesus' early ministry.
- Shrine of Our Lady of Guadalupe, Mexico City. Apparition of the Virgin Mary.
- St. Andrews, Scotland, it is said that Saint Andrew was given, by God, directions to the location of St Andrews
- St. Patrick's Purgatory, Donegal, Ireland
- St. Thomas Mount, India. Place where St. Thomas was martyed.
- Taizé Community, France, modern monastery that actively encourages pilgrimages to it
- Nidaros Cathedral, Norway
- Turin, Italy. Holy Shroud.
- Vailankanni, India. 16th-century Mary apparition site.
- Vierzehnheiligen, Germany.
- Walsingham, England. Virgin Mary apparition site.
- Wittenberg, Germany. Church of Martin Luther and centre of the Protestant Reformation.

Hinduism

Hindus are required to undertake pilgrimages during their lifetime. Most Hindus who can afford to go on such journeys travel to numerous sites including those below:

- Badrinath

- Kedarnath
- Gangotri
- Yamunotri
- Rishikesh
- Haridwar
- Benares
- Mandher Devi temple in Mandhradevi
- Vrindavan
- Mayapur
- Udupi
- Kateel
- Talapady
- Tirupati
- Palani
- Kukke Subramanya

The first four sites in the list above together comprise the Chardham, or four holy pilgrimage destinations. It is believed that travelling to these places leads to moksha, the release from samsara (cycle of rebirths). Vrindavan is most important place of pilgrimage for every Vaishnava, especially for the followers of Gaudiya Vaishnavism who regard Krishna as the original Personality of Godhead (God). Here one can attain love of God (prema).

Islam

Pilgrimage to Mecca-the Hajj-is one of the Five Pillars of Islam. It should be attempted at least once in the lifetime of all able-bodied Muslims who can afford to do so. It is the most important of all Muslim Pilgrimages.

Many Muslims also undergo ziyarat, which is a pilgrimage to sites associated with the prophet Muhammad, his companions, or other venerated figures in Islamic history, such as Shi'a imams or Sufi saints. Sites of pilgrimage include mosques, graves, battlefields, mountains, and caves. Local Pilgrimage traditions-those undertaken as ziarah visits to local graves, are also found throughout Muslim countries.

In some countries, the grave sites of heroes have very strong ziyarah traditions as visiting the graves at auspicious times is a display of national and community identity. Some traditions within Islam have negative attitudes towards grave visiting.

The third religiously sanctioned pilgrimage for Muslims is to the Al Quds mount in Jerusalem which hosts Al-Aqsa Mosque and the Dome of the Rock.

Judaism

Within Judaism, the Temple in Jerusalem was the center of the Jewish religion, until its destruction in 70 AD, and all who were able were under obligation to visit and offer sacrifices known as the korbanot, particularly during the Jewish holidays in Jerusalem.

Following the destruction of the Second Temple and the onset of the diaspora, the centrality of pilgrimage to Jerusalem in Judaism was discontinued. In its place came prayers and rituals hoping for a return to Zion and the accompanying restoration of regular pilgrimages (see Jerusalem, Jews and Judaism).

Until recent centuries, pilgrimage has been a fairly difficult and arduous adventure. But now, Jews from many countries make periodic pilgrimages to the holy sites of their religion.

The western retaining wall of the original temple, known as the Wailing Wall, or Western Wall remains in the Old City of Jerusalem and this has been the most sacred site for Zionist Jews. Pilgrimage to this area was off-limits from 1948 to 1967, when East Jerusalem was controlled by Jordan. Some Reform and Conservative Jews who no longer consider themselves exiles, still enjoy visiting Israel even if it is not an official "pilgrimage."

SACRED TRAVEL

Sacred travel, or metaphysical tourism, is a growing niche of the travel market. It attracts New Age believers, primarily middle-aged women, and involves tours and travel to "spiritual hotspots" on the Earth.

Destinations are often ancient sites where there is a mystery concerning their origin or purpose, such as Machu Picchu in Peru, The Pyramids of Egypt, or Stonehenge in England. Some Christian sites such as the locations of the Black Madonnas and the Rosslyn Chapel in Scotland are also popular.

These travelers see the journey as more than just tourism and take the trips in order to heal themselves and the world. Part of this may involve rituals involving, (supposedly), leaving their bodies, possession by spirits (channelling), and recovery of past life memories.

SAFARI

A safari is an overland journey. It usually refers to a trip by tourists to Africa, traditionally for a big-game hunt and in more modern times to watch and photograph big game and other wildlife as a safari holiday. There is a certain theme or style associated with the word, which includes khaki clothing, pith helmets, and animal skins-like leopard's skin.

Etymology

Entering the English language in the late 19th century, the word safari means 'journey' in Swahili language. Originally from the Arabic (safara) meaning travel The verb for "to travel" in Swahili is "safiri", the noun for the journey is "safari". These words are used for any type of journey e.g. by bus from Nairobi to Mombasa.

Touristic Usage

Most people in the West still believe that a true safari can only be in East Africa, that is Kenya and Tanzania, and not in Africa as a whole. That is to say that if you were in South Africa doing some big game watching, you wouldn't be "on safari" even though the word is broadly used, because the word "safari" comes from the Swahili-speaking people who can be found along the Swahili Coast. Today the word is used generally to mean anything from big game viewing, photography, or even game hunting.

VIRTUAL TOURISM

Virtual tourism refers to pre-planning alternative touristic activity before your departure, by integrating multiple digital resources to explore regions of the world without having to physically travel. It helps focus attention onto people, places and exploring changes over time.

By using the internet, travel literature (travel guides and travelogues), Journals, Papers and television visual learning courseware graphically shows information necessary to make an informed decision about which places to visit and historic or scenic byways to explore.

It is an economical activity that employs people from several different specific areas, such as journalists and photographers, geographers, editors, cameras, writers, etc... and it is one activity related to promoting nature-based or people-powered outdoor recreation involving adventure-based tourism.

VOLUNTEER VACATION

Volunteer vacations are an opportunity for people to make a positive difference in the lives of others or to help improve or contribute to society, culture, or the environment while on vacation.

It is also a chance for people of nearly any age to immerse themselves in foreign or challenging circumstances, experience a different culture first-hand, and learn more about the world they live in.

According to the Travel Industry Association of America, more than 55 million Americans have participated in a volunteer vacation, and about 100 million more are considering taking one. Volunteer vacations attract people from all walks of life and all age groups-students on break or who take a year off between high school and college, singles, couples, families with young children, and older adults.

Despite obvious differences among these people, they typically share a desire to "do something good" while also experiencing new places and challenges in locales they might not otherwise visit.

Choosing a Volunteer Vacation

People choose to take a volunteer vacation for a variety of reasons, and often more than one applies. First and foremost is a desire to help-be it children, the elderly, the handicapped, animals, or the natural environment.

Some people have a specific cause in mind; say, protecting endangered gorillas or preserving the coral reefs off the coast of Australia, and they target organizations that offer such opportunities.

Other people have a more general idea of what they want to do; for example, help alleviate hunger or teach children to read.

Along with an altruistic reason for volunteering there are often others, such as a desire to see exotic or unusual places, an opportunity to experience new challenges, a chance to practice a foreign language, having an experience that will enhance their resume and/or job opportunities, and the fact that such trips usually provide a substantial tax deduction.

When choosing a volunteer vacation opportunity, prospective travelers should consider several questions.

- Where to go? Volunteer vacation opportunities are available in every corner of the world, from the United States to Australia, China, Iceland, and the Amazon.
- How much does it cost? The program fees participants pay to take part in volunteer vacations typically (but not always) include room and board, project fees, travel

medical insurance, and travel within the country in which the volunteer activity occurs. The fees usually do not include transportation to the country. Potential volunteers should check with the sponsoring organization to determine which costs are included in the program fee, and to learn how much of the fee is tax deductible.

- How challenging is it? Some volunteer vacations require a certain level of physical strength and stamina, especially those that involve working outdoors. Potential volunteers should always clearly understand the physical expectations and requirements and be sure they are medically capable of meeting them.
- What are the accommodations? Lodging options vary widely and may involve pitching a tent, living in unheated huts, staying with native families, sharing a dormitory-type residence, or checking into a comfortable hotel. Questions about food, water, linens, availability of power (including computer and cell phone access), medical care, and local transportation should be addressed during the evaluation process.
- How long? Most volunteer vacations last from one to four weeks; some can extend on for months. The vast variety of volunteer vacation opportunities usually means people can find more than one vacation that fits their needs.
- Any special skills needed? People who have special skills-teachers, nurses, veterinarians, biologists, accountants, lawyers, photographers, farmers-are always welcome and in fact urgently needed in some locations. Most volunteer opportunities, however, only ask that people have a desire to help and a willingness to learn and follow directions.
- Is language a barrier? Since so many volunteer vacations are in remote, foreign locations, knowledge of another language in addition to English can be helpful and in some cases, strongly recommended. However, most

potential volunteers do not need to know a second language.

- What about free time? The amount of time volunteers have to spend sightseeing or doing other activities away from their volunteer tasks varies with each assignment, as do the types of activities that are available. This information is usually provided by the sponsoring organization, and it can be helpful to talk or correspond with other people who have volunteered in the location previously.
- Who can participate? Volunteer vacations are available for singles, couples, students, families, and older adults. The age limitation is typically 16 to 18 years of age; a parent or guardian usually must accompany any person younger than 16. Volunteer vacations geared for families with younger children have their own special regulations.

HOW TO FIND A VOLUNTEER VACATION

Both for-profit and nonprofit organizations and companies offer volunteer vacations. Some organizations sponsor opportunities that focus on a specific issue, such as saving sea turtles or building homes for the needy, while others offer a broad spectrum of projects that center on areas such as education, poverty, public health, endangered species, and habitat preservation. While some organizations have projects in only a few countries, others offer options in dozens of locations on nearly every continent.

People interested in learning more about volunteer vacations in general or selecting one in particular can begin by exploring volunteer vacation directories or targeting organizations that offer specific opportunities.

Volunteer Vacation Directories

People who are uncertain about the type of volunteer vacation they want to take may find it best to start by checking a directory of opportunities by category. Charity Guide is a nonprofit that provides information on volunteer vacations in several different categories: environmental protection, children's issues, animal welfare, and health and safety.

Travel with a Challenge provides a directory that caters to mature volunteers (age 45 years and older). Transitions Abroad is a portal for volunteer vacations involving social issues around the globe.

Organizations that Sponsor Volunteer Vacations

Potential volunteers can also scour the opportunities offered by organizations that sponsor volunteer vacations. Airline Ambassadors International distributes medical and other aid to children, families, and underprivileged communities around the world.

Global Service Corp. focuses its efforts in two countries, Tanzania and Thailand, and offers projects that last from two weeks up to six months. People interested in environmental and animal issues can choose from more than 130 projects in 47 countries offered by the nonprofit group Earthwatch. Cross Cultural Solutions has projects lasting from one to twelve weeks located in eleven countries.

One-week opportunities are the mainstay of Globe Aware, which sponsors projects in nine countries. Community development, conservation, and teaching are just a few of the types of projects offered by i-to-i in more than two dozen countries. One unique type of organization is Peace Villages Foundation, a Non-Profit Franchise run and paid for entirely by volunteers.

People who don't find what they're looking for with a sponsoring organization or who have a pet cause or favorite charity can contact the particular group or charity on their own and ask about volunteer vacation opportunities.

WINE TOURISM

Wine tourism refers to tourism whose purpose is or includes the tasting, consumption, or purchase of wine, often at or near the source. Wine tourism can consist of visits to wineries, vineyards, and restaurants known to offer unique vintages, as well as organized wine tours, wine festivals, or other special events.

Many wine regions around the world have found it financially beneficial to promote such tourism; accordingly, growers associations and others in the hospitality industry in wine regions have spent significant amounts of money over the years to promote such tourism.

The National Wine Centre of Australia is a tourism venue that showcases the entire Australian wine industry. It is an education hub for tourists, the general public and full time students.

The National Wine Centre is a teaching centre for wine-related academic programs of The University of Adelaide, Australia. The University of Adelaide, "the wine university", is one of the top two educators in the world for wine studies along with the University of California-Davis.

Flinders University in Australia offers a degree program in food and wine tourism.

SUSTAINABLE TOURISM

There are many different definitions of sustainable tourism, or responsible tourism, that have been developed over the last decade. Most tend to assume that all tourists are responsible for respecting and conserving a location's economic, environmental, and socio-cultural balances.

Global economists forecast continuing international tourism growth, ranging between three and six percent annually, depending on the location.

As one of the world's largest and fastest growing industries, this continuous growth will place great stress on remaining biodiverse habitats, often used to support mass tourism.

Sustainable tourists are aware of these dangers and seek to protect their favorite destinations, and to protect tourism as an industry. Sustainable tourists face many responsibilities to reduce tourism's impact on communities, including:

- informing themselves of the culture, politics, and economy of the communities being visited.
- anticipating and respecting local cultures' expectations and assumptions.
- contributing to intercultural understanding and tolerance.
- supporting the integrity of local cultures by favoring businesses which conserve cultural heritage
- supporting local economies by purchasing local goods and participating with small, local businesses.
- conserving resources by seeking out businesses that are environmentally conscious, and by using the least possible amount of non-renewable resources.

The Multilateral Investment Fund MIF Focus on destinations where there is already a critical mass of tourism businesses, MIF projects aim to boost the competitiveness of locally owned small and medium enterprises, helping them to organize themselves and work toward the shared goals of increasing income, employment and economic develcpment.

See the Sustainable Tourism Action Plan and project proposal Guidelines.

Ecotourism

Ecotourism, according to Heather Robinson (2006), is a subset of sustainable tourism, differing by its focus on ecology.

Ecotourism is sustainable tourism that "contributes actively to the conservation of natural and cultural heritage; includes local and indigenous communities in its planning, development and operation, contributing to their well-being; interprets the natural and cultural heritage of the destination to visitors; and lends itself better to independent travellers, as well as to organized tours for small size groups. In simple words ecotourism means while practicing any kind of tourism one should not harm nature.

For today's fast changing world only the practice of ecotourism can save nature from ever growing human population. Ecotourism is the best way to practice any kind of tourism whether it is wildlife tourism, adventure tourism, or heritage tourism.

It is the duty of all mankind to preserve nature and different species, only then can they survive for a long time; mankind should respect nature and its rules.

Man should preserve nature for the upcoming generation, so they also feel the pleasure of being in nature as people of this and earlier generations felt.

Green Conventions, Meetings and Events

Large conventions, meetings and other major organized events drive the travel, tourism and hospitality industry.

Cities and convention centers compete to attract such commerce, commerce which has heavy impacts on resource use and the environment.

Major sporting events, such as the Olympic Games, present special problems regarding environmental burdens and degradation. But burdens imposed by the regular convention industry can be vastly more significant.

Green conventions and events are a new but growing sector and marketing point within the convention and hospitality industry.

More environmentally aware organizations, corporations and government agencies are now seeking more sustainable event practices, greener hotels, restaurants and convention venues, and more energy efficient or climate neutral travel and ground transportation.

Additionally, some convention centers have begun to take direct action in reducing the impact of the conventions they host.

One example is the Moscone Center in San Francisco, California, which has a very aggressive recycling program, a large solar power system, and other programs aimed at reducing impact and increasing efficiency.

With the advent of the internet, some traditional conventions are being replaced with virtual conventions, where the attendees remain in their home physical location and "attend" the convention by use of a web-based interface programmed for the task.

This sort of "virtual" meeting eliminates all of the impacts associated with travel, accommodation, food wastage, and other necessary impacts of traditional, physical conventions.

BIBLIOGRAPHY

Abram, Simone: *Tourists and Tourism: Identifying with People and Places*, New York, Berg, 1997.

Andrew Holden: *Tourism: A New Perspective*, London, Prentice Hall, 1995.

Andronicou, Antonios: *Tourism in Cyprus*, New York, Oxford University Press, 1979.

Apostolopulos, Y., S. Lewadi: *The Sociology of Tourism*, New York, Routledge, 1996.

Ashworth, Gregory J.: *Marketing Tourism Places*, London, Routledge, 1990.

Bennett, O.: *Financing for Tourism Projects in Developing Countries*, England, Wiley, 1994.

Bevan, D. L., and D. W. Soskice: *Appraising Tourist Development in a Small Economy*, London, Heinemann, 1976.

Boissevain, Jeremy: *Coping with Tourists: European Reactions to Mass Tourism*, England, Berghahn, 1996.

Brass, Jane L.: *Community Tourism Assessment Handbook*, Corvallis, Oregon State University, 1996.

Brogan, E.: *Human Resource Development in Tourism: The Scottish Perspective*, England, Wiley, 1994.

Bruce, David : *Tourism Strategies for Rural Development*, Sackville, New Brunswick, 1993.

Chambers, Erve: *Tourism and Culture: An Applied Perspective*, Albany, State University of New York Press, 1997.

Cooper, C.: *Tourism: Principles and Practice*, London, Pitman, 1993.

Dane, Suzanne: *Share Your Heritage: Cultural Heritage Tourism Success Stories*, Washington, DC, National Trust for Historic Preservation, 2001.

Daniel, R.: *Recent Advances in Tourism Marketing Research*, New York, Hawthorne Press, 1996.

David Taylor: *Cost-Benefit Analysis of Local Tourism Development*, Corvallis, Oregon, 1994.

David W.: *Tourism Planning*, Chicago, Council of Planning Librarians, 1995.

David, L.: *International Tourism Policy*, New York, Van Nostrand Reinhold, 1990.

Davidson, R.: *European Business Travel and Tourism*, England, Wiley, 1994.

Douglas C.: *Heritage Tourism is in the Future of Many Alabama Communities*, Auburn Univ., Auburn, 1991.

Douglas, Pearce: *Change in Tourism: People, Places, Processes*, New York, Routledge, 1995.

Edward, M.: *In International Tourism: Identity and Change*, London, Sage, 1995.

Foley, M.: *In Tourism: The State of the Art*, England, Wiley, 1994.

Forbes, A. H.: *Tourism and Transport Policy in the European Union*, England, Wiley, 1994.

Fowler, Peter: *Heritage and Tourism*, New York, Routledge, 1993.

France, Lesley: *The Earthscan Reader in Sustainable Tourism*, California, Island, 1997.

Frew, E.: *International Charter Travel—a New Opportunity for Australian Tourism*, England, Wiley, 1994.

Garfield, Donald: *Partners in Tourism: Culture and Commerce*, Washington, DC, American Association of Museums, 1997.

Gimblett, Barbara: *Destination Culture: Tourism, Museums, and Heritage*, California, University of California, 1998.

Gorman, Michael: *Design for Tourism: An ICSID Interdesign Report*, New York, Oxford University Press, 1972.

Gunn, Clare A.: *Tourism Planning*, New York, Crane Russak, 1979.

Harrison, David: *Tourism and the Less Developed Countries*, London, Belhaven, 1992.

Haylock, R.: *Timeshare—the New Force in Tourism*, England, Wiley, 1994.

Heise, Dorothy: *Promoting Tourism in Rural American*, Maryland, National Agriculture Library, 1991.

Hitchcock, Michael: *Tourism in South-East Asia*, London, Routledge, 1993.

Holden, Andrew: *Tourism: A Commodity of Opportunity for Change?* Chichester, England, 1994.

Howard Green: *Tourism and the Environment: A Sustainable Relationship*, New York, Routledge, 1995.

Howard Green: *Tourism and the Environment: A Sustainable Relationship*, New York, Routledge, 1995.

Hudman, Lloyd E.: *Tourism: A Shrinking World*, Columbus, Grid, 1980.

Inskeep, E.: *Training for Tourism in Developing Countries*, Chichester, England, 1994.

James Makens: *Marketing for Hospitality and Tourism*: New Jersey, Prentice-Hall, 1998.

Jenkins, C. L.: *Tourism in Developing Countries: The Privatisation Issue*, Chichester, England, 1994.

Jenkins, J.: *Tourism and Recreation in Rural Areas*, Chichester, U.K., 1998.

John Sem: *A Training Guide for Rural Tourism Development*, Minnesota: Rural Tourism Center, 1995.

Julia, Sharpley: *Rural Tourism: An Introduction*, London, International Thomson Business Press, 1997.

Knox, J.: *Tourism Research Priorities in Hawaii and the Pacific*, Honolulu, University of Hawaii, 1979.

Komilis, P.: *Tourism and Sustainable Regional Development*, Chichester, England, 1994.

Koth, Barbara: *A Training Guide for Rural Tourism Development*, Minnesota: Rural Tourism Center, 1995.

Kotler, Philip: *Marketing for Hospitality and Tourism*: New Jersey, Prentice-Hall, 1998.

Leonard J.: *An Introduction to Tourism*, New York, Butterworth-Heinemann, 1997.

Margaret Whitla: *Tourism Strategies for Rural Development*, Sackville, New Brunswick, 1993.

Martinus J.: *Tourism by Train: Its Role in Alternative Tourism*, Philadelphia, University of Pennsylvania Press, 1992.

Mary, E.: *A Heritage Tourism Tool: National Register of Historic Places*, Radnor, Pennsylvania, 1993.

McConnell II, D. W.: *Nature-Based Tourism and Rural Coastal Development: Observations, Options, and Trends*, South Carolina, Clemson University, 1990.

Mieczkowski, Zbigniew: *Environmental Issues of Tourism and Recreation*, Lanham, University Press of America, 1995.

Muzaffer Uysal: *Recent Advances in Tourism Marketing Research*, New York, Hawthorne Press, 1996.

Richard, W.: *Tourism and Recreation in Rural Areas*, Chichester, U.K., 1998.

Ryan, Chris: *Recreational Tourism: A Social Science Perspective*, London, Routledge, 1991.

Sharpley, Richard: *Rural Tourism: An Introduction*, London, International Thomson Business Press, 1997.

Stabler, Michael J.: *Tourism and Sustainability: Principles to Practice*, New York, CAB International, 1997.

Stephen F.: *Linking Tourism, the Environment, and Sustainability*, Ogden, Utah, 1995.

Stephen, C.: *Tourism in the Navajo Country: Resources and Planning*, Winslow Rock, Navajo Tribe, 1967.

Suggs, C.: *Tourism Research Priorities in Hawaii and the Pacific*, Honolulu, University of Hawaii, 1979.

Valentine, Udoh: *Tourism Development: A Research Note on Africa*, Connecticut, Praeger, 1996.

Victor T. C.: *Sustainable Tourism: A Marketing Perspective*, Woburn, Massachusetts: Butterworth-Heinemann, 1998.

William W. Swart: *Planning for Tourism Development: Quantitative Approaches*, New York, Praeger, 1976.

INDEX

L

M

N

O

P

U

V

W

□□□